Keys to Success
Quick

Carol **Carter**   Joyce **Bishop**   Sarah **Lyman Kravits**

Boston   Columbus   Indianapolis   New York   San Francisco   Upper Saddle River
Amsterdam   Cape Town   Dubai   London   Madrid   Milan   Munich   Paris   Montreal   Toronto
Delhi   Mexico City   Sao Paulo   Sydney   Hong Kong   Seoul   Singapore   Taipei   Tokyo

Editor-in-Chief: Jodi McPherson
Development Editor: Charlotte Morrissey
Editorial Assistant: Clara Ciminelli
Executive Marketing Manager: Amy Judd
Production Editor: Gregory Erb
Editorial Production Service: Omegatype Typography, Inc.
Manufacturing Buyer: Megan Cochran
Electronic Composition: Omegatype Typography, Inc.
Interior Design: Omegatype Typography, Inc.
Photo Researcher: Annie Pickert
Cover Designer: John Wincek
Cover Administrator: Elena Sidorova

Credits and acknowledgments borrowed from other sources and reproduced, with permission, in this textbook appear on appropriate page within text or below.

Photo Credits: p. 1: Shutterstock; p. 14: Corey Sundahl/iStockphoto; p. 20: Universal Images Group/SuperStock; p. 29: Jeff Greenberg/PhotoEdit; p. 45: Andy Levin/Photo Researchers; p. 61: Hero Images Inc./Alamy; p. 77: Doug Martin/Photo Researchers; p. 90: Bonnie Kamin/PhotoEdit; p. 106: picsfive; p. 119: Yellow Dog Productions/Getty Images; p. 132: Rachel Epstein/PhotoEdit; p. 146: Comstock; p. 160: Stockbyte/Getty Images

Library of Congress Cataloging-in-Publication Data

Carter, Carol.
    Keys to success quick / Carol Carter, Joyce Bishop, Sarah Lyman Kravits.
        p.   cm.
    Includes bibliographical references and index.
    ISBN-13: 978-0-13-254171-8
    ISBN-10: 0-13-254171-8
  1. College student orientation—United States—Handbooks, manuals, etc.   2. Study skills—Handbooks, manuals, etc.   3. College students—United States—Life skills guides.
    I. Bishop, Joyce (Joyce L.).   II. Kravits, Sarah Lyman.   III. Title.
    LB2343.32.C38 2012
    378.1'98   dc22

                                                                2010033664

11   V011   15

www.pearsonhighered.com
ISBN-10: 0-13-254171-8
ISBN-13: 978-0-13-254171-8

Brief Contents

Contents

1 Welcome to College
Attitudes and Actions for Success   1

2 Goals and Time
Planning Your Future and Your Time Wisely   14

3 Learning How You Learn
Making the Most of Your Abilities   29

4 Critical, Creative, and Practical Thinking
Solving Problems and Making Decisions   45

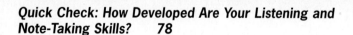

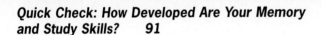

7 Memory and Studying
Retaining What You Learn   90

8 Test Taking
Showing What You Know   105

9 Diversity and Communication
Making Relationships Work   119

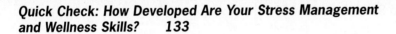

10 Wellness and Stress Management
Staying Healthy in Mind and Body   132

11 Managing Money
Living Within Your Means   146

It's not just what you know . . . It's what you know *how* to do.

Your time and money are valuable, limited resources—and this book will help you make the most of both. Our most streamlined student success text to date, *Keys to Success Quick* takes the skills and techniques instructors and students have come to love from our bestselling *Keys* series and condenses them into 174 pages of essential information.

Quick gets right to the point with each important topic, providing the tools you'll need to build top-notch academic, self-management, and thinking skills for use in college, career, and life. Other than putting all this in a super-short package, what makes *Quick* so special?

▶ *Critical, creative, and practical thinking skills.* The text is organized around these three active and goal-focused thinking skills, based on psychologist Dr. Robert Sternberg's research on the types of thinking necessary for goal achievement. They are introduced in the first chapter, reinforced in chapter exercises, and referenced throughout the text. Research proves that building these thinking skills increases student achievement, no matter what your age, culture, gender, or life experience.

▶ *Self-knowledge focus.* With self-assessments opening and closing the text, as well as chapter-focused self-assessments that begin each chapter, *Quick* promotes self-knowledge and awareness from start to finish.

This text is designed with features that deepen and solidify learning. *Quick* features include:

QUICK CHECK. This brief self-assessment helps gauge knowledge and awareness of each chapter's material before it starts. It asks questions designed to inspire thinking about what readers will learn.

quick!
CHECK

How Developed Are Your Self-Management Skills?

For each statement, circle the number that best describes how true the statement is for you, from 1 for "not at all true for me" to 5 for "very true for me."

▶ Periodically, I take time to think through academic and personal goals.

▶ I read each syllabus carefully to understand the course goals.
1 2 3 4 5

▶ I have a system for reminding myself of what my goals are.
1 2 3 4 5

▶ I find ways to motivate myself when I am working toward a goal.
1 2 3 4 5

▶ When I set a long-term goal, I break it down into a series of short-term goals.
1 2 3 4 5

▶ I've been looking into majors that might appeal to me.
1 2 3 4 5

▶ I know myself as a time manager and which strategies work best for me.
1 2 3 4 5

1 2 3 4 5

THINK ACTIVITIES. Three activities appearing in each chapter—Think Practically, Think Creatively, and Think Critically—apply chapter skills immediately to everyday life. Through a mixture of brainstorming, journaling, and action, readers are encouraged to think outside of the box and put their developing skills to work in real-world applications.

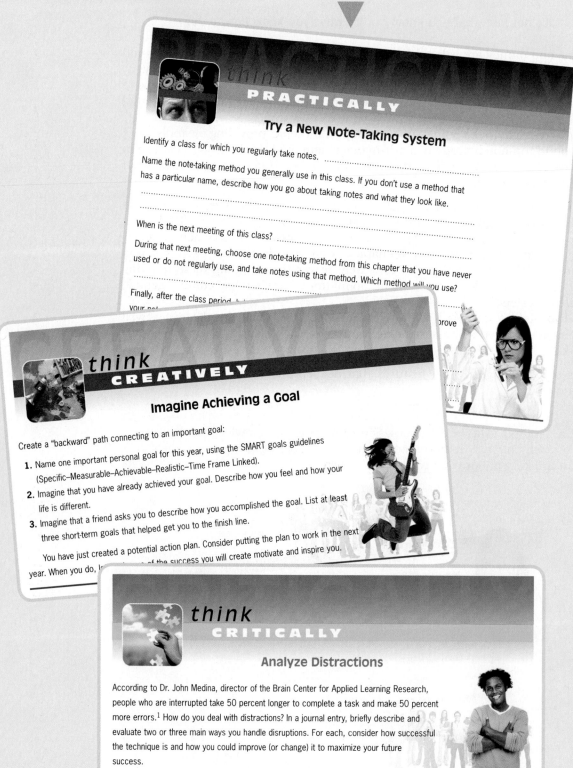

think
PRACTICALLY

Try a New Note-Taking System

Identify a class for which you regularly take notes.

Name the note-taking method you generally use in this class. If you don't use a method that has a particular name, describe how you go about taking notes and what they look like.

When is the next meeting of this class?

During that next meeting, choose one note-taking method from this chapter that you have never used or do not regularly use, and take notes using that method. Which method will you use?

Finally, after the class period, ... your ... prove

think
CREATIVELY

Imagine Achieving a Goal

Create a "backward" path connecting to an important goal:

1. Name one important personal goal for this year, using the SMART goals guidelines (Specific–Measurable–Achievable–Realistic–Time Frame Linked).
2. Imagine that you have already achieved your goal. Describe how you feel and how your life is different.
3. Imagine that a friend asks you to describe how you accomplished the goal. List at least three short-term goals that helped get you to the finish line.

You have just created a potential action plan. Consider putting the plan to work in the next year. When you do, ... of the success you will create motivate and inspire you.

think
CRITICALLY

Analyze Distractions

According to Dr. John Medina, director of the Brain Center for Applied Learning Research, people who are interrupted take 50 percent longer to complete a task and make 50 percent more errors.[1] How do you deal with distractions? In a journal entry, briefly describe and evaluate two or three main ways you handle disruptions. For each, consider how successful the technique is and how you could improve (or change) it to maximize your future success.

THINK BACK. This end-of-chapter synthesis activity provides an opportunity to review the text for understanding, prepare for tests, and pursue personal growth. Task one involves revisiting the chapter-opening questions, and task two builds on one of those questions to create and map out a personal goal.

quick! SKILL BUILDING

Think Back

Solidify your knowledge and prepare for tests with this review. Answer the following questions on a separate sheet of paper or electronic file.

▶ Revisit the chapter-opening questions on page 77. Scan the chapter and write a short answer for each.

▶ As you review the chapter, take notes on the first section of material using an informal outline. For the second section, use a visual method, such as the mind map or charting method.

Analyze, Create, Practice

Identify Listening and Note-Taking Conditions That Work for You

Put your thinking skills to work to improve your listening and note-taking skills:

Analyze. Describe a recent class in which you were able to listen effectively and take notes (course title, type of classroom setting, and so forth).

....
....

Describe the instructor's style (lecture, group discussion, Q&A) and any listening barriers.

....
....

ANALYZE, CREATE, PRACTICE. This multistep, end-of-chapter exercise is an opportunity to apply the three thinking skills to chapter material in a way that relates directly to personal, real-life needs. The yellow portfolio icon signals an activity that you can use to build a personal portfolio demonstrating skills and self-knowledge you've acquired in the course.

MULTIPLE INTELLIGENCES IN ACTION. This end-of-chapter exercise encourages the development of practical strategies relating to strongest and weakest intelligences. Building on the information and self-assessment results from the learning styles chapter, this activity encourages both creative thinking and problem-solving skills while addressing day-to-day needs.

Multiple Intelligences in action

Write three intelligences in the left-hand column—two that are highly developed for you and one you would like to build. Then, in the right-hand column, brainstorm a strategy for listening and/or note taking that relates to each intelligence.

Intelligence	Use MI Strategies to Come Up with Solutions
Example: Naturalistic	*Use the chart method to categorize pieces of information your instructor discusses. Later, identify relationships among the points.*

Keys to Success *Quick*
Because your time is valuable.

Acknowledgments

This significant revision has been produced through the efforts of an extraordinary team. Many thanks to:

▶ Our reviewers, for their responsiveness and invaluable input: Sheryl Blahnik, Richland Community College; Castell Burton, Valencia Community College; Gary Corona, Florida Community College at Jacksonville; Mo Cuevas, West Texas A&M University; Russell Davis, Southwest College, HCC; Karen Droms, Luzerne County Community College; Lewis Gray, Middle Tennessee State University; Lois Hassan, Henry Ford Community College; Angie Rataj, University of Missouri; Amy Reese, Baton Rouge Community College; Kerri A. Sleeman, Michigan Technological University; Iris Strunc, Okaloosa-Walton College; Voltaire Villanueva, Foothill College; and Candace Whitney, Gavilan College.

▶ Robert J. Sternberg, Dean of the School of Arts and Sciences at Tufts University, for his groundbreaking work on thinking and intelligence and for his gracious permission to use and adapt that work for this text.

▶ Chelsey Emmelhainz, editorial assistant to the author team, for her insightful comments and hard work.

▶ Our editor Sande Johnson, her editorial assistant Clara Ciminelli, and developmental editor Charlotte Morrissey for their dedication, vision, and efforts.

▶ Our production team for their patience, flexibility, and attention to detail, especially production editor Greg Erb, director of production Elaine Ober, cover designer John Wincek, and Diana Neatrour and the entire team at Omegatype.

▶ Our marketing gurus, especially Amy Judd, Executive Marketing Manager; Margaret Waples, Vice President, Director of Marketing; and our sales director team—Connie James, Director of Sales Programs; Deb Wilson, Senior Sales Director; and Sean Wittmann, Missy Bittner, Lynda Sax, Chris Cardona, and Hector Amaya, Sales Directors.

▶ Editor-in-Chief of Student Success and Career Development Jodi McPherson, President of Pearson Teacher Education and Student Success Nancy Forsyth, CEO of Teacher Education & Development Susan Badger, and Prentice Hall President Tim Bozik, for their interest in the *Keys* series.

▶ The Pearson representatives and the management team led by Brian Kibby, Senior Vice President Sales/Marketing.

▶ The staff at LifeBound for their hard work and dedication: Heather Brown, Kelly Carson, and Cynthia Nordberg.

▶ Our families and friends, who have encouraged us and put up with our commitments.

▶ Special thanks to Judy Block, who contributed research and writing to this book.

Finally, for their ideas, opinions, and stories, we would like to thank all of the students and professors with whom we work. Joyce in particular would like to thank the thousands of students who have allowed her, as their professor, the privilege of sharing part of their journey through college. We appreciate that, through reading this book, you give us the opportunity to learn and discover with you—in your classroom, at home, on a bus or train, and wherever else learning takes place.

Supplemental Resources

INSTRUCTOR SUPPORT
Resources to simplify your life and support your students.

Book-Specific Resources

Instructor's Resource Manual and Test Bank (ISBN: 0-13-138209-8). This online manual is intended to give instructors a framework or blueprint of ideas and suggestions to assist them in providing their students with activities, journal writing, thought-provoking situations, and group activities. The test bank, organized by chapter, includes multiple choice, true/false, short answer, and essay questions that support the key features in the book. Each test item is correlated to a chapter learning objective and is given a level of difficulty based on Bloom's taxonomy. This downloadable version of the Instructor's Resource Manual is available from the Pearson Instructor's Resource Center (IRC) at www.pearsonhighered.com/irc.

Online PowerPoint Presentation (ISBN: 0-13-13138205-5). A comprehensive set of PowerPoint slides that can be used by instructors for class presentations or by students for lecture preview or review. The presentation includes visuals from the textbook. The presentation also contains bullet point slides for each chapter that highlight the important points to help students understand the concepts within each chapter. Instructors may download these PowerPoint presentations from the IRC at www.pearsonhighered.com/irc.

MyTest Bank (ISBN: 0-13-138206-3). Pearson MyTest offers instructors a secure online environment and quality assessments to easily create print exams, study guide questions, and quizzes from any computer with an Internet connection.

Premium Assessment Content
▶ Draw from a rich library of question test banks that complement your Pearson textbook and your course's learning objectives.
▶ Edit questions or tests to fit your specific teaching needs.

Instructor-Friendly Features
▶ Easily create and store your own questions, including images, diagrams, and charts using simple drag-and-drop and Word-like controls.
▶ Use additional information provided by Pearson, such as the question's difficulty level or learning objective, to help you quickly build your test.

Time-Saving Enhancements
▶ Add headers or footers and easily scramble questions and answer choices all from one simple toolbar.
▶ Quickly create multiple versions of your test or answer key, and when ready, simply save to Word or PDF format and print!
▶ Export your exams for import to Blackboard 6.0, CE (WebCT), or Vista (WebCT)!
▶ Additional information is available at www.pearsonmytest.com.

 Are you teaching online, in a hybrid setting, or looking to infuse exciting technology into your classroom for the first time? Then be sure to refer to the MyStudentSuccessLab section on pages xxiii–xxv to learn more. This online solution, designed to help students build the skills they need to succeed, is at www.mystudentsuccesslab.com.

Other Resources

Easy access to online, book-specific teaching support is now just a click away!

Instructor Resource Center. Register. Redeem. Login. Three easy steps open the door to a variety of print and media resources in downloadable, digital format. Available to instructors exclusively through the Pearson IRC: www.pearsonhighered.com/irc.

Choose from a wide range of video resources for the classroom!

Pearson Reference Library: Life Skills Pack (ISBN: 0-13-127079-6). Contains all four videos, which may also be requested individually as follows:

- ▶ Learning Styles and Self-Awareness (ISBN: 0-13-028502-1)
- ▶ Critical and Creative Thinking (ISBN: 0-13-028504-8)
- ▶ Relating to Others (ISBN: 0-13-028511-0)
- ▶ Personal Wellness (ISBN: 0-13-028514-5)

Pearson Reference Library: Study Skills Pack (ISBN: 0-13-127080-X). Contains all six videos, or they may be requested individually as follows:

- ▶ Reading Effectively (ISBN: 0-13-028505-6)
- ▶ Listening and Memory (ISBN: 0-13-028506-4)
- ▶ Note Taking and Research (ISBN: 0-13-028508-0)
- ▶ Writing Effectively (ISBN: 0-13-028509-9)
- ▶ Effective Test Taking (ISBN: 0-13-028500-5)
- ▶ Goal Setting and Time Management (ISBN: 0-13-028503-X)

Pearson Reference Library: Career Skills Pack (ISBN: 0-13-118529-2). Contains all three videos, which may also be requested individually as follows:

- ▶ Skills for the 21st Century—Technology (ISBN: 0-13-028512-9)
- ▶ Skills for the 21st Century—Math and Science (ISBN: 0-13-028513-7)
- ▶ Managing Money and Career (ISBN: 0-13-028516-1)

Complete Reference Library—Life/Study Skills/Career Video Pack on DVD (ISBN: 0-13-501095-0). Our reference library of thirteen popular video resources has now been digitized onto one DVD so students and instructors alike can benefit from the array of video clips. Featuring Life Skills, Study Skills, and Career Skills, the videos help to reinforce the course content in a more interactive way.

Faculty Video Resources
- ▶ Teacher Training Video 1: Critical Thinking (ISBN: 0-13-099432-4)
- ▶ Teacher Training Video 2: Stress Management & Communication (ISBN: 0-13-099578-9)
- ▶ Teacher Training Video 3: Classroom Tips (ISBN: 0-13-917205-X)
- ▶ Student Advice Video (ISBN: 0-13-233206-X)
- ▶ Study Skills Video (ISBN: 0-13-096095-0)

Current Issues Videos
- ▶ ABC News Video Series: Student Success, Second Edition (ISBN: 0-13-031901-5)
- ▶ ABC News Video Series: Student Success, Third Edition (ISBN: 0-13-152865-3)

MyStudentSuccessLab Videos on DVD (ISBN: 0-13-514249-0). Our six most popular video resources have been digitized onto one DVD so students and instructors alike can benefit from the array of video clips. Featuring Technology, Math and Science, Managing Money and Career, Learning Styles and Self-Awareness, Study Skills, and Peer Advice, the videos help to reinforce the course content in a more interactive way. They are also accessible through our MSSL and course management offerings and available on VHS.

Assessments

Through partnership opportunities, we offer a variety of assessment options!

LASSI (Paper ISBN: 0-13-172315-4; Online ISBN: 0-13-172316-2). The LASSI is a 10-scale, 80-item assessment of students' awareness about and use of learning and study strategies. Addressing skill, will, and self-regulation, the focus is on both covert and overt thoughts, behaviors, attitudes, and beliefs that relate to successful learning and that can be altered through educational interventions. Available in paper and online (access card) formats

Noel Levitz/RMS (Paper Long Form A ISBN: 0-13-512066-7; Paper Short Form B ISBN: 0-13-512065-9; Online ISBN: 0-13-098158-3). This retention tool measures Academic Motivation, General Coping Ability, Receptivity to Support Services, PLUS Social Motivation. It helps identify at-risk students, the areas with which they struggle, and their receptiveness to support. Available in paper or online formats, as well as short and long versions.

Robbins Self-Assessment Library. This compilation teaches students to create a portfolio of skills. S.A.L. is a self-contained, interactive library of 49 behavioral questionnaires that help students discover new ideas about themselves, their attitudes, and their personal strengths and weaknesses. Available in paper, CD-ROM, and online (access card) formats.

Readiness for Education at a Distance Indicator (READI) (ISBN: 0-13-188967-2). READI is a web-based tool that assesses the overall likelihood for online learning success. READI generates an immediate score and a diagnostic interpretation of results, including recommendations for successful participation in online courses and potential remediation sources. Please visit www.readi.info for additional information.

Pathway to Student Success CD-ROM (ISBN: 0-13-239314-X). The CD is divided into several categories, each of which focuses on a specific topic that relates to students and provides them with the context, tools, and strategies to enhance their educational experience.

The Golden Personality Type Profiler (ISBN: 0-13-706654-6). The Golden Personality Type Profiler™ helps students understand how they make decisions and relate to others. By completing the Golden Personality Type Profiler™, students develop a deeper understanding of their strengths, a clearer picture of how their behavior impacts others, and a better appreciation for the interpersonal style of others and how to interact with them more effectively. Using these results as a guide, students will gain the self-awareness that is key to professional development and success.

Pearson Custom Publishing

For a truly tailored solution that fosters campus connections and increases retention, talk with us about custom publishing.

Pearson Custom Publishing is the largest custom provider for print and media shaped to your course's needs. Please visit us at www.pearsoncustom.com to learn more.

STUDENT SUPPORT
Tools to help make the grade now, and excel in school later.

PEARSON mystudentsuccesslab Today's students are more inclined than ever to use technology to enhance their learning. Refer to the **MyStudentSuccessLab** section on pages xxiii–xxv to learn about our revolutionary resource (www.mystudent successlab.com). This online solution is designed to help students build the skills they need to succeed.

Time Management

Time management is the #1 challenge students face. We can help.

Pearson Planner. A basic planner that includes a monthly and daily calendar plus other materials to facilitate organization. 8.5 × 11 trim size.

Premier Annual Planner. This specially designed, annual four-color collegiate planner includes an academic planning/resources section, monthly planning section (two pages/month), and a weekly planning section (48 weeks; July start date), which facilitate short-term as well as long-term planning. Spiral bound, 6 × 9 trim size. Customization is available.

Journaling

Journaling activities promote self-discovery and self-awareness.

Through the **Student Reflection Journal,** students are encouraged to track their progress and share their insights, thoughts, and concerns. 8.5 × 11 trim size. 90 pages.

The Student Orientation Series

Includes short booklets on specialized topics that facilitate greater student understanding.

S.O.S. Guides help students understand what these opportunities are, how to take advantage of them, and how to learn from their peers while doing so. They include:

▶ Connolly: *Learning Communities* (ISBN: 0-13-232243-9)
▶ Hoffman: *Stop Procrastination Now! 10 Simple and SUCCESSFUL Steps for Student Success* (ISBN: 0-13-513056-5)
▶ Jabr: *English Language Learners* (ISBN: 0-13-232242-0)
▶ Watts: *Service Learning* (ISBN: 0-13-232201-0)

For Students!

Why is this course important?

This course will help you transition to college, introduce you to campus resources, and prepare you for success in all aspects of college, career, and life. You will:
- Develop Skills to Excel in Other Classes
- Apply Concepts from College to Your Career and Life
- Learn to Use Media Resources

How can you get the most out of the book and online resources required in this class?

Purchase your book and online resources before the First Day of Class. Register and log in to the online resources using your access code.

Develop Skills to Excel in Other Classes
- Helps you with your homework
- Prepares you for exams

Apply Concepts from College to Your Career and Life
- Provides learning techniques
- Helps you achieve your goals

Learn to Use Media Resources
- **www.mystudentsuccesslab.com** helps you build skills you need to succeed through peer-led videos, interactive exercises and projects, journaling and goal setting activities.
- Connect with real students, practice skill development, and personalize what is learned.

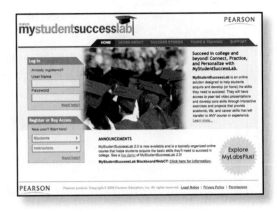

Want to get involved with Pearson like other students have?

Join www.PearsonStudents.com
It is a place where our student customers can incorporate their views and ideas into their learning experience. They come to find out about our programs such as the **Pearson Student Advisory Board**, **Pearson Campus Ambassador**, and the **Pearson Prize** (student scholarship!).

Here's how you can get involved:

- Tell your instructors, friends, and family members about **PearsonStudents**.
- To get daily updates on how students can boost their resumes, study tips, get involved with Pearson, and earn rewards:

  f Become a fan of **Pearson Students on Facebook**

  t Follow **@Pearson_Student on Twitter**

- Explore **Pearson Free Agent**. It allows you get involved in the publishing process, by giving student feedback.

See you on **PearsonStudents** where our student customers live. When students succeed, we succeed!

Succeed in college and beyond!
Connect, practice, and personalize with MyStudentSuccessLab.

www.mystudentsuccesslab.com

MyStudentSuccessLab is an online solution designed to help students acquire the skills they need to succeed. They will have access to peer-led video presentations and develop core skills through interactive exercises and projects that provide academic, life, and career skills that will transfer to ANY course.

It can accompany any Student Success text, or be sold as a stand-alone course offering. To become successful learners, students must consistently apply techniques to daily activities.

How will MyStudentSuccessLab make a difference?

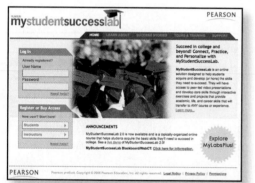

Is motivation a challenge, and if so, how do you deal with it?
Video Presentation — Experience peer led video 'by students, for students' of all ages and stages.

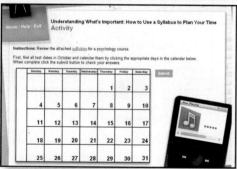

How would better class preparation improve the learning experience?
Practice activities — Practice skills for each topic — beginning, intermediate, and advanced — leveled by Bloom's taxonomy.

What could you gain by building critical thinking and problem-solving skills in this class? **Apply (final project)** — Complete a final project using these skills to create 'personally relevant' resources.

MyStudentSuccessLab Feature set:

Topic Overview: Module objectives.

Video Presentation – Connect: Real student video interviews on key issues.

Practice: Three skill–building exercises per topic provide interactive experience and practice.

Apply – Personalize: Apply what is learned by creating a personally relevant project and journal.

Resources: Plagiarism Guide, Dictionary, Calculators, and Assessments (Career, Learning Styles, and Personality Styles).

Additional Assignments: Extra suggested activities to use with each topic.

Text–Specific Study Plan (available with select books): Chapter Objectives, Practice Tests, Enrichment activities, and Flashcards.

MyStudentSuccessLab Topic List –

1. Time Management/Planning
2. Values/Goal Setting
3.   Learning How You Learn
4. Listening and Taking Class Notes
5. Reading and Annotating
6. Memory and Studying
7. Critical Thinking
8. Problem-Solving
9. Information Literacy
10. Communication
11. Test Prep and Test Taking
12. Stress Management
13. Financial Literacy
14. Majors and Careers

MyStudentSuccessLab Support:

• **Demos, Registration, Log-in** – www.mystudentsuccesslab.com under "Tours and Training" and "Support."

• **Email support** – Send an inquiry to MyStudentSuccessLab@pearson.com

• **Online Training** – Join one of our weekly WebEx training sessions.

• **Peer Training** – Faculty Advocate connection for qualified adoptions.

• **Technical support** – 24 hours a day, seven days a week, at http://247pearsoned.custhelp.com

chapter

1

Welcome to College

Attitudes and Actions for Success

Going to college offers benefits—in exchange for effort, money, and time. As you read this chapter, think about what you want out of this course and out of your college education— and what you are willing to do to make sure that you get it.

In this chapter, you'll explore answers to the following questions:

What does college offer and expect of you?

p. 2

What thinking skills can help you achieve your goals?

p. 5

How can a "growth mindset" help you succeed?

p. 7

How can you work effectively with others?

p. 10

How does college prepare you for work and life success?

p. 11

How Prepared Are You for College?

For each statement, circle the number that best describes how true the statement is for you, from 1 for "not at all true for me" to 5 for "very true for me."

▶ I feel ready to handle college-level work. **1 2 3 4 5**

▶ I can identify how college culture differs from high school and the workplace. **1 2 3 4 5**

▶ When I need help, I can find—and use—resources that can help me academically, financially, and socially. **1 2 3 4 5**

▶ I aim to build thinking skills to be more able to reach my most important goals. **1 2 3 4 5**

▶ I believe that I can grow my intelligence with effort and focus. **1 2 3 4 5**

▶ When I learn information or a skill, I consider how it may help me in the future. **1 2 3 4 5**

▶ I can explain the value of acting with academic integrity in college. **1 2 3 4 5**

▶ I am able to perceive my own emotions as well as those of others. **1 2 3 4 5**

▶ I relate effectively to others and can work successfully in a team. **1 2 3 4 5**

▶ As I learn information or a skill, I consider how it may help me in the workplace. **1 2 3 4 5**

If your total ranges from 41–50, you consider yourself ready to make the most of college.
If your total ranges from 24–40, you consider yourself fairly ready to make the most of college.
If your total is less than 24, you think you need to become more prepared for college.

Now total your scores.

REMEMBER No matter how prepared you are to succeed in college, you can improve with effort. Read the chapter to learn new ways to prepare effectively, and practice by doing the activities.

What DOES COLLEGE OFFER AND EXPECT OF YOU?

You've entered a new phase of your life—enrolling in college, finding a way to pay for it, signing up for courses, and showing up for class. You've earned the opportunity to be here and to build a better future. Now that you *have* the opportunity, how can you *use* it to reach your goals and dreams? Start by looking at what college offers and what faculty and others will expect of you in terms of college culture, finding resources, and preparing for academic success.

The Culture of College

In high school, you most likely read assignments, listened to teachers review them in class, memorized study guides, and then took tests on that material. You took in the information but didn't necessarily put it to work. The result? You may have forgotten much of it.

College instruction and learning are different and give you the opportunity to take things to a new, more meaningful level. What are some key elements of college culture?

Independent learning College offers you the chance to learn with a great deal of freedom and independence. In exchange, though, instructors expect you to calendar and remember key deadlines in your syllabus, keep up with the reading, attend class, and complete projects without much guidance.

Fast pace College courses move faster, with more papers, homework, reading, and projects than you probably had in high school or on the job. The pace can be demanding, although it can also energize and motivate you, especially if you did not feel inspired by high school assignments.

Challenging work Although challenging, college-level work offers an enormous opportunity to learn and grow. College texts often have more words per page, higher-level terminology, and more abstract ideas than high school texts. In addition to difficult reading, college often involves challenging assignments, projects, lab work, and tests.

More out-of-class time to manage The freedom of the college schedule requires more management on your part. You might have days when your classes end at noon or don't begin until two in the afternoon—or don't meet at all. You will need to make use of these blocks of time for studying and other responsibilities, including perhaps a job and family.

Diverse culture Typically, you will encounter different ideas and diverse people in college. Your fellow students may differ from you in age, life experience, ethnicity, political mindset, family obligations, values, and much more. Also, if you commute to school or attend class with others who do, you may find it challenging to connect with others.

Higher-level thinking You'll be asked to move far beyond recall. Instead of just summarizing and taking the ideas of others at face value, you will interpret, evaluate, generate new ideas, and apply what you know to new situations (more on thinking skills later in this chapter).

College offers a range of resources to help you academically, financially, socially, and emotionally. Your end of the bargain is that you are expected to find the resources you need.

Connect with People

Learning who can help you—and reaching out to those people—will help you become more successful in college and beyond.

You Have Much to Gain from College

Studies show the following benefits of a college education:[1]

▶ **Increased income.** College graduates earn, on average, around $20,000 more per year than those with a high school diploma.

▶ **Increased chances of finding and keeping a job.** The unemployment rate for college graduates is less than half that of high school graduates.

▶ **Better health.** With the knowledge and increased self-awareness that college often brings, both college graduates and their children are more likely to stay healthy.

▶ **More money for the future.** College graduates, on average, put away more money in savings.

▶ **Broader thinking.** College graduates tend to be more open-minded and less prejudiced. They generally have more understanding of diverse cultures and more knowledge of the world.

▶ **Better decision making.** As consumers, college graduates tend to think more carefully and comprehensively about the pros and cons of a purchase before diving in.

Getting through the day-to-day activities of college demands basic computer know-how as well as an understanding of the school's research and communication technology.

© iStockPhoto

more efficiently. Key 1.1 offers more ideas about who can help you when you need it.

Mentors

A *mentor*—defined as a wise and trusted guide—is a person with qualities you admire who takes a particular interest in you and in your growth. A mentor can come to you as part of an organized program (found in many schools and organizations that have "mentoring" programs pairing mentors with students). More often, students may find a mentor in a more casual way, discovering a teacher, administrator, more experienced student, supervisor, or other person who reaches out to them and offers advice and support. Think about the people who guide and support you every day. If someone stands out to you, seek that person's advice and try it out. You may find a true mentor who can help you through the ups and downs of college life.

Faculty and Staff

Faculty and staff are among the most valuable—but underused—sources of help, as a recent survey shows: Only 25 percent of students asked a teacher for advice outside of class at any time during the term.[2] Instructors can help you learn more—and

Connect with Technology and Written Resources

The booklets, papers, and e-mails you get at the start of college and every term often have key information. Instead of pitching them into the recycling bin or your electronic "trash" file, read them carefully.

Key 1.1 **Human Resources Are There to Help**

People Who Can Help You	How They Can Help
Instructors and teaching assistants	Contact instructors during office hours, by e-mail, or use voice mail. To clarify material presented in class, get help with homework, find out how to prepare for a test, ask about a paper you are drafting, discuss grades, or get advice about majors or careers.
Academic advisors	In most colleges, every student is assigned an advisor who is the student's personal connection with the college. Your advisor will help you choose courses, plan your academic program, and understand graduation requirements. You may be required to meet with your advisor once each term.
Tutors and academic centers	If you feel you could benefit from a tutor, ask your instructor or academic advisor for a recommendation. If your school has one or more academic centers, you may find a tutor there. Academic centers, offering assistance in reading, writing, math, and study skills, help students improve skills at all levels.
Counselors	College counselors provide confidential services that can help you address academic problems, stress, or psychological problems.
Other offices and departments	People in the financial aid office, student health center, libraries, and other offices have expertise and are there to help you.

Following are some ways to put these resources to use.

Class and Course Information

Your *syllabus* is one of your most important resources. In nearly all courses, instructors hand them out the first day. The syllabus tells you everything you need to know about your course—when to read chapters and materials, dates of exams and due dates for assignments, how your final grade is calculated, and more. Make use of it by calendaring key dates, spotting time crunches, and getting a sense of how much time you need to set aside to study. Keep it handy—or bookmark the online version—so you can refer to it throughout the term.

Also, consult your *student handbook* and *course catalog* for information about school procedures and policies—registration, requirements for majors, transferring, and so on. These publications are usually available both in hard copy and on your school's website.

Technology

You will be expected to connect to and use your college's network for a variety of purposes, including research and communication. How can you make the most of it?

- *Get started right away.* Register for an e-mail account and connect to the college network. In addition, register your cell phone number with the school so you can get emergency alerts.
- *Use the system.* Communicate with instructors and fellow students using e-mail. If you don't know how, find someone to show you.
- *Save and protect your work.* Save electronic work periodically onto a primary or backup hard drive, CD, or flash drive. Use antivirus software if your system needs it.
- *Stay on task.* During study time, try to limit Internet surfing, instant messaging, visiting Facebook or other social networking sites, and playing computer games.

It also pays to follow e-mail etiquette when communicating with instructors, rather than abbreviating with the same e-mail shorthand you would use with friends. Key 1.2 shows two versions of the same message. Which would an instructor find more appropriate?

Now that you've considered how to find helpful resources, think more broadly about how your thinking skills can set you up for success in your college experience and beyond.

Key 1.2 Appropriate E-Mail Format Gets Results

TO: ESantos@school.edu
FROM: Disastergirl@yahoo.com
SUBJECT: Need to meet

Hey FYI, I missed the last two class mtgs because I was sick so I'm behind. I need to meet with you ASAP to see if I can turn in my project next wk instead of tomorrow. Bye 4 now.

TO: ESantos@school.edu
FROM: Helen_Miller@school.edu
SUBJECT: Need to discuss change in project due date for ENG 115 (Tu/Th 11 am section)

Hello Dr. Santos,

I missed both class meetings last week due to illness. May I meet with you to discuss the possibility of submitting my project after tomorrow's deadline? Do you have any time available today after class or during your 4–5 pm office hours? Please let me know.

Thanks—

Helen Miller

What THINKING SKILLS CAN HELP YOU ACHIEVE YOUR GOALS?

How can you shift to college-level work successfully? The first step is to know that you have the ability to *grow* as a thinker. Research by prominent psychologists such as Robert Sternberg, Carol Dweck, and others suggests that intelligence is not fixed; people have the capacity to *increase* intelligence as they learn.[3] Recent brain research shows that when you are learning through questioning, answering, and action, your brain and nerve cells (neurons) are forming new connections (synapses) by growing new branches (dendrites).[4]

The second step is to understand, and use, the types of thinking that encourage that kind of growth and move you toward achieving your most important goals.

The Three Thinking Skills

Three types of thinking will help you to make information meaningful so that you learn it, retain it, and use it: *critical thinking, creative thinking,* and *practical thinking.*[5] The three thinking skills not only help you learn information more deeply, but also teach you about yourself, how you think and process information, and what you value.

Critical thinking starts by engaging with information through asking questions (Why is this important? Does it make sense? How can I define or explain it? What seems true about it—or not?) and then searching for answers to those questions by analyzing and evaluating information without bias. It often involves comparing, contrasting, and cause-and-effect thinking.

Creative thinking concerns generating new and different ideas and approaches to problems, and, often, viewing the world in ways that disregard convention. It often involves imagining and considering different perspectives. Creative thinking also means taking information that you already know and thinking about it in a new way.

Practical thinking means applying what you've learned. By putting what comes from critical and creative thinking into action to solve a problem or make a decision, you can work effectively with others and overcome obstacles. Practical thinking often involves learning from experience as well as emotional intelligence (see p. 10).

How Thinking Skills Move You Toward Your Goals

If you can train your brain to think critically, creatively, and practically, you will be more able to reach your goals in college and at work. Consider: If you sit in class just waiting for a lecture to end, you aren't likely to achieve any academic or learning goal. If you were to take a similar passive approach to a job, you probably wouldn't hold that job for long. You are investing time and money in this experience. Use your thinking power to work toward your goal for that investment—self-knowledge, information, and useful skills—and you will gain more from your classes and prepare more effectively for the workplace.

Consider the following example about a science concept:

• *Think critically.* After reading about the human respiratory system and hearing about it in class, you ask questions: What are the parts? Why is the system important? What role does each part play? Then you investigate your

notes and work with a study partner to understand each part and its relationship to the whole system, considering how the information relates to other anatomy or general science concepts that you already understand.

• *Think creatively.* To motivate yourself, you come up with ideas about what learning this information will help you achieve in this course, other courses, or maybe a major or career area. You broaden your brainstorming to life experiences—for example, you realize that this information could help you the next time you run three miles and your breathing gets ragged.

• *Think practically.* You apply what you've learned to study questions and assignments. When the next test comes, use your knowledge to complete it successfully. If your interest goes beyond this course, you can use your knowledge on the running track, in the anatomy and physiology course you plan to take next year, in a major in physiology, or in a career as a medical researcher.

Compare the results of using all three thinking skills to what a student focusing on recall might experience in the same situation. He memorizes the names of the parts of the respiratory system, completes assigned work, and when the test comes around, gets a C+. Ultimately, he passes the course but doesn't feel connected to the material and doesn't retain much of it. He doesn't even think about pursuing any major or job that requires the knowledge of anatomy.

What's the difference? Using the thinking skills available to you, not only do you have more chance of retaining the information, but you have also learned something about what you might want—or not want—to pursue as a major or career. The recall-focused student has closed the door on careers in biology or medicine. On a basic level, he has also missed out on the chance to understand himself and the world a little better.

Because thinking is a skill that you can develop as you can any other, all kinds of learners can use it to move toward personal goals, no matter what their "natural" abilities may be. Everyone can find room—and ways—to grow. The features in each chapter of this book will help in the following ways:

1. The chapter opening objectives questions and Quick Check self-assessment help you think about chapter material while building self-awareness and perhaps inspiring questions of your own.
2. The main part of each chapter is designed to engage your critical, creative,

Analyze the Effect of Education

"Of all the factors linked to a long and healthy life, education is the most beneficial."[6]

In a journal entry, analyze this statement by comparing education to other factors such as health care, marital status, good genes, satisfaction at work, and so on (for ideas, think about people you know who have lived long and well and what seems to have helped them). Explain whether you think the statement is accurate. Then apply it to your life. How do you think college will help you stay healthy while growing personally?

---

and practical thinking skills as you search for answers, make connections, relate information to what you already know or can imagine, and act on what you learn.

3. The Think Critically journal prompt in each chapter is an opportunity to apply critical thinking to current information and to your life.

4. The Think Creatively exercise in each chapter is designed to inspire brainstorming, shifting perspectives, or other creative thinking activities on a chapter-related topic, helping you to grow your ability to generate ideas.

5. The Think Practically exercise in each chapter gives you the chance to apply what you've learned to accomplish something specific and useful.

6. At the end of each chapter, the Analyze, Create, Practice exercise gives you a chance to put all your thinking skills together toward a goal.

Although thinking skills provide tools for achieving goals, you need motivation to put them to work and grow from your efforts. Explore a mindset that will motivate you.

How CAN A "GROWTH MINDSET" HELP YOU SUCCEED?

Although you cannot control what happens around you, you *can* control your attitude, or *mindset,* and the actions that come from that mindset. Based on years of research, Carol Dweck has determined that the perception that talent and intelligence can develop with effort—what she calls a *growth mindset—*promotes success. "This view creates a love of learning and resilience that is essential for great accomplishment," reports Dweck. People with a growth mindset "understand that no one has ever accomplished great things—not Mozart, Darwin, or Michael Jordan—without years of passionate practice and learning."[7]

By contrast, people with a *fixed mindset* believe that they have a set level of talent and intelligence. They think their ability to succeed matches what they've been born with, and they tend to resist effort. As Dweck reports, "In one world [that of the fixed mindset], effort is a bad thing. It . . . means you're not smart or talented. If you were, you wouldn't need effort. In the other world [growth mindset], effort is what *makes* you smart or talented."[8]

For example, two students do poorly on an anatomy midterm. One blames the time of day of the test and his dislike of the subject, whereas the other feels that he didn't study enough. The first student couldn't change the subject or meeting time, of course, and didn't change his approach to the material (no extra effort). As you may expect, he did poorly on the final. The second student put in more study time after the midterm (increased, focused effort) and improved his grade on the final as a result. This student knows that "smart is as smart does."

You don't have to be born with a growth mindset. *You can build one.* "You have a choice," says Dweck. "Mindsets are just beliefs. They're powerful beliefs, but they're just something in your mind, and you can change your mind."[9] One way to change your mind is through specific actions that demonstrate what you want to believe. Three such actions are being responsible, practicing academic integrity, and facing your fears.

Be Responsible

Taking responsible action produces results that help build self-esteem and support your belief that intelligence can grow. The more you develop a growth mindset, the more encouraged you will feel to put in effort and face challenges. Action and belief form an energizing cycle—the more you do, the more you believe you *can* do, which leads you to do more yet again.

Being a responsible student means taking the basic actions that form the building blocks of success (see Key 1.3). Consider this example: Two students start the term feeling pretty confident. One puts in the effort to get to class, keep up with assignments, and study regularly. The other does the minimum necessary to get by. Although they both pass, one student probably has far more of a growth mindset by the end of the term—plus a much greater command of a valuable set of skills and habits that will be useful throughout life.

Practice Academic Integrity

Choosing to act with *integrity*—by one definition, meaning that you are honest, trustworthy, fair, respectful, and responsible—increases your self-esteem and earns respect from those around you. It gives you more of a chance to retain what you learn and builds positive habits that you will have for life. In the current workplace, where high-level misconduct by major companies or individuals has

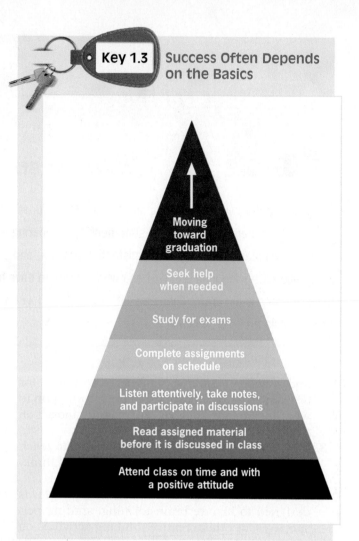

Key 1.3 Success Often Depends on the Basics

Moving toward graduation

Seek help when needed

Study for exams

Complete assignments on schedule

Listen attentively, take notes, and participate in discussions

Read assigned material before it is discussed in class

Attend class on time and with a positive attitude

think CREATIVELY

Imagine Your Potential

Imagine your vision of the ideal student. What does he do each day? What does she do each night to prepare for what's coming next? Ask what if . . . *you* were this student? With this image in your mind, come up with a do-able list of specific, personal actions for your own everyday academic success. Post it in a high-traffic location where you live, in your date book or electronic organizer, or on your computer where you will see it every day.

Key 1.4 Types of Cheating Common in College

- Exchanging text messages with key information or listening to information on an MP3 player during a test

- Paying to download a paper from an Internet site and turning it in as your own work

- Employing a service to write a paper for you—or writing one for someone else

- Studying from old tests unless the instructor provides them as study materials

- Copying lab notes for an experiment you did not perform

cost people, charities, and business billions of dollars, being honest and trustworthy has more value than ever.

Despite the benefits, the principles of *academic integrity* (acting with integrity in your dealings with information and people as a college student) are frequently violated (see Key 1.4). In a recent survey, three of four undergraduate students admitted to cheating at least once during college,[10] despite the risk of losing grade points, failing a course, or suspension or expulsion.

What does academic integrity have to do with a growth mindset? Well, first of all, being fair, honest, and responsible takes effort and choice. Second, and more important, academic integrity comes naturally to students who aim to grow and see struggle and failure as opportunities to learn. If you want to learn something, you know that cheating is likely to keep you from reaching your goal. In this sense, maintaining a growth mindset actually promotes academic integrity and makes the reasons for its worth that much more obvious.

Think carefully about your actions and their potential consequences. Read your school's code of honor or academic integrity policy in your student handbook or online—when you enrolled, you agreed to abide by it. And know that making an ethical choice is not only "the right thing" but also gives you more of what you came here for—skills and information you understand, own, and take with you into the world.

Face Your Fears

Anything unknown—starting college, meeting new people—can provoke fear. Facing fear with a growth mindset will allow you to proceed with courage as you reignite your motivation and learn. Following a step-by-step approach in a process can help you deal with your feelings.

1. *Acknowledge fears.* Naming your fear can begin to release its hold on you. "I'm worried about understanding a Shakespeare play I have to read."
2. *Examine fears.* Determine what exactly is causing your fear. Sometimes deeper fears emerge. "I feel that if I don't understand the play, I won't do well on the test and it will affect my GPA. That could cause trouble with my financial aid or my major."
3. *Develop and implement a plan.* Come up with ways to manage your fear, choose how to move forward, and put the plan into action. "I will rent a film of the play and watch it after I read. I will talk to my instructor about my concerns."

When you've put your plan into action, you've done what a growth mindset gives you the power to

The more you work and communicate with others, the more you will learn and develop teamwork skills.

© Mary Kate Denny/PhotoEdit

do—take action and learn from the experience. Then perhaps the next time you face a similar situation, your fear may not be as strong.

CAN YOU WORK EFFECTIVELY WITH OTHERS?

How

Your ability to interact with others is an essential skill for success in college, work, and life. What helps you study in a group will also help you achieve goals in a work team and in personal relationships. Understanding the concept of emotional intelligence will help you relate more effectively to others in all spheres of activity.

Emotional Intelligence

Success in a diverse world depends on relationships, and effective relationships demand *emotional intelligence*. Psychologists John Mayer, Peter Salovey, and David Caruso define emotional intelligence (EI) as the ability to understand "one's own and others' emotions and the ability to use this information as a guide to thinking and behavior."[11] Emotional intelligence helps you *understand* what you and others feel as a way to choose how to *think* and how to *act*.

You might think of emotional intelligence as *thinking skills applied to relationships*. Putting emotional intelligence to work means taking in and analyzing how you and others feel, creating new ways of thinking based on these feelings, and taking action in response—all with the purpose of achieving a goal in your interpersonal relations.

The Abilities of Emotional Intelligence

Emotional intelligence is a set of skills or abilities:[12]

PERCEIVING EMOTIONS
Recognizing how you and others feel.

UNDERSTANDING EMOTIONS
Determining what the emotions involved in a situation tell you, seeing how they affect your thinking and mindset, and considering how you can adjust your mindset or direct thinking in a productive way.

MANAGING EMOTIONS
Using what you learn from your emotions and those of others to choose behavior and actions that move you toward positive outcomes.

These skills allow you to create the best possible outcomes from your interactions with people. Given that you will interact with others in almost every aspect of school, work, and life, EI is a pretty important tool.

How Emotional Intelligence Promotes Success

Research has indicated the following benefits for emotional intelligence:[13]

- Emotionally intelligent people are more competent in social situations and have higher-quality relationships.
- Managers in the workplace with high EI have more productive working relationships and greater personal integrity.
- Employees scoring high in EI were more likely to receive positive ratings and raises.

As an example, consider two students who are part of a group you are working with on a project. One always gets her share of the job done but has no patience for anyone who can't match her pace. She picks up tasks she thinks won't get done and criticizes group members. The other is sometimes prepared, sometimes not, but always has a sense of what is going on with the group and responds to it. She works to make up for it when she hasn't gotten everything done, and when she is on top of her tasks she helps others. Which person would you want to work with again? The bottom line is that more emotional intelligence means stronger relationships and more goal achievement.

Strategies for Study Group Success

In addition to emotional intelligence, a study group's success depends on personalities, the subject you study, the size of the group, and its commitment. The following general strategies can help your team thrive.

- *Set long-term and short-term goals.* At your first meeting, determine what the group wants to accomplish. At the start of each meeting, assign one person to compile a list of questions to address.
- *Determine a regular schedule and leadership rotation.* Meeting at least once a week sets a good rhythm. Rotate the leadership among those willing to lead to encourage active involvement.
- *Create study materials that aid learning.* Have group members teach information, quiz each other, or work on flash card drills. Write sample tests and review with one another.
- *Pool class and text notes.* Compare notes with group members and fill in what you don't have.

PRACTICALLY

Connect College to Career

Teamwork is high on the list of what employers look for in job candidates. The following list shows its place in a ranking of desirable qualities for employees.

1. Communication skills (verbal, written)
2. Teamwork skills (working with others)
3. Strong work ethic
4. Analytical skills
5. Flexibility/adaptability
6. Interpersonal skills (relating to others)
7. Motivation/initiative
8. Computer skills
9. Attention to detail

10. Organizational skills
11. Leadership skills
12. Self-confidence
13. Good manners/politeness
14. Friendly/outgoing personality
15. Tactfulness
16. Creativity
17. GPA (3.0 or better)
18. Entrepreneurial skills/risk-taker

Choose two qualities or skills from the list that you will work to improve this term and circle them. Then name a specific action you will take to make changes in each area and select calendar dates to check your progress with each action.

	Qualities/Skills	Actions for Change	Progress Check Dates
1.	....	....	....
2.	....	....	....
	....	....	....

Source: NACE Research, *Job Outlook*, 2006, p. 18.

Finally, don't wait until crunch time to start studying with others. Begin now to exchange phone numbers and e-mails, form groups, and schedule meetings. This will not only benefit you in class now, but also later in the world of work where almost everything happens in teams.

How DOES COLLEGE PREPARE YOU FOR WORK AND LIFE SUCCESS?

You are living in a time of rapid and major change. On a world level, technology, global communication, environmental concerns, and the shifting economy are some key factors that shape your college and work experience. Leading education and business researchers with the Partnership for 21st Century Skills have developed core competencies for success in college, work, and life, which have been organized into four specific areas as shown in Key 1.5.

Looking at this framework, you will see that success in today's workplace requires more than just knowing skills specific to an academic area or job. Your college experience, starting with this course and this book, is designed to build skills in all four areas—skills that will help you achieve your most

Core Areas

Global awareness

Financial, economic, business, and entrepreneurial literacy

Civic literacy—community service

Health literacy

Information, Media, and Technology Skills

Information literacy

Media literacy

Technology skills

Learning and Innovation Skills

Creativity and innovation

Critical thinking and problem solving

Communication and collaboration

Life and Career Skills

Flexibility and adaptability

Initiative and self-direction

Social and cross-cultural skills

Productivity and accountability

Leadership and responsibility

Source: The Partnership for 21st Century Skills, Framework for 21st Century Learning, www.21stcenturyskills.org.

important goals while delivering what the world needs workers to do.

Imagine that you are sitting in class with your *growth mindset,* open to learning. You are ready to use *critical* and *creative* skills to examine the knowledge you take in and come up with new ideas. You are motivated to use your *practical* skills to move toward your goals. Your *emotional intelligence* has prepared you to adjust to and work with all kinds of people. You're ready to grow. Use *Keys to Success Quick* to make it happen.

quick! SKILL BUILDING

Think Back

Solidify your knowledge and prepare for tests with this review. Answer the following questions on a separate sheet of paper or electronic file.

▶ Revisit the chapter-opening questions. Scan the chapter and write a short answer for each.

▶ Go back to the Quick Check self-assessment. From the list, choose one item that you want to develop further. Set a specific goal based on what you have read in the chapter. Describe your goal and plan in a short paragraph, including a time frame and specific steps.

Analyze, Create, Practice

Assess and Build Motivation

Active thinkers share some characteristics that keep them moving toward their most important goals.[14] The self-assessment below will help you measure your level of motivation.

Analyze. How well do I get, and stay, motivated? Take this self-assessment to explore your beliefs and experiences.

	1 Not at All Like Me	2 Somewhat Unlike Me	3 Not Sure	4 Somewhat Like Me	5 Definitely Like Me
Please highlight or circle the number that best represents your answer:					
1. I am able to translate ideas into action.	1	2	3	4	5
2. I am able to maintain confidence in myself.	1	2	3	4	5
3. I can stay on track toward a goal.	1	2	3	4	5
4. I complete tasks and have good follow-through.	1	2	3	4	5
5. I avoid procrastination.	1	2	3	4	5
6. I accept responsibility when I make a mistake.	1	2	3	4	5
7. I independently take responsibility for tasks.	1	2	3	4	5
8. I work hard to overcome personal difficulties.	1	2	3	4	5
9. I create an environment that helps me to concentrate on my goals.	1	2	3	4	5
10. I can delay gratification to receive the benefits.	1	2	3	4	5

Create. Choose one item that you rated a 5. Brainstorm a list showing how you demonstrate motivation in this area. Then choose an item that you rated a 1 or 2. Brainstorm a list of ideas about how you might improve in this area.

Practice. For the item that you rated a 5, write down on paper or electronically a brief description of past activities that demonstrate your motivation in this area. Include a work sample (if you have one) and a personal reference who can confirm some of your abilities, skills, or accomplishments. For the item that you rated a 1 or 2, write down a specific plan aimed at developing this quality by the end of the term. Include specific actions you plan to take and the dates by which you intend to complete each action.

chapter

2

Success in your academic pursuits and future career involves understanding your goals and placing them in time. This chapter will encourage you to explore your most important short-term and long-term goals, how you plan to achieve them, and how to schedule and manage your time.

In this chapter, you'll explore answers to the following questions:

How do goals help you strive for success?

p. 15

How can you create and achieve realistic goals?

p. 17

How can you effectively manage your time?

p. 19

Goals and Time

Planning Your Future and Your Time Wisely

How Developed Are Your Self-Management Skills?

For each statement, circle the number that best describes how true the statement is for you, from 1 for "not at all true for me" to 5 for "very true for me."

▶ Periodically, I take time to think through academic and personal goals.   1 2 3 4 5

▶ I read each syllabus carefully to understand the course goals.   1 2 3 4 5

▶ I have a system for reminding myself of what my goals are.   1 2 3 4 5

▶ I find ways to motivate myself when I am working toward a goal.   1 2 3 4 5

▶ When I set a long-term goal, I break it down into a series of short-term goals.   1 2 3 4 5

▶ I've been looking into majors that might appeal to me.   1 2 3 4 5

▶ I know myself as a time manager and which strategies work best for me.   1 2 3 4 5

▶ I record my tasks, events, and responsibilities and refer regularly to my notes.   1 2 3 4 5

▶ When I procrastinate, I know how to get back on track.   1 2 3 4 5

▶ I set priorities, making sure I focus first on which is most important every day.   1 2 3 4 5

If your total ranges from 41–50, you consider your goal-setting and time management skills to be well developed.
If your total ranges from 24–40, you consider your goal-setting and time management skills to be somewhat developed.
If your total is less than 24, you consider your goal-setting and time management skills to be underdeveloped.

Now total your scores.

REMEMBER No matter how developed your goal-setting and time management skills, you can improve them with effort. Read the chapter to learn new ways to build these skills, and practice by doing the activities.

How DO GOALS HELP YOU STRIVE FOR SUCCESS?

There's an old saying: "How do you know when you've arrived if you don't know where you're going?" Goal setting is all about determining your destination throughout the days, weeks, months, and years of your life. In fact, you probably set goals all the time and don't even know it. For example, you may not say, "My goal is to get up by 7:00 A.M. tomorrow," but if you set your alarm clock for that time, you've set a goal.

The Definition of a Goal

A *goal* is a dream with a deadline; it is a result you want to achieve. Goals are choices you make about what you want in various areas of your life, as in the following examples.

- *Fitness.* Improve eating habits; run 2 miles every other day
- *School.* Decide on a major by June; get an A in chemistry
- *Finances.* Save up enough money to buy a car

Long-Term Goals

Long-term goals are objectives that sit out on the horizon, at least 6 months to a year away. They're goals that you can imagine and maybe even visualize, but they're too far out for you to touch. These ambitions reflect who you are and what is important to you. The more you know about yourself, the better able you are to set and work toward meaningful long-term goals, as in the following list by a student who loves reading books and enjoys writing:

1. Declare my major in writing and literature by the end of the year
2. Intern with a publisher my junior year
3. Get a bachelor's degree in writing and literature in 4 years
4. Get a master's of fine arts in creative writing in 5 years
5. Find an editing job with a publisher

Most long-term goals are far more achievable if you break them into smaller chunks, which then become short-term goals.

Short-Term Goals

A *short-term goal* is a step that moves you closer to a long-term goal, making your long-range pursuit seem clearer and easier to reach. A short-term goal may last only a few hours or days, or it may take weeks or even months.

For example, suppose you have a long-term goal of graduating and becoming a nurse. You may decide to set the following short-term goal, with three supplemental short-term goals:

1. Meet with a study group 3 hours a week to better understand the skeletal and muscular system
   - *By the end of today:* Call study partners and find out when they can meet
   - *1 week from today:* Schedule each weekly meeting for the month
   - *2 weeks from today:* Hold the first meeting

Notice in Key 2.1 how long-term and short-term goals are linked to one another.

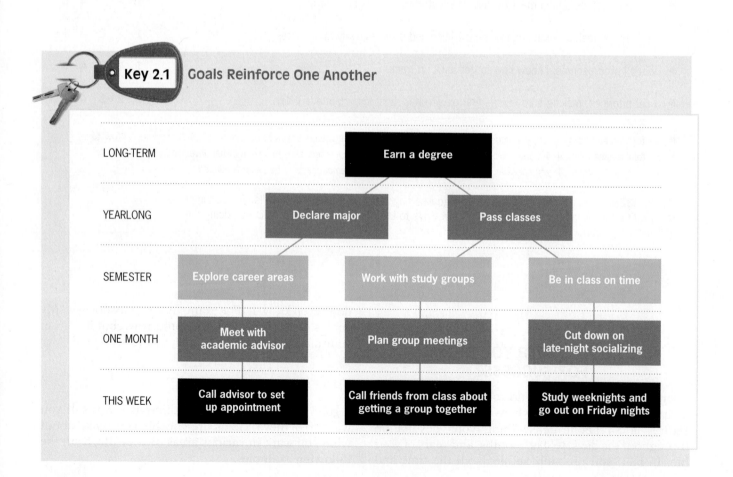

Key 2.1   **Goals Reinforce One Another**

LONG-TERM		Earn a degree	
YEARLONG	Declare major		Pass classes
SEMESTER	Explore career areas	Work with study groups	Be in class on time
ONE MONTH	Meet with academic advisor	Plan group meetings	Cut down on late-night socializing
THIS WEEK	Call advisor to set up appointment	Call friends from class about getting a group together	Study weeknights and go out on Friday nights

Goals take effort and planning to reach. This music producer spends days, and even weeks, adjusting equipment and recording tracks on the way to the production of just one song.

© UpperCut Images/Getty Images

How CAN YOU CREATE AND ACHIEVE REALISTIC GOALS?

How many goals have you thought about, and even jotted down, that you never reached? To help you set and reach goals successfully, focus on setting *effective* goals by following two basic steps:

1. Get to know yourself
2. Set SMART goals

Now let's look at each step in detail, using the example of thinking about your major.

Get to Know Yourself

How well do you know yourself? Getting in touch with yourself might mean thinking back to when you were a child and asking yourself some questions:

What was I interested in? What did I like to do? What was I good at? Those interests and talents are still inside you, even if you have to dig a little deeper to find them. They may lend themselves to something bigger now that you're older. You may even choose to make them into a major and later a career.

Looking into majors is one useful way to get to know yourself better. Choosing or changing a major or academic emphasis is an important goal—and an achievable one. (For the sake of simplicity, this text will use the term *major* to refer to any kind of academic emphasis, whether for a bachelor's, associate's, or technical degree.) Throughout this section, you will see how to apply goal-setting techniques for picking a major or readjusting your academic focus to include a new major.

When you set about declaring or changing a major, consider the fact that success in school and the workplace is more likely when you're doing something you're interested in and using your innate talents. When you study subjects that interest you, you're more likely to have a positive attitude and perform at your highest level.

To pinpoint the areas that spark your interest, think about the following questions:

- What are my favorite courses? What do these courses have in common?
- What subjects do I like to read about?
- What activities do I look forward to?
- What interests me?
- Am I a "natural" in any academic or skill area?
- What do others say I do well?

Set SMART Goals

Setting goals doesn't mean you'll achieve them. If you set "SMART" goals, however, you'll be more likely to succeed. SMART is an acronym for a five-part process that makes your goals more concrete and improves your chances of achieving them.

Specific. Make sure your goal includes as many details as possible to make it concrete. Focus on behaviors and events that are under your control and map out specific steps that will get you there.

Measurable. Define your goal in a way that lets you measure it and create a way to evaluate your progress. This could mean keeping a journal, an alarm system on your phone or computer, or reporting to a friend. Don't leave progress up to chance.

Achievable. To see if you have what it takes to achieve the goal, first determine whether it aligns with your hopes, interests, abilities, and values. Then reflect on whether you have the skills or resources needed to make it happen. If you're missing something, plan out how to get it.

R **ealistic.** Make sure you define the goal in a way that makes it realistic to you. Create specific deadlines that will help you stay on track without making you feel rushed. If the challenge or risk is too great and the timeline too short, you'll probably fail.

T **ime Frame Linked.** All goals need a time frame so you have something to work toward. If a goal is "a dream with a deadline," then without the deadline, your goal is only a dream.

The following example shows a rather vague goal, followed by a more concrete SMART goal:

Original goal: I will choose a major.

This goal leaves a lot of unanswered questions. When are you going to do this? How will you do it? Why are you doing it? The following SMART goal answers the questions raised by the vague goal.

SMART goal: I will choose and declare a major this term by speaking with an academic advisor, consulting with students in the major, and researching possible career paths from it. This will help me make an educated decision about the direction of my academic path.

The difference between these goals lies in the details of the second goal, based on the SMART process:

S **pecific.** By saying that you will "choose and declare a major" you are defining the nature of this task.

M **easurable.** By adding the "and declare" to the goal, you provide a way to measure the completion of it.

A **chievable.** Including other resources you might look into like academic advisors and research illustrates what obstacles you might encounter and provides a way to move past them.

R **ealistic.** The reasoning for choosing the goal in the last sentence serves two purposes: to solidify the goal as an attainable action and to reinforce the benefits associated with completing the task.

T **ime Frame Linked.** You have set from now through the end of the term as your time frame.

Work Toward Goals

Now that you have a sense of how to set goals, it's time to focus on how to *reach* them. To do so, follow the basic steps in Key 2.2.

think
CREATIVELY

Imagine Achieving a Goal

Create a "backward" path connecting to an important goal:

1. Name one important personal goal for this year, using the SMART goals guidelines (Specific–Measurable–Achievable–Realistic–Time Frame Linked).

2. Imagine that you have already achieved your goal. Describe how you feel and how your life is different.

3. Imagine that a friend asks you to describe how you accomplished the goal. List at least three short-term goals that helped get you to the finish line.

You have just created a potential action plan. Consider putting the plan to work in the next year. When you do, let the image of the success you will create motivate and inspire you.

- *Commit to the goal.* You need to believe 100 percent in the goal and feel a sense of energy and enthusiasm around it. Your commitment becomes the engine that drives you when times get tough.

- *Identify your resources.* When you commit to a goal, take stock of where you are today so you can identify resources for moving forward, such as books, instructors, advisors, teachers, or other students.

- *Build your support team.* Find people who can both help you *and* hold you accountable. Share your goal with them so it becomes more concrete. However, make sure you share your goal with supportive people who will not judge you harshly if progress is erratic or slow.

- *Make an action plan.* How do you plan to reach your goal? Brainstorm with your support team about ways to get to the finish line. A common way to create an action plan is to break up the goal into subgoals or milestones and then map out the steps to achieve each milestone.

- *Identify deadlines and establish a timeline.* If you've created a SMART goal, you've established an end date for accomplishing your goal. Now, work backward from that date and create a realistic timeline that includes specific milestones and the steps to achieve them.

- *Track your progress and be accountable.* Set aside time to review how you're doing. Make adjustments to your plan if you need to.

- *Celebrate!* It's important to recognize your progress and accomplishments—you might even choose to reward yourself when you've achieved your goal.

Of course, things don't always go as planned. Obstacles will almost always pop up along the way. Although you can't often control the roadblocks that stop you in your tracks, you *can* control your response when you encounter them. What can you do if you get stuck on the way?

- Continue to remind yourself of the benefits of your goal.
- Discuss your challenges with someone who can offer support or help. Don't invite negative feedback from people who will drag you down.
- Replace your inner critic with your inner cheerleader. This means replacing negative thoughts with positive self-talk every day.

How CAN YOU EFFECTIVELY MANAGE YOUR TIME?

No matter how well you define your goals and develop your action plans, you still have to deal with time. You only have 24 hours in a day, and 8 or so of those hours involve sleeping (or should, if you want to remain healthy and alert enough to achieve your goals).

Although the idea of "managing time" may seem impossible, think of it instead as *behavioral management*—adjusting what you do to meet your needs in the time you have available. You can't manage how time passes, but you *can* manage how you use it. Time management is key to feeling in control of your situation. The first step in time management is to figure out your time profile and preferences.

Identify Your Time Profile and Preferences

People have unique body rhythms and habits that affect how they deal with time. Some people are night owls who have lots of energy late at night. Others are early birds who do their best work early in the day. Some people are chronically late, whereas others get everything done with time to spare.

The more you're aware of your own time-related behaviors, the better able you'll be to create a schedule that maximizes your strengths and reduces stress. The following steps can help you get in touch with your own inner time clock:

- *Consider your personal time profile.* A personal time profile is an individualized schedule created to best fit your natural rhythm. It can help you schedule your time in a way that takes advantage of your

think
CRITICALLY

Analyze Distractions

According to Dr. John Medina, director of the Brain Center for Applied Learning Research, people who are interrupted take 50 percent longer to complete a task and make 50 percent more errors.[1] How do you deal with distractions? In a journal entry, briefly describe and evaluate two or three main ways you handle disruptions. For each, consider how successful the technique is and how you could improve (or change) it to maximize your future success.

peak energy levels throughout the day. For example, consider the following time profile:

- I go to bed late and get up late. I feel tired in the morning and don't get going until 10:00 A.M. I have lots energy in the late afternoon and early evening.
- I like to work on one thing for a while until I'm tired of it and then work on something else. I don't like to have too many things to do or I get overwhelmed.

Managing time effectively often means taking advantage of opportunities whenever they arise. This student, also a mother, fits schoolwork in during naptime.

© **Universal Images Group/SuperStock**

- *Establish the schedule preferences that match your profile.* Based on the time profile you develop, list your preferences—or map out an ideal schedule as a way of illustrating them, as in the following:

  - Mondays, Wednesdays, and Fridays: Afternoon classes bunched together
  - Tuesdays and Thursdays: Free for studying, research, or other activities

Next, build a schedule that takes this information into account as much as possible. Do your best to maximize your strengths and compensate for your weaker time management areas.

Use Schedules and Planners

Goals and tasks don't get done on their own; you have to think about when you want to accomplish them. That's where schedules come in. Schedules provide some structure so you feel more in control of events life throws at you. They accomplish this by performing two important duties:

1. Reminding you of tasks, events, due dates, responsibilities, and deadlines
2. Mapping out segments of time for working on goal-related tasks

Planners will help you manage and use your time to its fullest potential. Time management expert Paul Timm says that "rule number one in a thoughtful planning process is: Use some form of a planner where you can write things down."[2] Paperback and hardbound planners, which can be found at office supply stores, are useful for hands-on and visual learners. Technology tools such as smart phones allow you to keep your schedule with you at all times. However, remember that electronics fail occasionally due to software or battery problems. Be sure to print or back up your schedules on a regular basis as a safeguard.

The first step in creating a schedule is to identify all known events and commitments that affect you, including the following:

- Test and quiz dates
- Due dates for papers, projects, and presentations
- School breaks
- Club, organizational, and personal meetings

Remember that it's important to include class prep time in your planner. This includes reading, studying, writing, and working on assignments and projects. According to one formula, you should schedule at least 2 hours of preparation time for every hour of class. For example, if you take 12 credits, you should spend 24 hours or more a week on course-related activities outside of class.

Once you have your schedule established, *use it*. Review and update it regularly so that you know where to be when and what to work on. Key 2.3 shows parts of both a daily and a weekly schedule.

Make To-Do Lists and Prioritize

Many people find it useful to create a daily or weekly *to-do list* and check off the items as they are completed. A to-do list can be useful on an especially busy

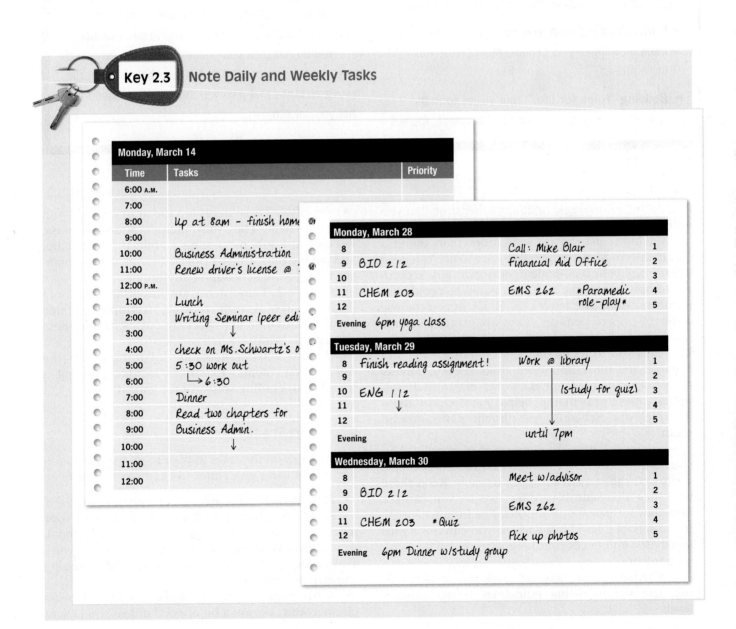

Key 2.3 Note Daily and Weekly Tasks

Monday, March 14

Time	Tasks	Priority
6:00 A.M.		
7:00		
8:00	Up at 8am - finish home or	
9:00		
10:00	Business Administration	
11:00	Renew driver's license @	
12:00 P.M.		
1:00	Lunch	
2:00	Writing Seminar (peer edi	
3:00	↓	
4:00	check on Ms. Schwartz's o	
5:00	5:30 work out	
6:00	↳ 6:30	
7:00	Dinner	
8:00	Read two chapters for	
9:00	Business Admin.	
10:00	↓	
11:00		
12:00		

Monday, March 28

8		Call: Mike Blair	1
9	BIO 212	Financial Aid Office	2
10			3
11	CHEM 203	EMS 262 *Paramedic	4
12		role-play*	5
Evening	6pm yoga class		

Tuesday, March 29

8	finish reading assignment!	Work @ library	1
9			2
10	ENG 112	(study for quiz)	3
11	↓		4
12			5
Evening		until 7pm	

Wednesday, March 30

8		Meet w/advisor	1
9	BIO 212		2
10		EMS 262	3
11	CHEM 203 *Quiz		4
12		Pick up photos	5
Evening	6pm Dinner w/study group		

You choose what to do, what to believe, what to buy, how to act, and more based on your personal *values*—principles or qualities that you consider important. Your choice to pursue a degree, for example, reflects that you value the personal and professional growth that come from a college education. Being on time for your classes shows that you value punctuality. Paying bills regularly and on time shows that you value financial stability.

Values play a key role in your drive to achieve important goals, helping you in the following ways:

▶ **Understanding what you want out of life.** Your most meaningful goals should reflect what you value most.

▶ **Building "rules for life."** Your values form the foundation for your decisions and behavior. You will return repeatedly to them to help you decide what you want to achieve.

Because what you value often determines the choices you make, it also shapes how you spend your time. Ideally, you should spend on the bulk of your time on what you value most. For example, valuing a solid education might lead a student to schedule adequate study time; valuing family might lead a parent to make sure that school and work don't crowd out time with the children. Once you look carefully at how you actually spend your time over a weeklong period, examine the results carefully to see whether what you do matches your values. If you are surprised to see that reality doesn't match your beliefs, consider making changes that give you more time to spend on what you value most.

day, during exam week, or at any other time that you anticipate being overloaded.

Making a list, however, is more than doing a "brain dump" of everything you have to do. You need to *prioritize* your list—code it, or organize it, according to how important each item is. Some people use numbers, some use letters (A, B, C), and some use different-colored pens or, if they are using electronic planners, highlighting and font color tools. Prioritizing helps you to focus the bulk of your energy and time on the most important tasks. Because many top-priority items (classes, work) occur at designated times, prioritizing helps you lock in these activities and schedule less urgent items around them.

Prioritizing isn't just for time management. You should also prioritize your long-term and short-term goals and the steps leading up to each. Keep these priorities alongside your daily lists so you can see how they influence one another. For instance, arriving at school a half hour early so you can meet with an advisor influences your long-term goal of deciding on a major.

Whether it's a task or goal you're scheduling, use the following guidelines to set priority levels.

- *Priority 1.* These items are the most crucial—you must do them. They may include attending class, working at a job, picking up a child from day care, and paying bills. Enter Priority 1 items in your planner first, before scheduling anything else.
- *Priority 2.* These items are important but more flexible parts of your routine. Examples include library study time and working out. Schedule these around the Priority 1 items.
- *Priority 3.* These items are least important—the "nice to do" items. Examples include phoning a friend or upgrading software for your iPod.

Plan and Track

As you work on the tasks in your to-do lists and planner, follow these guidelines to keep you focused:

- *Plan regularly.* Set aside a regular time each day to plan your schedule (right before bed, with your morning coffee, on your commute to or from school, or whatever time and situation works best for you). This reduces stress and saves the hassle of forgetting something important.
- *Actively manage your schedule.* The most detailed planner won't do you a bit of good unless you look at

it. Check your schedule at regular intervals throughout the day or week.

• *Use monthly and yearly calendars at home.* A standard monthly or yearly wall calendar is a great place to keep track of your major commitments. A wall calendar such as the monthly calendar in Key 2.4 gives you the "big picture" overview you need.

• *Try not to put off tasks.* If you can get a task done ahead of time, get it done. You'll feel less pressure later.

• *Avoid time traps.* Stay away from situations that eat up time. Learn to say no when you just don't have time for an extra responsibility. Curb use of anything that distracts you from your task such as your cell phone, social networking site, or Twitter account.

• *Check things off.* Each time you complete a task, check it off your to-do list, delete it from your electronic scheduler, or crumple up the Post-it note where you wrote it. This physical action promotes the feeling of confidence that comes from getting something done.

• *Schedule downtime.* It's easy to get so caught up in completing tasks that you forget to relax and breathe. Even a half hour of downtime a day will refresh you and improve your productivity when you get back on task.

• *Don't forget to put sleep into your schedule.* Sleep-deprived bodies and minds have a hard time functioning, and research reports that one-quarter of all college students are chronically sleep-deprived.[3] Figure out how much sleep you need and do your best to get it. With time for relaxation, your mind is better able to manage stress, and your schoolwork is likely to improve.

Key 2.4   **Keep Track of Your Time with a Monthly Calendar**

MARCH

SUNDAY	MONDAY	TUESDAY	WEDNESDAY	THURSDAY	FRIDAY	SATURDAY
	1	2 Turn in English paper topic WORK	3 Dentist 2pm	4	5 WORK	6
7 Frank's birthday	8 Psych Test 9am WORK	9	10 6:30 pm Meeting @ Acad. Ctr	11	12 WORK	13 Dinner @ Ryan's
14	15 English paper due WORK	16 Western Civ paper	17	18 Library 6 pm	19 Western Civ makeup class WORK	20
21	22 WORK	23 2 pm meeting, psych group	24 Start running: 2 miles	25	26 WORK Run 2 miles	27
28 Run 3 miles	29 WORK	30 Western Civ paper due	31 Run 2 miles			

Define Yourself as a Time Manager

Answer the following questions about your time preferences:

1. When do you have the most energy during the day? The least energy?

....
....
....

2. Do you tend to be early, on time, or late for appointments?

....
....
....

3. Do you focus well for long stretches or need more frequent breaks?

....
....
....

4. Do you like to work on one thing at a time or switch back and forth between tasks?

....
....
....

5. Do you like to study every day between classes? On specific days? Whenever you feel like it?

....
....
....

Based on what you've described, name one change you can make that would better suit your time management style.

....
....
....
....

Put it into practice and see whether it makes a difference.

Confront Procrastination

Even the most motivated person occasionally puts things off. It's only human to leave difficult or undesirable tasks until later. However, if taken to the extreme, *procrastination*—the act of putting off a task until another time—can develop into a habit that causes serious problems. For example, procrastinators who don't get things done in the workplace may prevent others from doing their work—and may lose a promotion or even be terminated because of it.

According to procrastination experts Jane B. Burka and Lenora M. Yuen, some people procrastinate in order to avoid the truth about what they can achieve. "As long as you procrastinate, you never have to confront the real limits of your ability, whatever those limits are."[4] A fixed mindset naturally leads to procrastination; "I can't do it," the person with the fixed mindset thinks, "so what's the point of trying?"

Here are some helpful strategies to avoid procrastination and its associated problems:

- *Analyze the effects.* What may happen if you continue to put off a task? Chances are you will benefit more in the long term facing the task head-on.
- *Set reasonable goals.* Unreasonable goals intimidate and immobilize you. If you concentrate on achieving one small step at a time, the task becomes less burdensome.
- *Get started whether you "feel like it" or not.* The motivation techniques from Chapter 1 might help you take the first step. Once you start, you may find it easier to continue.
- *Ask for help.* Once you identify what's holding you up, find someone to help you face the task. Another person may come up with an innovative method to get you moving again.
- *Don't expect perfection.* People learn by starting at the beginning, making mistakes, and learning from them. If you avoid mistakes, you deprive yourself of learning and growth.
- *Reward yourself.* Boost your confidence when you accomplish a task. Celebrate progress with a reward—a break, a movie, whatever feels like a treat to you.

Working toward goals and managing time are lifelong tasks. Your ability to successfully perform these tasks rises and falls according to your circumstances. Remember that you are not in this alone. When you seek help from the resources your college provides, especially the people who are in place to support your progress, you give yourself the best chance for success.

quick! SKILL BUILDING

Think Back

Solidify your knowledge and prepare for tests with this review. Answer the following questions on a separate sheet of paper or electronic file.

▶ Revisit the chapter-opening questions on page 14. Scan the chapter and write a short answer for each.

▶ Create an outline or think link (mind map, visual organizer) of what you consider the top ten time management strategies found in this chapter.

Analyze, Create, Practice

Discover How You Spend Your Time

Analyze. Take the first step in critical thinking—gathering information—by spending a week recording exactly how you spend your time. Before you begin, however, make a written estimate of how much time you spend per week on the following activities: studying, sleeping, and interacting with media and technology for nonschool purposes. Then put your estimate aside and turn to the chart on pages 26 and 27, which is divided into blocks showing half-hour increments. As you go through the week, write in what you do each hour, indicating when you started and when you stopped. Don't forget activities that don't involve much "activity," such as sleeping, relaxing, and watching TV. Finally, be sure to record your actual activities instead of how you *wish* you had, or think you *should* have, spent your time. There are no wrong answers.

TIME	Monday activity	Tuesday activity	Wednesday activity	Thursday activity
6:00 A.M.				
6:30 A.M.				
7:00 A.M.				
7:30 A.M.				
8:00 A.M.				
8:30 A.M.				
9:00 A.M.				
9:30 A.M.				
10:00 A.M.				
10:30 A.M.				
11:00 A.M.				
11:30 A.M.				
12:00 P.M.				
12:30 P.M.				
1:00 P.M.				
1:30 P.M.				
2:00 P.M.				
2:30 P.M.				
3:00 P.M.				
3:30 P.M.				
4:00 P.M.				
4:30 P.M.				
5:00 P.M.				
5:30 P.M.				
6:00 P.M.				
6:30 P.M.				
7:00 P.M.				
7:30 P.M.				
8:00 P.M.				
8:30 P.M.				
9:00 P.M.				
9:30 P.M.				
10:00 P.M.				
10:30 P.M.				
11:00 P.M.				
11:30 P.M.				
12:00 A.M.				
12:30 A.M.				
1:00 A.M.				
1:30 A.M.				
2:00 A.M.				

TIME	Friday activity	Saturday activity	Sunday activity
6:00 A.M.			
6:30 A.M.			
7:00 A.M.			
7:30 A.M.			
8:00 A.M.			
8:30 A.M.			
9:00 A.M.			
9:30 A.M.			
10:00 A.M.			
10:30 A.M.			
11:00 A.M.			
11:30 A.M.			
12:00 P.M.			
12:30 P.M.			
1:00 P.M.			
1:30 P.M.			
2:00 P.M.			
2:30 P.M.			
3:00 P.M.			
3:30 P.M.			
4:00 P.M.			
4:30 P.M.			
5:00 P.M.			
5:30 P.M.			
6:00 P.M.			
6:30 P.M.			
7:00 P.M.			
7:30 P.M.			
8:00 P.M.			
8:30 P.M.			
9:00 P.M.			
9:30 P.M.			
10:00 P.M.			
10:30 P.M.			
11:00 P.M.			
11:30 P.M.			
12:00 A.M.			
12:30 A.M.			
1:00 A.M.			
1:30 A.M.			
2:00 A.M.			

After a week, go through the chart and add up how many hours you spent on the various activities rounded off to the nearest half hour. List the activities as shown in the first column of the table below. Tally the times in the second column of the table, using straight tally marks for hours and a short tally mark for any additional half hour. In the third column, total the hours for each activity. Leave the "Ideal Time in Hours" column blank for now.

Activity	Time Tallied Over One-Week Period	Total Time in Hours	Ideal Time in Hours
Example: Class	ͰͰͰ ͰͰͰ ͰͰͰ ǁ	*16.5*	
Class			
Work			
Studying			
Sleeping			
Eating			
Family time/child care			
Commuting/traveling			
Chores and personal business			
Friends and important relationships			
Telephone time			
Leisure/entertainment			
Spiritual life			
Other			

Add the totals in the third column to find your grand total. At this point, take your previously written estimate and compare your grand total to your estimated grand total; compare your actual activity hour totals to your estimated activity hour totals. Use a separate sheet of paper to answer the following questions:

- What matches and what doesn't? Describe the most interesting similarities and differences.
- Where do you waste the most time? What do you think that is costing you?

Now evaluate what kinds of changes might improve your ability to achieve goals. Analyze what you do daily, weekly, and monthly. Ask yourself the following questions:

- On what activities do you think you should spend more or less time?
- What are you willing to change, and why do you think that change will make a difference?

Create. Go back to the table and indicate how you *want* to spend your time by filling in the "Ideal Time in Hours" column. Looking at the difference between actual hours and ideal hours, come up with three changes you can make to move closer to your ideal. Describe what goals you are aiming for, and map out how you plan to put the changes into action.

Practice. Put your three ideas into action over the next week. You might consider writing them in your planner for quick access if needed. At the end of the week, answer the following questions:

- Which solution worked best for you? Why?
- Which solution wasn't as successful? Why?
- If one or more solutions didn't work, come up with some replacement techniques for them. Write them down or put them into your planner.
- What did you learn about yourself from this activity?
- If another student were to ask you for time management advice, what strategies would you share after doing this activity?

Learning How You Learn

Making the Most of Your Abilities

No one is good at everything, and no one likes every course, instructor, classmate, or co-worker. In this chapter, you will first get to know yourself better as a learner, and then build your ability to adjust to environments and people, whether they suit your strengths or present new challenges to you.

In this chapter, you'll explore answers to the following questions:

Why explore who you are as a learner?

p. 30

What tools can help you assess how you learn and interact with others?

p. 31

How can you use your self-knowledge?

p. 37

How Aware Are You of How You Learn?

For each statement, circle the number that best describes how true the statement is for you, from 1 for "not at all true for me" to 5 for "very true for me."

▶ I believe I can develop my skills and abilities through self-knowledge and hard work. 1 2 3 4 5

▶ I have a pretty clear idea of my strengths and abilities. 1 2 3 4 5

▶ I understand which subjects and situations make it more difficult for me to succeed. 1 2 3 4 5

▶ In my work in the classroom and out, I try to maximize what I do well. 1 2 3 4 5

▶ I recognize that being comfortable with the subject matter isn't necessarily enough to succeed in a particular course. 1 2 3 4 5

▶ I recognize that it's better to have people with different strengths working together to accomplish goals. 1 2 3 4 5

▶ I assess an instructor's teaching style and make adjustments so that I can learn effectively. 1 2 3 4 5

▶ I choose study techniques that tap into how I learn best. 1 2 3 4 5

▶ I try to use technology that works well with how I learn. 1 2 3 4 5

▶ I've taken a skills and/or interests inventory to help find a major or career area that suits me. 1 2 3 4 5

If your total ranges from 41–50, you consider your awareness of how you learn to be fairly well developed.
If your total ranges from 24–40, you consider your awareness of how you learn to be somewhat developed.
If your total is less than 24, you consider your awareness of how you learn to be underdeveloped.

Now total your scores.

REMEMBER No matter how well you know yourself as a learner, you can improve with effort. Read the chapter to learn new ways to build self-knowledge, and practice by doing the activities.

Why EXPLORE WHO YOU ARE AS A LEARNER?

Have you thought about how you learn? Now, as you begin college, is the perfect time for thinking about how you learn, think, and function in the world. Thinking about thinking is known as *metacognition* (something you are building with each chapter-opening self-assessment). Building metacognition and self-knowledge will help you become a better stu-

dent and decision maker because the more you know about yourself, the more effectively you can analyze courses, study environments, and study partners. Self-knowledge can also help you come up with ideas about your academic path as well as make practical choices about what, how, and where to study.

As you discover more about how you learn, keep in mind your growth mindset. Picture a bag of rubber bands of different sizes: Some are thick, some are thin; some are long, some are short—*but all of them can stretch.* A small rubber band, stretched out, can reach the length of a larger one that lies unstretched. With work, you can grow, to some extent, whatever raw material you have at the start.

Use Assessments to Learn About Yourself

Ask yourself: Who am I right now? Where could I be, and where would I like to be, in 5 years? Assessments focused on how you learn and interact with others can help you start to answer these big questions. Assessments have a different goal than tests. A test seeks to identify a level of performance, whereas an assessment gives you feedback about potential skills, abilities, traits, or interests.

The assessments you will take in this chapter provide questions that get you thinking actively about your strengths and weaknesses. As you search for answers, you are gathering important information about yourself. The material presented after the assessments will then help you think practically about how to maximize what you do well as well as how to compensate for challenging areas. Understanding yourself as a learner will also help you appreciate how people differ, allowing you to use what you know about learning differences to improve communication and teamwork.

Assess to Grow, Not to Label

As you complete this chapter's assessments, resist the impulse to treat your responses as permanent labels that lock you into one style of learning. An assessment is simply a starting point, a snapshot of where you are at a given moment. There are no "right" answers, no "best" scores. Additionally, your learning patterns are apt to change as you gain experience, build skills, and

learn more. You may want to take the assessments again in the future to see if your results are different.

Keep in mind, too, that one of the goals of education is to stretch your knowledge and abilities. Learning in different ways can be like cross-training for the brain. Educators will often challenge you to learn in ways that aren't as comfortable for you. With an understanding of different learning styles, you will be ready for the challenge.

What TOOLS CAN HELP YOU ASSESS HOW YOU LEARN AND INTERACT WITH OTHERS?

Many different tools can help you become more aware of how you think, process information, and relate to others. Some focus on learning preferences, some on areas of potential, and some on personality type. This chapter briefly describes one assessment that measures learning modes (VAK) and then examines two assessments in depth. The first—*Multiple Pathways to Learning*—is a learning preferences assessment focusing on eight areas of potential, based on Howard Gardner's Multiple Intelligences (or MI) theory. The second—the *Personality Spectrum*—is a personality type assessment based on the Myers-Briggs Type Indicator and helps you evaluate how you react to people and situations.

The VAK questionnaire assesses three learning modes: Visual (information in maps, charts, writing, and other representations of words), Auditory (information heard or spoken), and Kinesthetic (information gathered through experience and practice). If you would like further information about

think CRITICALLY

Analyze the Value of Lifelong Learning

Currently, nearly half of all U.S. adults are involved in some formal type of lifelong learning.[1] Also, it is now common to have more than one career, and perhaps several, over your lifetime. Consider, and describe in a journal entry, how you think an understanding of how you learn will help you in *any* career. Then, looking at one career area that interests you, analyze what kind of lifelong learning may be necessary for success in that area, perhaps comparing and contrasting with the demands of other career areas.

VAK, search online using the keywords "VAK assessment." The MI assessment in this chapter encompasses the VAK areas through three of the eight "intelligences"—visual-spatial, verbal-linguistic, and bodily-kinesthetic. Auditory learners who learn and remember best through listening should note that their strength is part of two MI dimensions:

- Many auditory learners have strong *verbal intelligence* but prefer to hear words (in a lecture or discussion or on a recording) instead of reading them.
- Many auditory learners have strong *musical intelligence* and remember and retain information based on sounds and rhythms.

When reading about the application of verbal and musical intelligences throughout this chapter, auditory learners should pay attention to suggestions in both categories. If you tend to absorb information better through listening, try study suggestions for these two intelligences. Podcasts are especially helpful to auditory learners, and an increasing number of instructors are converting their lectures into digital format for downloading.

Assess Your Multiple Intelligences with Pathways to Learning

In 1983, Howard Gardner changed the way people perceive intelligence and learning with his theory of multiple intelligences. Gardner believed that the traditional view of intelligence—based on mathematical, logical, and verbal measurements—did not comprehensively reflect the range of human ability. His research led him to identify eight unique "intelligences," or areas of ability. These include the aptitudes traditionally associated with the term *intelligence*—logic and verbal skills—but go beyond, to include a wide range of potentials of the human brain.

Gardner defines an *intelligence* as an ability that is valued by a group of people for what it can produce.[2] As mountain Tibetans prize the bodily-kinesthetic ability of a top-notch Himalayan guide, for example, so Detroit automakers appreciate the visual-spatial talents of a master car designer. Different cultures and situations need different abilities.

You have your own personal "map" of abilities, which is a combination of what you were born with and what you have worked to develop. When you find a task or subject easy, you are probably using a more fully developed intelligence. When you have trouble, you may be using a less developed intelligence. Note that you almost never use only one intelligence at a time. Gardner emphasizes that, with few exceptions, intelligences work together.[3] As you read the descriptions of the intelligences in Key 3.1, remember that everyone has some level of ability in each area.

Gardner believes your levels of development in the eight intelligences can grow or recede throughout

Know How to Identify Learning Disabilities

Any kind of learner can experience a learning disability. The National Center for Learning Disabilities (NCLD) defines *learning disabilities* as neurological disorders that interfere with one's ability to store, process, and produce information.[4] According to the NCLD, persistent problems in any of the following areas may indicate a learning disability:[5]

- ▶ Reading or reading comprehension
- ▶ Math calculations, understanding language and concepts
- ▶ Social skills or interpreting social cues
- ▶ Following a schedule, being on time, meeting deadlines
- ▶ Reading or following maps

- ▶ Balancing a checkbook
- ▶ Following directions, especially on multistep tasks
- ▶ Writing, sentence structure, spelling, and organizing written work

If you are diagnosed with a learning disability, get informed about it. Look up the NCLD at www.ncld.org or LD Online at www.ldonline.org, or call NCLD at 1-888-575-7373. Then talk to your advisor about how your school can help you. You may have received an Individualized Education Program or IEP (a document describing your disability and recommended strategies) that you can share with your advisor. Finally, build a positive attitude. Rely on support and know that it will give you the best possible chance to learn and grow.

Intelligence		Description	High-Achieving Example
Verbal-Linguistic		Ability to communicate through language; listening, reading, writing, speaking	• Author J. K. Rowling • Orator and President Barack Obama
Logical-Mathematical		Ability to understand logical reasoning and problem solving; math, science, patterns, sequences	• Physicist Stephen Hawking • Mathematician Svetlana Jitomirskaya
Bodily-Kinesthetic		Ability to use the physical body skillfully and to take in knowledge through bodily sensation; coordination, working with hands	• Gymnast Nastia Liukin • Survivalist Bear Grylls
Visual-Spatial		Ability to understand spatial relationships and to perceive and create images; visual art, graphic design, charts and maps	• Artist Walt Disney • Designer Stella McCartney
Interpersonal		Ability to relate to others, noticing their moods, motivations, and feelings; social activity, cooperative learning, teamwork	• Media personality Ellen DeGeneres • Former Secretary of State Colin Powell
Intrapersonal		Ability to understand one's own behavior and feelings; self-awareness, independence, time spent alone	• Animal researcher Jane Goodall • Philosopher Friedrich Nietzsche
Musical		Ability to comprehend and create meaningful sound; sensitivity to music and musical patterns	• Singer and musician Alicia Keys • Composer Andrew Lloyd Webber
Naturalist		Ability to identify, distinguish, categorize, and classify species or items, often incorporating high interest in elements of the natural environment	• Social activist Wangari Maathai • Bird cataloger John James Audubon

Multiple Pathways to Learning

Each intelligence has a set of numbered statements. Consider each statement on its own. Then, on a scale from 1 (lowest) to 4 (highest), rate how closely it matches who you are right now and write that number on the line next to the statement. Finally, total each set of six questions.

1. rarely   2. sometimes   3. usually   4. always

1. ____ I enjoy physical activities.
2. ____ I am uncomfortable sitting still.
3. ____ I prefer to learn through doing.
4. ____ When sitting I move my legs or hands.
5. ____ I enjoy working with my hands.
6. ____ I like to pace when I'm thinking or studying.
____ TOTAL for **BODILY-KINESTHETIC**

1. ____ I enjoy telling stories.
2. ____ I like to write.
3. ____ I like to read.
4. ____ I express myself clearly.
5. ____ I am good at negotiating.
6. ____ I like to discuss topics that interest me.
____ TOTAL for **VERBAL-LINGUISTIC**

1. ____ I use maps easily.
2. ____ I draw pictures/diagrams when explaining ideas.
3. ____ I can assemble items easily from diagrams.
4. ____ I enjoy drawing or photography.
5. ____ I do not like to read long paragraphs.
6. ____ I prefer a drawn map over written directions.
____ TOTAL for **VISUAL-SPATIAL**

1. ____ I like math in school.
2. ____ I like science.
3. ____ I problem solve well.
4. ____ I question how things work.
5. ____ I enjoy planning or designing something new.
6. ____ I am able to fix things.
____ TOTAL for **LOGICAL-MATHEMATICAL**

1. ____ I listen to music.
2. ____ I move my fingers or feet when I hear music.
3. ____ I have good rhythm.
4. ____ I like to sing along with music.
5. ____ People have said I have musical talent.
6. ____ I like to express my ideas through music.
____ TOTAL for **MUSICAL**

1. ____ I need quiet time to think.
2. ____ I think about issues before I want to talk.
3. ____ I am interested in self-improvement.
4. ____ I understand my thoughts and feelings.
5. ____ I know what I want out of life.
6. ____ I prefer to work on projects alone.
____ TOTAL for **INTRAPERSONAL**

1. ____ I like doing a project with other people.
2. ____ People come to me to help settle conflicts.
3. ____ I like to spend time with friends.
4. ____ I am good at understanding people.
5. ____ I am good at making people feel comfortable.
6. ____ I enjoy helping others.
____ TOTAL for **INTERPERSONAL**

1. ____ I like to think about how things, ideas, or people fit into categories.
2. ____ I enjoy studying plants, animals, or oceans.
3. ____ I tend to see how things relate to, or are distinct from, one another.
4. ____ I think about having a career in the natural sciences.
5. ____ As a child I often played with bugs and leaves.
6. ____ I like to investigate the natural world around me.
____ TOTAL for **NATURALISTIC**

Source: Developed by Joyce Bishop, PhD, Golden West College, Huntington Beach, CA. Based on Howard Gardner, Frames of Mind: The Theory of Multiple Intelligences, New York: Harper Collins, 1993.

your life, depending on your efforts and experiences. Although you will not become a world-class pianist if you have limited musical ability, for example, you still can grow what you have with focus and work. Conversely, even a highly talented musician will lose ability without practice. This reflects how the brain grows with learning and slows without it.

The Multiple Pathways to Learning assessment helps you determine the levels to which your eight intelligences are developed. Your goal is to

Scoring Grid for Multiple Pathways to Learning

For each intelligence, shade the box in the row that corresponds with the range where your score falls. For example, if you scored 17 in Bodily-Kinesthetic intelligence, you would shade the middle box in that row; if you scored a 13 in Visual-Spatial, you would shade the last box in that row. When you have shaded one box for each row, you will see a "map" of your range of development at a glance.

A score of 20–24 indicates a high level of development in that particular type of intelligence, 14–19 a moderate level, and below 14 an underdeveloped intelligence.

	20–24 (Highly Developed)	14–19 (Moderately Developed)	Below 14 (Underdeveloped)
Bodily-Kinesthetic			
Visual-Spatial			
Verbal-Linguistic			
Logical-Mathematical			
Musical			
Interpersonal			
Intrapersonal			
Naturalistic			

identify what your levels are now, work your strongest intelligences to your advantage, and recognize where you can develop further. See Key 3.2 for specific skills that tend to be associated with the eight intelligences.

Assess Your Style of Interaction with the Personality Spectrum

Personality assessments help you understand how you respond to the world around you, including people, work, and school. In the early 1900s, psychologist Carl Jung focused his work on personality types, defining two aspects of personality:[6]

- *A person's preferred "world."* Jung said that extroverts tend to prefer the outside world of people and activities, whereas introverts tend to prefer the inner world of thoughts, feelings, and fantasies.
- *Different ways of dealing with the world, or "functions."* Jung laid out four ways of interacting: sensing (comprehending through what your senses take in), thinking (evaluating information rationally), intuiting (learning through instinct), and feeling (understanding information through emotional response).

Katharine Briggs and her daughter, Isabel Briggs Myers, developed an assessment based on Jung's work. Their Myers-Briggs Type Indicator or MBTI is one of the most widely used personality inventories in the

Students drawn to the sciences may find that they have strengths in logical-mathematical or naturalistic thinking.

© iStockPhoto

Verbal-Linguistic

- Remembering terms easily
- Mastering a foreign language
- Using writing or speech to convince someone to do or believe something

Musical

- Sensing tonal qualities
- Being sensitive to sounds and rhythms in music and in spoken language
- Using an understanding of musical patterns to hear music

Logical-Mathematical

- Recognizing abstract patterns
- Using facts to support an idea, and generating ideas based on evidence
- Reasoning scientifically (formulating and testing a hypothesis)

Visual-Spatial

- Recognizing relationships between objects
- Representing something graphically
- Manipulating images

Bodily-Kinesthetic

- Strong mind–body connection
- Controlling and coordinating body movement
- Using the body to create products or express emotion

Intrapersonal

- Accessing one's internal emotions
- Understanding feelings and using them to guide behavior
- Understanding self in relation to others

Interpersonal

- Seeing things from others' perspectives
- Noticing moods, intentions, and temperaments of others
- Gauging the most effective way to work with individual group members

Naturalistic

- Ability to categorize something as a member of a group or species
- Understanding of relationships among natural organisms
- Deep comfort with, and respect for, the natural world

Personality Spectrum

STEP 1 Rank-order all four responses to each question from most like you (4) to least like you (1) so that for each question you use the numbers 1, 2, 3, and 4 one time each. Place the numbers in the boxes next to the responses.

4. most like me   3. more like me   2. less like me   1. least like me

1. I like instructors who
   a. ☐ tell me exactly what is expected of me.
   b. ☐ make learning active and exciting.
   c. ☐ maintain a safe and supportive classroom.
   d. ☐ challenge me to think at higher levels.

2. I learn best when the material is
   a. ☐ well organized.
   b. ☐ something I can do hands-on.
   c. ☐ about understanding and improving the human condition.
   d. ☐ intellectually challenging.

3. A high priority in my life is to
   a. ☐ keep my commitments.
   b. ☐ experience as much of life as possible.
   c. ☐ make a difference in the lives of others.
   d. ☐ understand how things work.

4. Other people think of me as
   a. ☐ dependable and loyal.
   b. ☐ dynamic and creative.
   c. ☐ caring and honest.
   d. ☐ intelligent and inventive.

5. When I experience stress I would most likely
   a. ☐ do something to help me feel more in control of my life.
   b. ☐ do something physical and daring.
   c. ☐ talk with a friend.
   d. ☐ go off by myself and think about my situation.

6. I would probably not be close friends with someone who is
   a. ☐ irresponsible.
   b. ☐ unwilling to try new things.
   c. ☐ selfish and unkind to others.
   d. ☐ an illogical thinker.

7. My vacations could be described as
   a. ☐ traditional.
   b. ☐ adventuresome.
   c. ☐ pleasing to others.
   d. ☐ a new learning experience.

8. One word that best describes me is
   a. ☐ sensible.
   b. ☐ spontaneous.
   c. ☐ giving.
   d. ☐ analytical.

STEP 2 Add up the total points for each letter.

TOTAL FOR   a. ____ Organizer   b. ____ Adventurer   c. ____ Giver   d. ____ Thinker

STEP 3 Plot these numbers on the brain diagram on page 38.

world. People completing the MBTI will find that they fall into one of sixteen possible types. David Keirsey and Marilyn Bates created an assessment called the Keirsey Sorter that simplifies the MBTI into four temperaments. You can take these assessments through your counseling center if it offers them; if not, the MBTI is available online for a fee (www.myersbriggs .org) and the Keirsey Temperament Sorter II can be found online for free (www.keirsey.com).

The Personality Spectrum assessment in this chapter is based on the MBTI and Keirsey Sorter, adapting the material to indicate four personality types—Thinker, Organizer, Giver, and Adventurer. It was developed by Dr. Joyce Bishop, one of the authors of *Keys to Success Quick*. With this assessment, you can identify the kinds of interactions that are most—and least—comfortable for you. As with multiple intelligences, personality results may change over time in reaction to new experiences, efforts, and practice. Look at Key 3.3 (p. 39) to see skills that tend to be characteristic of each personality type.

Scoring Diagram for Personality Spectrum

Write your scores from page 37 in the four squares just outside the brain diagram—Thinker score at top left, Giver score at top right, Organizer score at bottom left, and Adventurer score at bottom right.

Each square has a line of numbers that go from the square to the center of the diagram. For each of your four scores, place a dot on the appropriate number in the line near that square. For example, if you scored 15 in the Giver spectrum, you would place a dot between the 14 and 16 in the upper right-hand line of numbers. If you scored a 26 in the Organizer spectrum, you would place a dot on the 26 in the lower left-hand line of numbers.

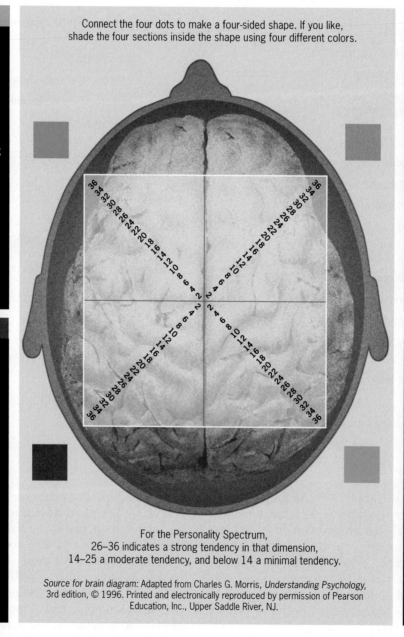

THINKER

Technical
Scientific
Mathematical
Dispassionate
Rational
Analytical
Logical
Problem solving
Theoretical
Intellectual
Objective
Quantitative
Explicit
Realistic
Literal
Precise
Formal

ORGANIZER

Tactical
Planning
Detailed
Practical
Confident
Predictable
Controlled
Dependable
Systematic
Sequential
Structured
Administrative
Procedural
Organized
Conservative
Safekeeping
Disciplined

GIVER

Interpersonal
Emotional
Caring
Sociable
Giving
Spiritual
Musical
Romantic
Feeling
Peacemaker
Trusting
Adaptable
Passionate
Harmonious
Idealistic
Talkative
Honest

ADVENTURER

Active
Visual
Risking
Original
Artistic
Spatial
Skillful
Impulsive
Metaphoric
Experimental
Divergent
Fast-paced
Simultaneous
Competitive
Imaginative
Open-minded
Adventuresome

Connect the four dots to make a four-sided shape. If you like, shade the four sections inside the shape using four different colors.

For the Personality Spectrum,
26–36 indicates a strong tendency in that dimension,
14–25 a moderate tendency, and below 14 a minimal tendency.

Source for brain diagram: Adapted from Charles G. Morris, *Understanding Psychology*, 3rd edition, © 1996. Printed and electronically reproduced by permission of Pearson Education, Inc., Upper Saddle River, NJ.

Thinker

- Solving problems
- Developing models and systems
- Analytical and abstract thinking

Organizer

- Responsibility, reliability
- Neatness, organization, attention to detail
- Comprehensive follow-through on tasks

Giver

- Successful, close relationships
- Making a difference in the world
- Negotiation; promoting peace

Adventurer

- Courage and daring
- Hands-on problem solving
- Active and spontaneous style

How CAN YOU USE YOUR SELF-KNOWLEDGE?

Now that you've developed a clearer picture of who you are as a learner, use it to choose effective strategies in the classroom, during study time, for your career, and with technology.

Learn to Work with Different Teaching Styles

With all the factors you have to consider in choosing courses—completing core curriculum, taking courses in your major, finding times that fit into your jam-packed schedule—you probably aren't able to think much about who's teaching and how they teach. However, an instructor's style can have a significant effect on your classroom experience. Instructors may favor one or more styles, such as the following:

- *Word-focused lecture.* Instructor speaks to the class for the entire period, with little class interaction. Lesson is taught primarily through words, spoken or written on the board, on PowerPoints, in handouts, or in books.
- *Small-group work.* Instructor presents material and then breaks class into small groups for discussion or project work.
- *Visual focus.* Instructor uses visual elements such as PowerPoint slides, diagrams, photographs, drawings, transparencies, and videos.
- *Logical presentation.* Instructor organizes material in a logical sequence, such as by steps, time, or importance.
- *Random presentation.* Instructor tackles topics in no particular order and may jump around a lot or digress.

Even if you cannot choose an instructor, you can choose how you *interact* with your instructor and function in the classroom. After several class meetings, you should have an idea of each instructor's dominant teaching styles. With this information, you can use what you know about your own learning and interaction styles to get the most from the course.

Add a new dimension to your experience of a course, and your learning, by talking to your instructor outside of class time.

© ThinkStock

and listen to them on an MP3 player. (Some institutions have rules about using recording devices. Be sure to check with your school's code of conduct before recording a lecture.)

• *Work to strengthen weaker areas.* A visual learner reviewing notes from a structured lecture course could use logical-mathematical strategies such as outlining notes or thinking about cause-and-effect relationships within the material.

• *Ask your instructor for help.* If you are having trouble with coursework, communicate with your instructor through e-mail or during office hours. This is especially important in large lectures where you are anonymous unless you speak up. A visual learner, for example, might ask the instructor to recommend graphs or videos that illustrate the lecture.

No instructor of a diverse group of learners can provide exactly what each one needs. However, adjusting to instructors' teaching styles builds flexibility that you need for career and life success. Just as you can't hand-pick your instructors, you will rarely, if ever, be able to choose your work colleagues or their ways of working or interacting with others.

Although styles vary, the word-focused lecture is still the norm. For this reason, the traditional college classroom is generally a happy home for the verbal or logical learner. However, many students learn best when interacting with other students. What can you do when your preferences don't match up with how your instructor teaches? Here are three suggestions:

• *Play to your strengths.* For example, a musical learner whose instructor delivers material in a random way might record lecture highlights digitally

Make Smart Study Choices

Start now to use what you have learned about yourself to choose the best study techniques. For example, if you tend to learn successfully from a linear, logical presentation, you can look for order (for example, a *chronology*—information organized sequentially

think CREATIVELY

Connect with an Instructor

Think about the instructors teaching your courses this term. Consider the instructor that you connect with the *least* right now. First, come up with possible explanations for the lack of connection. Then brainstorm some actions you can take to improve the situation. To help generate ideas, try to come up with at least one action that will address each of your explanations. For example, to address a sense that you don't know an instructor well, schedule a friendly meeting during office hours.

Link How You Learn to Coursework and Major

Summarize how you see yourself as a learner in a short paragraph. Focus on what you learned about yourself from the chapter assessment.

....

....

....

....

....

....

Next, schedule a meeting with your academic advisor. Write the time and date of the meeting in your calendar and here:

....

Give the advisor an overview of your learning strengths and challenges, based on your summary. Ask for advice about courses and majors that might interest you. Take notes.

Indicate two courses to consider in the next year and note the majors to which they are linked.

1. ....

2. ....

Finally, create a separate to-do list of how you plan to explore one course and one major. Set a deadline for each task.

according to event dates—or a problem–solution structure) as you review notes. If you are strong in interpersonal intelligence, try to work in study groups whenever possible.

When you study with others, you and the entire group will be more successful if you understand the different learning styles in the group, as in the following examples.

- An interpersonal learner could take the lead in teaching material to others.
- A naturalistic learner might clarify ideas by organizing facts into categories.

Look at Keys 3.4 and 3.5 for study strategies that suit each intelligence and Personality Spectrum dimension. Because you have some level of ability in each area, and because there will be times that you need to boost your ability in a weaker area, you may find useful suggestions under any of the headings. Try different techniques, analyze how effective they are for you, and use what works best for you. In grids found in Chapters 4 through 12, you will indicate learning styles–based strategies that you believe will help you master specific skills from each chapter.

Verbal-Linguistic

- Read text; highlight selectively
- Use a computer to retype and summarize notes
- Outline chapters
- Recite information or write scripts/debates

Musical

- Create rhythms out of words
- Beat out rhythms with hand or stick while reciting concepts
- Write songs/raps that help you learn concepts
- Chant or sing study material along with a favorite tune as you listen

Logical-Mathematical

- Organize material logically; if it suits the topic, use a spreadsheet program
- Explain material sequentially to someone
- Develop systems and find patterns
- Analyze and evaluate information

Visual-Spatial

- Develop graphic organizers for new material
- Draw mind maps/think links
- Use a computer to develop charts and tables
- Use color in notes to organize

Bodily-Kinesthetic

- Move while you learn; pace and recite
- Rewrite or retype notes to engage "muscle memory"
- Design and play games to learn material
- Act out scripts of material

Intrapersonal

- Reflect on personal meaning of information
- Keep a journal
- Study in quiet areas
- Imagine essays or experiments before beginning

Interpersonal

- Study in a group
- Discuss material over the phone or send instant messages
- Teach someone else the material
- Make time to discuss assignments and tests with your instructor

Naturalistic

- Break down information into categories
- Look for ways in which items fit or don't fit together
- Look for relationships among ideas, events, facts
- Study in a natural setting if it helps you to focus

Thinker

- Convert material into logical charts, flow diagrams, and outlines
- Reflect independently on new information
- Learn through problem solving
- Design new ways of approaching material or problems

Organizer

- Define tasks in concrete terms
- Use a planner to schedule tasks and dates
- Organize material by rewriting and summarizing class and text notes
- Create or find a well-structured study environment

Giver

- Study with others in person, on the phone, or using instant messages
- Teach material to others
- Seek out tasks, groups, and subjects that involve helping people
- Connect with instructors, advisors, and tutors

Adventurer

- Look for environments or courses that encourage nontraditional approaches
- Find hands-on ways to learn
- Use or develop games or puzzles to help memorize terms
- Ask to do something extra or perform a task in a more active way

Use Technology That Works for Your Learning Style

Technology plays a significant role in academic settings, where you may encounter any of the following:

- Instructors who require students to communicate via e-mail
- Courses that have their own websites where you can access the syllabus and connect with resources and classmates
- Textbooks with websites that you can, or are required to, use to complete assignments, which you then e-mail to your instructor

Knowing your strengths and challenges as a learner can help you make decisions about how to approach technology. Are you strong in the logical-mathematical intelligence? Working with an online tutorial may be a good choice. Are you an interpersonal learner? Find a tech savvy classmate to help you get the hang of it. Finally, make choices that will help you demystify technology and get you up to speed.

Transfer Self-Knowledge to the Workplace

The self-knowledge you build in this chapter will help you succeed at work in several ways.

- You can find ways to use your strengths on the job more readily. For tasks that require you to use less developed skills, you will be more able to compensate in ways such as seeking help from colleagues or a supervisor.
- You can make effective decisions about how best to contribute to a team project. Knowing how you relate to others improves your ability to work with team members.
- You will be more focused on what works for you—and what doesn't—as you search for jobs and internships and plan a career.

As you continue through this text, through college, and into your life, use your metacognition to stay in touch with how you think and learn. Always give yourself the chance to grow.

Think Back

Solidify your knowledge and prepare for tests with this review. Answer the following questions on a separate sheet of paper or electronic file.

▶ Revisit the chapter-opening questions on page 29. Scan the chapter and write a short answer for each.

▶ Create a study sheet that helps you remember Gardner's eight intelligences and the four Personality Spectrum dimensions. You can give each an image, a word, a color, or create an acronym for each set (see Chapter 7 on memory)—whatever works for you.

Analyze, Create, Practice

Improve Your Classroom Experience

Analyze. Consider first what you know about yourself as a learner. Then reflect on your instructors' teaching styles this term. Consider which instructors' styles mesh well with how you learn and which do not. Make notes about your most challenging situation.

Course: ....

Instructor style: ....

Your view of the problem:

....

....

....

....

....

....

Create. Next, brainstorm three actions you can take to improve the situation. Note the intelligence (or intelligences) on which each action is based (refer to Keys 3.4 and 3.5 for ideas):

1. ....

....

2. ....

....

3. ....

....

Practice. Finally, choose one and put it to work. Note what happened. Were there improvements?

....

....

....

....

....

....

Critical, Creative, and Practical Thinking

Solving Problems and Making Decisions

Problems and decisions, both big and small, come into your life every day. This chapter will develop your critical, creative, and practical thinking skills. Separately and together, these skills will help you solve problems and make decisions carefully and comprehensively.

In this chapter, you'll explore answers to the following questions:

Why is it important to ask and answer questions?

p. 46

How can you improve critical thinking skills?

p. 47

How can you improve creative thinking skills?

p. 50

How can you improve practical thinking skills?

p. 52

How can you solve problems and make decisions effectively?

p. 54

How Developed Are Your Thinking Skills?

For each statement, circle the number that best describes how true the statement is for you, from 1 for "not at all true for me" to 5 for "very true for me."

▶ I discover information, make decisions, and solve problems by asking and answering questions.   **1 2 3 4 5**

▶ I don't take everything I read or hear as fact; I question how useful, truthful, and logical information is before I decide whether I can use it.   **1 2 3 4 5**

▶ I look for biased perspectives when I read or listen because I am aware of how they can lead me in the wrong direction.   **1 2 3 4 5**

▶ Even if it seems like there is only one way to solve a problem, I brainstorm to think of other options.   **1 2 3 4 5**

▶ I try not to let the idea that things have *always* been done a certain way stop me from trying different approaches.   **1 2 3 4 5**

▶ When I work in a group, I try to manage my emotions and notice how I affect others.   **1 2 3 4 5**

▶ I think about different solutions before I choose one and take action.   **1 2 3 4 5**

▶ I spend time researching different possibilities before making a decision.   **1 2 3 4 5**

▶ I avoid making decisions on the spur of the moment.   **1 2 3 4 5**

▶ When I make a decision, I consider how my choice will affect others.   **1 2 3 4 5**

If your total ranges from 41–50, you consider your thinking, problem-solving, and decision-making skills to be fairly well developed.

If your total ranges from 24–40, you consider your thinking, problem-solving, and decision-making skills to be somewhat developed.

If your total is less than 24, you consider your thinking, problem-solving, and decision-making skills to be underdeveloped.

Now total your scores.

REMEMBER No matter how developed your thinking skills, you can improve them with effort. Read the chapter to learn new ways to build these skills, and practice by doing the activities.

Why IS IT IMPORTANT TO ASK AND ANSWER QUESTIONS?

As a college student as well as a human being, you ask questions and search for answers every day. Common activities such as the following involve you in a process of questioning.

- Choosing a term paper topic by looking at the topic list, thinking about available research sources, and considering your own interests
- Deciding between two banking plans by reading brochures and talking to the bank manager

- Offering an opposing opinion after listening to a friend's point of view

You may not consider asking questions to be that important, and you may even feel that the more intelligent and educated you are, the less you have to ask questions. But consider this: The act of thinking *depends* on questioning. According to experts, thinking is what happens when you ask questions and move toward the answers.[1] "Questions define tasks, express problems and delineate issues," says Richard Paul of the Center for Critical Thinking and Moral Critique, *"Only students who have questions are really thinking and learning."*[2]

As you explore answers to questions, you transform pieces of information into knowledge you can act on. For example, a computer programming student may ask how a certain code can make software perform a task. A pharmacy technology student may question which drug works best for a particular illness. Questioners seek information that they will use to achieve goals.

Knowing *why* you are questioning also helps you *want* to think. "Critical-thinking skills are different from critical-thinking dispositions, or a willingness to deploy these skills," says cognitive psychologist D. Alan Bensley of Frostburg State University in Mary-

land.[3] In other words, having the skills isn't enough— you also need the desire to use them. If you know and understand your goal, you will more willingly put your skills to work to achieve that goal.

Achieving your goals in college requires you to think in ways that move you beyond memorizing what you learn. You will be expected to think *critically, creatively,* and *practically.* Asking questions opens the door to all three.

How CAN YOU IMPROVE CRITICAL THINKING SKILLS?

Critical thinking is the process of gathering information, breaking it into parts, examining and evaluating those parts, and making connections for the purposes of gaining understanding, solving a problem, or making a decision.

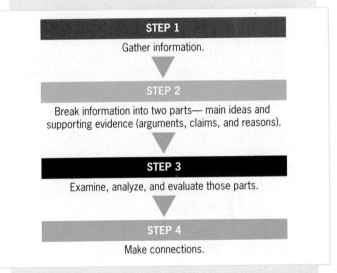

STEP 1
Gather information.

▼

STEP 2
Break information into two parts— main ideas and supporting evidence (arguments, claims, and reasons).

▼

STEP 3
Examine, analyze, and evaluate those parts.

▼

STEP 4
Make connections.

Through the critical thinking process, you will look for how pieces of information relate to one another, setting aside any pieces that are unclear, unrelated, unimportant, or biased. You may also form new questions that change your direction. Be open to them and to where they may lead you.

Gather Information

Information is the raw material for thinking. Gathering information means analyzing how much and what type of information you need, where to search for it, how much time to spend gathering it, and whether it is relevant. Say, for instance, that you have to write a paper on one aspect of the media (TV, radio, Internet) and its influence on a particular

Many types of work, such as the elevation drawings this engineering student is working on, involve analytical thinking.

© Shutterstock

▶ **What** are the reasons for this?

▶ **Does** the evidence make sense?

▶ **Are** there examples that might disprove the idea?

▶ **Is** this fact or opinion?

▶ **How** important is this information?

▶ **What** is similar to this information, and what is different?

group. Here's how critical thinking can help you gather information for that paper:

- Reviewing the assignment terms, you note two important items: The paper should be approximately ten pages and describe at least three significant points of influence.
- At the library and online, you find thousands of articles in this topic area. After scanning the titles and noticing the number of articles that concentrate on certain aspects of the topic, you decide to focus your paper on how the Internet influences young teens (ages 13–15).
- Examining the summaries of six comprehensive articles leads you to three in-depth, credible sources.

In this way you achieve a subgoal—a selection of useful materials—on the way to your larger goal of writing a well-crafted paper.

Break Information into Parts

The next step is to search for the two most relevant parts of the information: the main idea or ideas (also called the *argument* or *viewpoint*) and the evidence that supports them (also called *reasons* or *supporting details*).

- *Separate the ideas.* Identify each of the main ideas conveyed in what you are reading. You can use lists or a mind map to visually separate ideas from one another. For instance, if you are reading about how teens ages 13 to 15 use the Internet, you could identify the goal of each method of access they use (websites, blogs, instant messaging).
- *Identify the evidence.* For each main idea, identify the evidence that supports it. For example, if an article claims that young teens rely on instant messaging three times more than on e-mails, note the facts, studies, or other evidence cited to support the truth of the claim.

Examine and Evaluate

The third step is by far the most significant and lies at the heart of critical thinking. Examine the information to see whether it is going to be useful for your purposes. Be sure to keep your mind open to all pertinent information, even if it conflicts with your personal views. Answering the following four questions will help you examine and evaluate effectively.

Do examples support ideas?

When you encounter an idea or claim, examine how it is supported with examples or *evidence*—facts, expert opinion, research findings, personal experience, and so on (see Key 4.1 for an illustration). How useful an idea is to your work may depend on whether, or how well, it is backed up with solid evi-

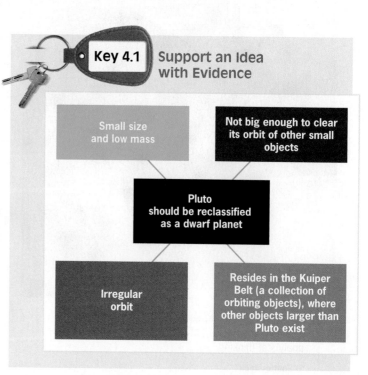

Key 4.1 Support an Idea with Evidence

Small size and low mass

Not big enough to clear its orbit of other small objects

Pluto should be reclassified as a dwarf planet

Irregular orbit

Resides in the Kuiper Belt (a collection of orbiting objects), where other objects larger than Pluto exist

dence or made concrete with examples. Be critical of the information you gather; don't take it at face value.

For example, a blog written by a 12-year-old may make statements about what kids do on the Internet. The word of one person, who may or may not be telling the truth, is not adequate support. However, a study of youth technology use by the Department of Commerce under the provisions of the Children's Internet Protection Act may be more reliable.

Is the supporting information factual and accurate, or is it opinion?

A *statement of fact* is information presented as objectively real and verifiable ("The Internet is a research tool"). In contrast, a *statement of opinion* is a belief, conclusion, or judgment that is inherently difficult, and sometimes impossible, to verify ("The Internet is always the best and most reliable research tool"). When you critically evaluate materials, one test of the evidence is whether it is fact or opinion. Key 4.2 defines important characteristics of fact and opinion.

Do causes and effects link logically?

Look at the reasons given for a situation or occurrence (causes) and the explanation of its consequences (effects, both positive and negative). For example, an article might detail what causes young teens to use the Internet after school and the effects that this has on their family life. The cause-and-effect chain should make sense to you. It is also important that you analyze carefully to seek out *key* or *"root" causes*—the most significant causes of a problem or situation. For example, many factors may be involved in young teens' Internet use, but on careful examination one or two factors may seem more significant than others.

Is the evidence biased?

Evidence with a *bias*—a preference or leaning that may prevent even-handed judgment—is evidence that is slanted in a particular direction. Searching for a bias involves looking for hidden *perspectives* or *assumptions* that lie within the material.

A *perspective* is a characteristic way of thinking about something and can be broad (such as a generally optimistic or pessimistic view of life) or more

Key 4.2   Examine How Fact and Opinion Differ

Facts include statements that . . .

. . . deal with actual people, places, objects, or events. Example: "In 2002, the European Union introduced the physical coins and banknotes of a new currency—the euro—that was designed to be used by its member nations."

. . . use concrete words or measurable statistics. Example: "The charity event raised $50,862."

. . . describe current events in exact terms. Example: "Mr. Barrett's course has 378 students enrolled this semester."

. . . avoid emotional words and focus on the verifiable. Example: "Citing dissatisfaction with the instruction, seven out of the twenty-five students in that class withdrew in September."

. . . avoid absolutes. Example: "Some students need to have a job while in school."

Opinions include statements that . . .

. . . show evaluation. Any statement of value indicates an opinion. Words such as *bad, good, pointless,* and *beneficial* indicate value judgments. Example: "The use of the euro has been beneficial to all the states of the European Union."

. . . use abstract words. Complicated words like *misery* and *success* usually indicate a personal opinion. Example: "The charity event was a smashing success."

. . . predict future events. Statements about future occurrences are often opinions. Example: "Mr. Barrett's course is going to set a new enrollment record this year."

. . . use emotional words. Emotions are unverifiable. Words such as *delightful* and *miserable* express an opinion. Example: "That class is a miserable experience."

. . . use absolutes. Absolute qualifiers, such as *all, none, never,* and *always,* often express an opinion. Example: "All students need to have a job while in school."

Source: Adapted from Ben E. Johnson, Stirring Up Thinking, New York: Houghton Mifflin, 1998, pp. 268–270.

Topic: How teens' grades are affected by Internet use

Statement by a Teaching Organization	Statement by a PR Agent for an Internet Search Engine	Statement by a Professor Specializing in New Media
"Too much Internet equals failing grades and stolen papers."	"The Internet allows students access to a plethora of information, which results in better grades."	"The effects of the Internet on young students are undeniable and impossible to overlook."

focused (such as an attitude about whether students should commute or live on campus). Perspectives are often associated with *assumptions*—judgments influenced by experience or values. For example, the perspective that people can maintain power over technology leads to assumptions such as "Parents can control children's exposure to the Internet." Having a particular experience with children and the Internet can build or reinforce such a perspective. Examining perspectives and assumptions helps you judge whether material is *reliable*. The less bias you can identify, the more reliable the information. Key 4.3 shows an example of how perspectives and assumptions can affect what you read or hear through the media.

After the questions: What information is most useful to you?

You've examined your information, looking at its evidence, validity, perspective, and any underlying assumptions. Now, based on that examination, you evaluate whether an idea or piece of information is important or unimportant, relevant or not, strong or weak, and why. You then set aside what is not useful and use the rest to form an opinion, possible solution, or decision.

In preparing your paper on young teens and the Internet, for example, you've analyzed a selection of information and materials to see how they apply to the goal of your paper. You then selected what you believe will be most useful, in preparation for drafting.

Make Connections

The last part of critical thinking, after you have broken information apart, is to find new and logical ways to connect pieces together. This step is crucial for research papers and essays because it is where your original ideas are born—and it is also where

your creative skills get involved (more on that in the next section). When you begin to write, focus on your new ideas, supporting them in a persuasive way with information you've learned from your analysis.

Following are some ways to make connections.

- *Compare and contrast.* Look at how ideas are similar to, or different from, each other. You might explore how different young teen subgroups (boys vs. girls, for example) have different purposes for setting up pages on sites such as Facebook or MySpace.
- *Look for themes, patterns, and categories.* Note connections that form as you look at how bits of information relate to one another. For example, you might see patterns of Internet use that link young teens from particular cultures or areas of the country together into categories.

Stay open-minded, ready to hear and read new ideas, think about them, and make informed decisions about what you believe. The process will educate you, sharpen your thinking skills, and give you more information to work with as you encounter life's problems.

HOW CAN YOU IMPROVE CREATIVE THINKING SKILLS?

Some researchers define *creativity* as combining existing elements in an innovative way to create a new purpose or result. Others see creativity as the ability to generate new ideas from looking at how things are related. Psychologist Robert Sternberg notes that creative people tend to have ideas that go against the norm—ideas that are often rejected at first but later are widely accepted.[5]

However it is defined, creative thinking is a skill that can be developed if you keep a flexible mind.

think
CRITICALLY

Analyze a Statement

The Internet is the best place to find information about a topic.

Analyze this statement in a journal entry by answering the following questions.

- Is this statement fact or opinion? Why?
- What examples can you think of that support, or argue against, this statement?
- What bias(es) show in the statement?
- What perspective(s) or point(s) of view seem to guide this statement?
- What is your evaluation of this statement?

Here are some techniques that will help you build creative thinking.

Brainstorm

When you *brainstorm,* you come up with ideas without thinking about how useful they are (considering how to use them comes later). Brainstorming works well in groups, because group members inspire one another and make creative use of one another's ideas.[6]

When you brainstorm, don't get hooked on finding the one "right" answer. Questions may have many answers. Some may prove more useful than others and some may work better for certain people than for other people. Also, don't stop when you think you

have the best answer—keep going until you are out of steam.[7] Ideas often arrive at random times, so get in the habit of writing them down on paper or into your computer so that you don't lose creative thoughts when they pop up.

Try a New Approach

Here are some ways to change how you tackle a situation or problem:

- *Break the mold.* Don't assume something has to be done a certain way because it has *always* been done that way. Experiment. Vary how you complete a task and see what you learn.
- *Shift your perspective.* Ask others what they think; research new ways to approach a question or

To Think Creatively, Ask Questions Like These

▶ **What** if . . . ?

▶ **How** could I do this in a totally unconventional way?

▶ **What** would be interesting and new to try, see, read?

▶ **What** are the craziest ideas I can think of?

▶ **How** would someone else do this or view this?

▶ **What** is a risky approach to this, and what could happen if I take it?

Consider Where Risk May Take You

Grace Murray Hopper, a Navy admiral as well as an accomplished mathematician, once said, "A ship in port is safe, but that's not what ships are built for." What does this say to you about your creativity, imagination, and willingness to take risks? Imagine taking the risk of sending *your* ship out of port, and describe what your ship is built for.

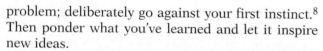

problem; deliberately go against your first instinct.[8] Then ponder what you've learned and let it inspire new ideas.

• *Ask "what if" questions.* For example: "What if money were not an issue? What if I didn't have a time limit?" See what ideas come from those questions and then consider how you might make those ideas happen.

• *Take risks.* Open yourself to the learning that comes from mistakes. When a pharmaceutical company attempted but failed to develop a new treatment for multiple sclerosis, the CEO said, "You have to celebrate the failures. If you send the message that the only road to career success is experiments that work, people won't ask risky questions, or get any dramatically new answers."[9]

CAN YOU IMPROVE PRACTICAL THINKING SKILLS?

Practical thinking refers to how you adapt to the environment, or shape or change the environment to adapt to you, while pursuing your goals. As important as critical thinking can be in the classroom, achieving your goals both in school and in the real world also requires this kind of "street smarts."[10]

To Think Practically, Ask Questions Like These

▶ **What** did I learn from that conversation, experience, event?

▶ **What** would I repeat, or do differently, the next time—and why?

▶ **What** have I done or seen others do that would be helpful in this situation?

▶ **How** can I make the most of what I do well in this situation?

▶ **How** did others react to what I said or did?

▶ **What** outcome do I want from this interaction?

Your success in a sociology class, for example, may depend as much on finding a way to get along with your instructor (practical thinking) as on knowing how to handle multiple-choice questions on exams (critical thinking).

You gain much of your practical thinking ability from personal experience rather than from formal training.[11] Experience answers "how" questions—how to talk, how to behave, how to proceed in any situation.[12] For example, after completing several papers for a course, your experience may have taught you practical lessons about what your instructor expects and what you have to do to get a good grade.

Put Emotional Intelligence to Work

Experience is a large part of what helps you develop the emotional intelligence you need to "navigate" personal emotions and social interactions in a way that achieves your goals. As you saw in Chapter 1, *emotional intelligence* is the ability to perceive emotions, understand what they mean and how you can adjust your thinking about them, and use what you've learned to choose behavior and actions that create a positive result.

Emotional intelligence gives you steps you can take to promote success. For example, if you are fuming about a low grade on an assignment, engage emotional intelligence to make the best of the situation.

- *Recognize* your emotion (anger, frustration).
- *Understand* what your emotion tells you. (Does it tell you that you feel you earned a higher grade—or that you agree with the grade and are angry with yourself for doing a low-quality job?)

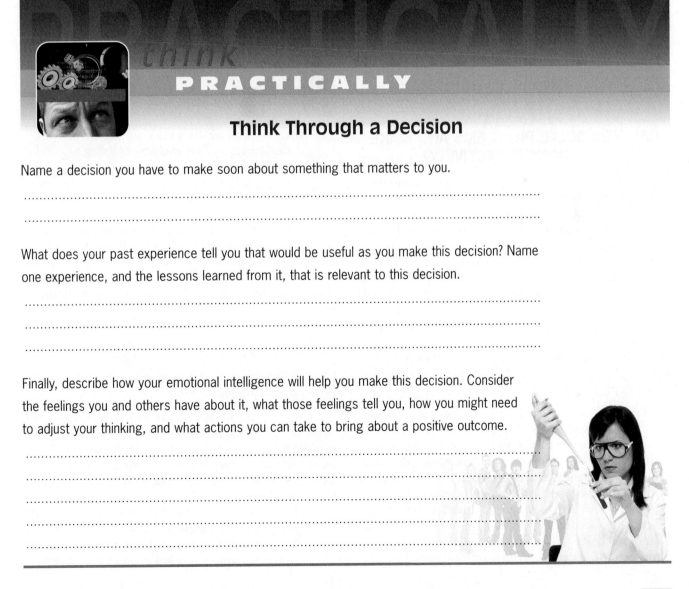

PRACTICALLY

Think Through a Decision

Name a decision you have to make soon about something that matters to you.

....

....

What does your past experience tell you that would be useful as you make this decision? Name one experience, and the lessons learned from it, that is relevant to this decision.

....

....

....

Finally, describe how your emotional intelligence will help you make this decision. Consider the feelings you and others have about it, what those feelings tell you, how you might need to adjust your thinking, and what actions you can take to bring about a positive outcome.

....

....

....

....

- *Adjust* your thinking. (Noticing that you are ready to blame the instructor, back off from that thinking and prepare yourself to focus on and ask questions about how you feel.)
- *Manage* emotions. (You choose to cool off first, schedule a meeting with the instructor, calmly make your points at the meeting, listen carefully to the response, and politely request whether a rewrite or extra assignment is possible.)

Practical actions like these make it more likely that you and your instructor will communicate well and come up with a useful plan.

Take Action

Action is practical. Basic student success strategies that promote action—staying motivated, making the most of your strengths, managing time, getting help from instructors and advisors, and believing in yourself—will keep you moving toward your goals.

Practical thinking is also powered by questioning. Asking yourself what would work in a situation while also considering other perspectives often will lead to more effective choices.

How CAN YOU SOLVE PROBLEMS AND MAKE DECISIONS EFFECTIVELY?

You've thought about how to analyze information critically, think creatively, and learn from practical experience. Now, put it all together to find the most effective way to solve the problems and make the decisions, both large and small, that come up every day of your life. This is the most important goal of active thinking and of all of your different thinking skills. When you combine critical, creative, and practical thinking skills, you have a powerful tool set for solving problems and making decisions.

Problem solving and decision making follow similar paths, although they differ in important ways.

- Problem solving generally requires that you focus on coming up with possible solutions. (My car is at the repair shop for two days—how can I get to and from campus?) In contrast, when you have a decision to make, your choices are often determined. (Which of these three lab sections should I choose?)
- A problem exists when a situation has negative effects, and problem solving aims to remove or counteract those effects. In contrast, decision making aims to fulfill a need.

When you solve problems in a group, the variety of ideas gives you a better chance of finding a workable solution.

© iStockPhoto

Both require you to identify and analyze a situation, generate possible solutions, choose one, follow through, and evaluate its success. Key 4.4 shows the path that you can use to map out both problems and decisions, while also indicating how to think about each step.

Solve a Problem

Use the following strategies as you move through the problem-solving path.

- *Use probing questions to define problems.* Ask what the problem is as well as what is *causing* the problem. Engage your emotional intelligence. If you determine that you are not motivated to do your work for a class, for example, you could ask questions like these:
  1. Do my feelings stem from how I interact with my instructor or classmates?
  2. Is the subject matter difficult? Uninteresting? Is the volume of work too much?

Problem Solving	Thinking Skill	Decision Making
Define the problem: Recognize that something needs to change, identify what's happening, look for true causes.	Step 1 *Define*	**Define the decision:** Identify your goal (your need) and then think though a decision that will help you get it.
Analyze the problem: Gather information, break it into pieces, verify facts, check the support, look for bias, evaluate information.	Step 2 *Analyze*	**Examine needs and motives:** Carefully consider layers of needs: Try to focus on what you really want.
Generate possible solutions: Use creative strategies to think of ways you could address the causes of this problem.	Step 3 *Create*	**Name and/or generate different options:** Use creative questions to come up with choices that would fulfill your needs.
Evaluate solutions: Look carefully at potential pros and cons of each, and choose what seems best.	Step 4 *Evaluate*	**Evaluate options:** Look carefully at potential pros and cons of each, and choose what seems best.
Put the solution to work: Persevere, focus on results, and believe in yourself as you move forward.	Step 5 *Choose and act*	**Act on your decision:** Go down the path and stay on target.
Evaluate how well the solution worked: Look at the effects of what you did.	Step 6 *Reevaluate*	**Evaluate the success of your decision:** Look at whether it accomplished what you had hoped.
In the future, apply what you learned: Use this solution, or a better one, in similar situations.	Step 7 *Apply results*	**In the future, apply what you learned:** Make this choice, or a better one, when a similar decision arises.

How you answer one or more of these questions may help you define the problem—and ultimately solve it.

• *Analyze carefully.* Consider how the problem is similar to or different from other problems. Clarify facts. Make sure your personal biases don't get in the way of clear thinking.

• *Generate possible solutions based on causes, not effects.* Addressing a cause provides a lasting solution, whereas "putting a Band-Aid" on an effect cannot. Say, for example, that your shoulder hurts when you type. Getting a massage is a helpful but temporary solution, because the pain returns whenever you go back to work. Changing your keyboard height is a better idea and a lasting solution to the problem, because it eliminates the cause of your pain.

• *Consider how possible solutions affect you and others.* What would suit you best? What takes other people's needs into consideration?

• *Evaluate your solution and act on it in the future.* Once you choose a solution and put it into action, ask yourself: What worked that you would do again? What didn't work that you would avoid or change in the future?

Key 4.5 shows how one student facing a problem with an instructor uses his critical, creative, and practical thinking skills to find a solution.

Make a Decision

As you take each step of the path to make a decision, remember these strategies:

• *Look at the given options—then try to determine if there are any more.* Consider similar situations you've been in or heard about, the decisions that were made, and what resulted from those decisions.

• *Think about how your decision affects others.* For example, if you are thinking about transferring schools, you might consider the impact on family and friends.

• *Gather perspectives.* Talk with others who have made similar decisions. If you listen carefully, you may hear ideas you haven't thought about.

DEFINE PROBLEM HERE:	ANALYZE THE PROBLEM
I don't like my Sociology instructor	We have different styles and personality types—I am not comfortable working in groups and being vocal. I'm not interested in being there, and my grades are suffering from my lack of motivation.

Use boxes below to list possible solutions:

POTENTIAL POSITIVE EFFECTS	SOLUTION #1	POTENTIAL NEGATIVE EFFECTS
List for each solution: Don't have to deal with that instructor Less stress	Drop the course	List for each solution: Grade gets entered on my transcript I'll have to take the course eventually; it's required for my major
Getting credit for the course Feeling like I've honored a commitment	**SOLUTION #2** Put up with it until the end of the semester	Stress every time I'm there Lowered motivation Probably not such a good final grade
A chance to express myself Could get good advice An opportunity to ask direct questions of the instructor	**SOLUTION #3** Schedule meetings with advisor and instructor	Have to face instructor one-on-one Might just make things worse

Now choose the solution you think is best—circle it and make it happen.

ACTUAL POSITIVE EFFECTS	PRACTICAL ACTION	ACTUAL NEGATIVE EFFECTS
List for chosen solution: Got some helpful advice from advisor Talking in person with the instructor actually promoted a fairly honest discussion I won't have to take the course again	I scheduled and attended meetings with both advisor and instructor and opted to stick with the course.	List for chosen solution: Still have to put up with some group work I still don't know how much learning I'll retain from this course

FINAL EVALUATION: Was it a good or bad solution?
The solution has improved things. I'll finish the course, and I got the chance to fulfill some class responsibilities on my own or with one partner. I feel more understood and more willing to put my time into the course.

Source: Based on heuristic created by Frank T. Lyman Jr. and George Eley, 1985.

• *Look at the long-term effects.* As with problem solving, it's key to examine what happens after you put the decision into action. For important decisions, do a short-term evaluation and another evaluation after a period of time. Consider whether your decision sent you in the right direction or whether you should rethink your choice.

When you make important decisions too quickly, or base them on factors that seem important at the time but fade later on, you may regret them. If a student considering a transfer makes her decision because a close friend goes to the other school, but then finds that the school doesn't suit her, she may wish she had made a different choice. Key 4.6 shows how one student uses her critical and creative thinking and emotional intelligence to make an effective decision.

In school, in your personal life, and at work, you will face obstacles of all kinds. Use what you have learned in this chapter about questioning, thinking, problem solving, and decision making to work through these obstacles and move toward achieving your most important goals.

quick! SKILL BUILDING

Think Back

Solidify your knowledge and prepare for tests with this review. Answer the following questions on a separate sheet of paper or electronic file.

▶ Revisit the chapter-opening questions on page 45. Scan the chapter and write a short answer for each.

▶ Go back to the Quick Check self-assessment. From the list, choose one item that you want to develop further. Name the type of thinking it requires (critical, creative, practical, or a combination), go to that section in the chapter, and set a specific goal based on what you read. Describe your goal and plan in a short paragraph, including a time frame and specific steps.

Analyze, Create, Practice

Solve a Problem

Put the problem-solving process to work on something that matters. Write your answers in the empty problem-solving flowchart on page 59 (Key 4.7).

Analyze. Think about a problem that you need to solve soon. Ask questions: What is the problem? Why is it important to solve it? (Example: I do not have enough money to pay tuition for next term. I need to solve it because I need to stay in school and continue toward my degree.)

Create. First, brainstorm ways to solve the problem. Consider any ideas you can imagine, even if they seem crazy or impossible. List at least two. (Examples: Take fewer courses to make room in my schedule for a full-time job. Live with family members to save money.) Then consider what could be good or bad about each solution. Evaluate potential effects and write them on either side of your solutions.

Practice. Taking your exploration into account, decide which solution makes the most sense. Circle it and write it in the "action taken" box. Now put your solution to work and evaluate the result. Do you think you chose an effective solution? Why or why not? List actual positive and negative effects of your chosen solution, and write your thoughts about whether it worked or not and whether you would make the same choice again.

Key 4.6 — Making a Decision About Whether to Transfer Schools

DEFINE PROBLEM HERE:	EXAMINE NEEDS AND MOTIVES
Whether or not to transfer schools	My father has changed jobs and can no longer afford my tuition. My goal is to become a physical therapist, so I need a school with a full physical therapy program. My family needs to cut costs. I need to transfer credits.

Use boxes below to list possible solutions:

POTENTIAL POSITIVE EFFECTS	SOLUTION #1	POTENTIAL NEGATIVE EFFECTS
List for each solution: No need to adjust to a new place or new people Ability to continue course work as planned	Continue at the current college	List for each solution: Need to finance most of my tuition and costs on my own Difficult to find time for a job Might not qualify for aid
Many physical therapy courses available School is close so I could live at home and save room costs Reasonable tuition; credits will transfer	SOLUTION #2 Transfer to the community college	No personal contacts there that I know of Less independence if I live at home No bachelor's degree available
Opportunity to earn tuition money Could live at home Status should be intact	SOLUTION #3 Stop out for a year	Could forget so much that it's hard to go back Could lose motivation A year might turn into more

Now choose the solution you think is best—circle it and make it happen.

ACTUAL POSITIVE EFFECTS	PRACTICAL ACTION	ACTUAL NEGATIVE EFFECTS
List for chosen solution: Money saved Opportunity to spend time on studies rather than on working to earn tuition money Availability of classes I need	Go to community college for two years; then transfer to a four-year school to get a B.A. and complete physical therapy course work.	List for chosen solution: Loss of some independence Less contact with friends

FINAL EVALUATION: Was it a good or bad solution?

I'm satisfied with the decision. It can be hard being at home at times, but my parents are adjusting to my independence and I'm trying to respect their concerns. With fewer social distractions, I'm really getting my work done. Plus the financial aspect of the decision is ideal.

Source: Based on heuristic created by Frank T. Lyman Jr. and George Eley, 1985.

Key 4.7 Work Through a Problem Using This Flowchart

DEFINE PROBLEM HERE:

WHY IS IT IMPORTANT TO SOLVE?

Use boxes below to list possible solutions:

POTENTIAL POSITIVE EFFECTS

List for each solution:

SOLUTION #1

SOLUTION #2

SOLUTION #3

POTENTIAL NEGATIVE EFFECTS

List for each solution:

Now choose the solution you think is best—circle it and make it happen.

ACTUAL POSITIVE EFFECTS

List for chosen solution:

PRACTICAL ACTION

ACTUAL NEGATIVE EFFECTS

List for chosen solution:

FINAL EVALUATION: Was it a good or bad solution?

Source: Based on heuristic created by Frank T. Lyman Jr. and George Eley, 1985.

Multiple **Intelligences** *in action*

List three intelligences in the left-hand column—two that are highly developed for you and one you would like to build. Then in the right-hand column brainstorm a strategy for generating creative ideas that relates to each intelligence.

Intelligence

Example: Visual-Spatial

Use MI Strategies to Come Up with Solutions

Create a mind map using lines, shapes, and colors to identify relationships among ideas.

....

....

....

....

....

....

....

chapter

5

Reading and Information Literacy

Learning from Print and Online Materials

Taking a wide range of classes requires mastering a variety of reading and studying skills, depending on the content, the teacher, and even the media used. Strategies in this chapter will help you absorb the material you read, for any course and in any format.

In this chapter, you'll explore answers to the following questions:

What sets you up for reading comprehension?

p. 62

How can you respond critically to what you read?

p. 63

How can SQ3R help you own what you read?

p. 65

How can you be an information literate reader and researcher?

p. 70

How Developed Are Your Reading and Information Literacy Skills?

For each statement, circle the number that best describes how true the statement is for you, from 1 for "not at all true for me" to 5 for "very true for me."

▶ I preview a text before studying it by skimming and scanning front matter, chapter elements, and back matter for clues about content and organization. 1 2 3 4 5

▶ I develop questions to guide me before I begin to read. 1 2 3 4 5

▶ I practice reciting what I've learned from the reading by working with a study partner, taking notes, using flash cards, or some other study technique. 1 2 3 4 5

▶ I use different strategies to read texts in different academic areas. 1 2 3 4 5

▶ I use text highlighting and text note taking to turn my texts into study tools. 1 2 3 4 5

▶ I have a process for reading on-screen assignments and articles. 1 2 3 4 5

▶ I prioritize my reading assignments so that I focus on what is most important. 1 2 3 4 5

▶ When I get a research or writing assignment, I go first to general references for an overview. 1 2 3 4 5

▶ I don't just rely on the Internet for research; I also consult library materials. 1 2 3 4 5

▶ I evaluate every Internet source for signs of bias, validity, credibility, and reliability. 1 2 3 4 5

If your total ranges from 41–50, you consider your reading and information literacy skills to be fairly well developed.
If your total ranges from 24–40, you consider your reading and information literacy skills to be somewhat developed.
If your total is less than 24, you consider your reading and information literacy skills to be underdeveloped.

Now total your scores.

REMEMBER No matter how developed your reading and literacy skills, you can improve them with effort. Read the chapter to learn new ways to build these skills, and practice by doing the activities.

What SETS YOU UP FOR READING COMPREHENSION?

College reading assignments, whether textbook chapters or other materials, are often challenging, requiring greater focus than with other materials as well as new strategies to understand the material fully. Before you open a book or log onto your computer, how can you get ready to make the most of your reading?

Take an Active and Positive Approach

Build a useful growth mindset with the following steps and strategies:

- *Define your purpose.* Know *why* you are reading what you are reading. To comprehend concepts and details? To evaluate critically? To learn how to do something?
- *Have an open mind.* Be careful not to prejudge assignments as impossible or a waste of time before you even begin.

If you look carefully at your schedule, you may find useful segments of time in between classes. Try using such time for reading assignments.

© Spencer Grant/Photo Researchers

- *Plan for multiple readings.* Don't expect to master challenging material on the first pass. Get an overview of key concepts on the first reading, and go into more detail on the next.
- *Get help when reading is tough to understand.* Consult reference materials, talk to instructors, or get help from study group partners or tutors.

Organize Your Study Area for Maximum Focus

Where, when, and with whom you study has a significant effect on your success.

- *Choose locations that work.* Know yourself and choose a setting that distracts you least—whether in your room at home, at a library, outdoors, or in an empty classroom. If you spent over 20 percent of your time blocking out distractions at a particular location, try someplace different.
- *Choose times that work.* Try to read at the times when you tend to be most alert and focused—keeping your time preferences and schedule in mind.

- *Concentrate.* Understanding material takes active focus. When you pay attention to one thing and one thing only, you are *concentrating.* The following tips can help improve your focus:
  1. *Deal with internal distractions.* When worries come up, such as to-do list items for other projects, write them down to deal with later. Sometimes you may want to take a break to handle what's bothering you. Exercise may help, music may relieve stress, and a snack can reduce hunger.
  2. *Take control of technology.* Web surfing, e-mailing, instant messaging, and downloading songs onto your iPod are reading distractions. Wait for breaks or after you finish your work to spend time checking texts or downloading.
  3. *Structure your work session.* Set realistic goals and a specific plan for dividing your time. Tell yourself: "I'm going to read 30 pages and then go online for 30 minutes."
  4. *Manage family obligations.* Set up activities or child care if you have kids. Tell them, if they are old enough to understand, what your education will mean to them and to you.
  5. *Plan a reward.* Have something to look forward to. You deserve it!

Expand Your Course Vocabulary

Every subject has its own specialized vocabulary. Mastering the new terms will improve your reading speed and comprehension, so it's worth the time to learn them. Try making flash cards, creating an end-of-text glossary, or simply using the words in your own sentences. The more you work with new ideas, the more embedded they will become.

How CAN YOU RESPOND CRITICALLY TO WHAT YOU READ?

Although textbooks are apt to be the core of your college reading, many instructors also assign other written materials such as trade books, journal and newspaper pieces, Internet articles, and *primary sources* (documents created during the time being studied—such as letters, diaries, legal documents, or plays). Also, any time you're asked to research and write about a topic, you will search for information by reading through articles and other source materials. Being a *critical reader*—a questioning reader who does not simply accept a document as truth—is crucial, even with textbooks, which are supposed to be as accurate as possible.

Critical reading involves questioning, analysis, and evaluation. Think of the reading process as an archaeological dig. First, you excavate a site and uncover the artifacts. Then you separate out what you've found, make connections among ideas, and evaluate what is important. This process allows you to focus on the most important materials.

Different purposes engage different parts of critical reading. When you are reading to learn and retain information or to master a skill, you *focus on important information* (analyzing and evaluating how the ideas are structured, how they connect, and what is most crucial to remember). When you are reading to search for truth, you *ask questions to evaluate arguments* (analyzing and evaluating the author's point of view as well as the credibility, accuracy, reliability, and relevancy of the material).

Focus on Important Information

Analyzing and evaluating the ideas and information in what you read is important for both texts and other materials. The following tips will help you determine what is most important to focus on as you study. Check to see whether the information does the following:

- Contains headings, charts, tables, captions, key terms, definitions, an introduction, or a summary (for a textbook, check midchapter or end-of-chapter exercises)
- Offers definitions, crucial concepts, examples, an explanation of a variety or type, critical relationships, or comparisons

- Sparks questions and reactions as you read
- Surprises or confuses you
- Mirrors what your instructor emphasizes in class or in assignments

Ask Questions to Evaluate Arguments

An *argument* refers to a persuasive case—a set of connected ideas supported by examples—that a writer makes to prove or disprove a point. Many scholarly books and articles, in print form or on the Internet, are organized around particular arguments (look for *claims*—arguments that appear to be factual but don't have adequate evidence to support them). Critical readers evaluate arguments and claims to determine whether they are accurate and logical. When quality evidence combines with sound logic, the argument is solid.

It's easy—and common—to accept or reject an argument according to whether it fits with your point of view. If you ask questions, however, you can determine the argument's validity and understand it in greater depth (see Key 5.1). Evaluating an argument involves looking at several factors:

- The quality of the *evidence* (facts, statistics, and other materials supporting an argument)
- Whether the evidence fits the idea concept
- The logical connections

Now that you are prepared to think critically about what you read, explore a tool that will help you read materials—especially textbooks—carefully and effectively.

Key 5.1 Ask Questions to Evaluate Arguments

Evaluate the Validity of the Evidence

What is the source?

Is the source reliable and free of bias?

Who wrote this and with what intent?

What assumptions underlie this material?

Is this argument based on opinion?

How does this evidence compare with evidence from other sources?

Determine Whether the Evidence Supports the Concept

Is there enough evidence?

Do examples and ideas logically connect?

Is the evidence convincing?

Do the examples build a strong case?

What different and perhaps opposing arguments seem equally valid?

How CAN SQ3R HELP YOU OWN WHAT YOU READ?

One of the most successful comprehension techniques for college students was first developed by Francis Pleasant Robinson in 1946. SQ3R, an acronym for *Survey, Question, Read, Recite,* and *Review,* is a reading comprehension tool for the active thinker.

As you move through the stages of SQ3R, you will skim and scan your text, a process that will help you become familiar with the material before trying to absorb every detail. *Skimming* involves the rapid reading of chapter elements like section introductions and conclusions, boldface or italicized terms, pictures, tables, charts, and chapter summaries. The goal of skimming is a quick overview. In contrast, *scanning* involves a careful search for specific information. You might use scanning during the SQ3R review phase to locate particular facts.

Just like many strategies presented to you throughout your college career, SQ3R works best if you adapt it to your own needs. Explore techniques, evaluate what works, and then make the system your own. As you become familiar with the system, keep in mind that SQ3R works best with textbook-based courses like science, math, social sciences, and humanities. SQ3R is not recommended for literature courses.

Step 1: Survey

The first stage of SQ3R, *surveying,* involves previewing, or prereading, your assignment. Most textbooks include elements that provide a big-picture overview of the main ideas and themes.

Front Matter

Skim the *table of contents* for the chapter titles, the main topics in each chapter, and the order in which they will be covered, as well as special features. Then skim the *preface* in which the author tells you what the book will cover and its point of view.

Chapter Elements

Text chapters use various devices to structure the material and highlight content.

- *Chapter titles* establish the topic and often the author's perspective.
- *Chapter introductions or outlines* generally list objectives or key topics.
- *Level headings* (first, second, third), including those in question form, break down material into bite-size chunks.
- *Margin materials* can include definitions, quotes, questions, and exercises.
- *Tables, charts, photographs, and captions* illustrate important concepts in a visual manner.

Reading Online Materials

More students, whether taking traditional, online, or hybrid courses, are reading textbooks on computers or other electronic devices. Keep these specific tips in mind when reading your text material online.

▶ **Get comfortable with your online reading platform.** Before you read anything, explore the features of the system, learning how to view the table of contents, flip pages, switch from one chapter to another, highlight and take notes, and adjust the view. The more you know your platform, the less technology issues will interfere with your learning as you read.

▶ **Know whether you need an Internet connection.** Some textbooks "live" online, whereas others are downloaded to your computer or device. Make sure you have Internet access if you need it.

▶ **Watch your speed.** When people read on a screen they tend to move quickly, focusing on heads and subheads, keywords, bullet points, and color. Make sure you slow down and focus in the same way you would when reading a printed book.

▶ **Print out material you want to have on paper.** Sometimes you may want to read or study at a time or place that does not allow electronic access.

PRACTICALLY

Use Step 2 to Get a Step Ahead
on Your Homework

By now you undoubtedly have some reading to do in some of your classes. Choose a text you are currently using and a small section or brief chapter from it.

Ask Yourself What You Know

Before you start, take a few minutes to summarize in writing what you already know about the topic of this brief section, if anything.

....
....
....

Write Questions

Looking at any headings, write questions linked to them.

....
....
....

Consider What You've Identified

Looking over the questions you've created, are there any themes that stand out? What are your major areas of concern? Of knowledge? Write them here.

....
....
....

- *Sidebars or boxed features* are connected to text themes and introduce extra tidbits of information that supplement the text.
- *Different styles or arrangements of type* (**boldface,** *italics,* underlining, larger fonts, bullet points, boxed text) can flag vocabulary or important ideas.
- *End-of-chapter summaries* review chapter content and main ideas.
- *Review questions and exercises* help you understand and apply content in creative and practical ways.

Back Matter

These can include extra resources like a glossary, index, and bibliography.

Before you begin to read, ask yourself the following questions to help you gain a deeper understanding of the material:

- What do the front matter, table of contents, and preface tell you about the theme? About the book's approach and point of view?

- What devices structure and organize a typical chapter? (Pay special attention to tables and charts if you are a visual-spatial learner.)
- After skimming the chapter, what do you know about the material? What elements helped you skim quickly?
- What back matter elements can you identify? What do they tell you about the text?
- How do you plan to use each of these elements to learn when you start studying?

Step 2: Question

The next step is to ask questions about your assignment. Using the *questioning* process that follows leads you to discover knowledge on your own, making an investment in the material and in your own memory.

- *Ask yourself what you know.* Before you begin reading, think about—and summarize in writing if you can—what you already know about the topic, if anything. This step prepares you to apply what you know to new material.
- *Write questions linked to chapter headings.* Next, examine the chapter headings and, on a separate page or in the text margins, write questions linked to them. When you encounter a reading without headings, divide the material into logical sections and then develop questions based on what you think is the main idea of each section. Key 5.2 shows how this works. The column on the left contains primary and secondary headings from a section of *Out of Many*, a U.S. history text. The column on the right rephrases these headings in question form.

Step 3: Read

Your text survey and questions give you a starting point for *reading*, the first R in SQ3R. Retaining what you read requires an active approach.

- *Focus on the key points of your survey.* Pay special attention to points raised in headings, in boldface type, in chapter objectives and summary, and other emphasized text.
- *Focus on your Q-stage questions.* Read the material with the purpose of answering each question. Write down or highlight ideas and examples that relate to your questions.
- *Look for the main idea.* Understanding what you read depends on your ability to recognize *main ideas*—the core ideas in a paragraph, segment, or chapter—and link other ideas to them. You are likely to find main ideas at the beginning or end of a paragraph.
- *Mark up your text.* Write notes in the margins, circle main ideas, or underline supporting details to focus on what's important. For an e-book, use the "Insert comments" feature. These cues will boost memory and help you study for exams. Here are some tips for *annotating*—taking marginal notes on the pages of your text:
  - Use pencil so you can erase comments or questions that are answered later.
  - Write your Q questions in the margins next to text headings.
  - Mark critical sections with marginal notations such as "Def." for definition, "e.g." for helpful example, "Concept" for an important concept, and so on.
  - Write notes at the bottom of the page connecting the text to what you learned in class or in

Key 5.2 | **Link Questions to Chapter Headings**

The Meaning of Freedom	What did freedom mean for both slaves and citizens in the United States?
Moving About	Where did African Americans go after they were freed from slavery?
The African American Family	How did freedom change the structure of the African American family?
African American Churches and Schools	What effect did freedom have on the formation of African American churches and schools?
Land and Labor After Slavery	How was land farmed and maintained after slaves were freed?
The Origins of African American Politics	How did the end of slavery bring about the beginning of African American political life?

research. You can also attach adhesive notes with your comments.

- *Highlight your text. Highlighting* involves the use of special markers or regular pens or pencils to flag important passages. When working with e-books, make note of the highlighting function, which allows you to overlay a color on important text. When used correctly, highlighting is an essential learning technique. However, experts agree that you will not learn what to highlight unless you *interact* with the material through surveying, questioning, reciting, and review. Use the following tips to make highlighting a true learning tool:

1. *Develop a system and stick to it.* Decide whether you will use different colors to highlight different elements, brackets for long passages, or pencil underlining.

2. *Consider using a regular pencil or pen instead of a highlighter pen.* The text will be cleaner and may look less like a coloring book.

3. *Mark text carefully if you are using a rented book or a book to be resold.* Use pencil as often as possible and erase your marks at the end of the class. Make notes on sticky notes that you can remove. Make copies of important chapters or sections for marking. If you are renting, check with the rental service to see what they permit.

4. *Read an entire paragraph before you begin to highlight, and don't start until you have a sense of what is important.* Only then put pencil or highlighter to paper as you pick out the main idea, key terms, and crucial supporting details and examples.

5. *Avoid overmarking.* Too much color can be overwhelming. Try enclosing long passages with brackets and avoid underlining entire sentences, when possible.

Key 5.3, from an introduction to business textbook describing the concepts of target marketing and market segmentation, shows how to underline and take marginal notes.

- *Use specific techniques for different disciplines.* Just as not all teachers are the same, neither are all course materials. Math textbooks often move sequentially—in other words, your understanding of later material depends on how well you have learned concepts in earlier chapters—and are problem-and-solution based, so you may want to work through problem steps as you read. Science textbooks are packed with vocabulary and formulas, so you may want to use mnemonic devices to remember them as you go. For social sciences, humanities, and literature, look for themes and think through problems and solutions.

Step 4: Recite

Once you finish reading a topic, stop and answer the questions you raised in the second stage of SQ3R. Even if you have already done this during the reading phase, do it again now—with the purpose of learning and committing the material to memory by *reciting* the answers.

You can say each answer aloud, silently speak the answers to yourself, "teach" the answers to another person, or write them down. Consider your learning styles as you find what works best. Whatever your method, make sure you know how ideas connect to one another and to the general concept.

When do you stop to recite? Waiting for the end of a chapter is too late; stopping at the end of one paragraph is too soon. The best plan is to recite at the end of each text section, right before a new heading. Repeat the question–read–recite cycle until you complete the chapter. If you fumble for thoughts, reread the section until you are on solid ground.

Step 5: Review

Studies show that between 40 and 50 percent of material we read is lost within 15 minutes of reading it.[1] After spending so much time reading material, it seems counterproductive to lose it. By *reviewing* soon after you finish a chapter, you can increase your retention of the material up to 80 percent.[2] Reviewing both immediately and periodically in the days and weeks after you read will

Chapter 10: Understanding Marketing Processes and Consumer Behavior   **297**

How does target marketing and market segmentation help companies sell product?

■ TARGET MARKETING AND MARKET SEGMENTATION

Definitions

Marketers have long known that products cannot be all things to all people. Buyers have different tastes, goals, lifestyles, and so on. The emergence of the marketing concept and the recognition of consumer needs and wants led marketers to think in terms of **target markets**—groups of people with similar wants and needs. <u>Selecting target markets is usually the first step in the marketing strategy.</u>

Target marketing requires **market segmentation**—dividing a market into categories of customer types or "segments." <u>Once they have identified segments, companies may adopt a variety of strategies.</u> Some <u>firms market products to more</u> than one segment. General Motors (*www.gm.com*), for example, offers compact cars, vans, trucks, luxury cars, and sports cars with various features and at various price levels. GM's strategy is to provide an automobile for nearly every segment of the market.

In contrast, <u>some businesses offer a narrower range of products</u>, each aimed toward a specific segment. Note that segmentation is a strategy for analyzing consumers, not products. The process of fixing, adapting, and communicating the nature of the product itself is called *product positioning.*

target market
Group of people that has similar wants and needs and that can be expected to show interest in the same products

← *GM eg*

market segmentation
Process of dividing a market into categories of customer types

GM makes cars for diff. market segments

How do companies identify market segments?

Identifying Market Segments

By definition, <u>members of a market segment must share some common traits that affect</u> their <u>purchasing decisions.</u> In identifying segments, researchers look at several different influences on consumer behavior. Three of the most important are *geographic, demographic,* and *psychographic variables.*

What effect does geography have on segmentation strategies?

Geographic Variables Many buying decisions are affected by the places people call home. The heavy rainfall in Washington State, for instance, means that people there buy more umbrellas than people in the Sun Belt. Urban residents don't need agricultural equipment, and sailboats sell better along the coasts than on the Great Plains. **Geographic variables** are the geographical units, from countries to neighborhoods, that may be considered in a segmentation strategy.

These patterns affect decisions about <u>marketing mixes for a huge range of products.</u> For example, consider a plan to market down-filled parkas in rural Minnesota. Demand will be high and price competition intense. Local newspaper ads may be

Buying decisions influenced by where people live

geographic variables
Geographical units that may be considered in developing a segmentation strategy

- good eg - selling parkas in Minnesota

Thought
Geographical variables change with the seasons

Source: Ronald J. Ebert and Ricky W. Griffin, *Business Essentials, 5th edition,* © 2005. Printed and electronically reproduced by permission of Pearson Education, Inc., Upper Saddle River, NJ.

help you learn and memorize material and prepare for exams. If you close the book after reading it once, you will probably forget almost everything.

Here are some reviewing techniques (which will be expanded on in Chapter 7). Try them all and use what works best for you.

- Reread your notes. Then summarize them from memory.
- Make an outline of key ideas or related concepts and identify relationships.
- Answer end-of-chapter review, discussion, and application questions.
- Make flash cards with a word or concept on one side and a definition, examples, or other related information on the other. Test yourself.
- Quiz yourself, using the questions you raised in the Q stage.
- Discuss the concepts with a classmate or in a study group.
- Ask your instructor about difficult material.

Refreshing your knowledge is easier and faster than learning it the first time. Make a weekly review schedule and stick to it until you're sure you know everything.

Being proficient in SQ3R will benefit you in almost every research situation you encounter, even those that don't necessarily involve books or in-class reading. Read on to learn the importance of information literacy and how to make the most of your next visit to the library, a search engine, or online database.

CAN YOU BE AN INFORMATION LITERATE READER AND RESEARCHER?

How

Although most students' first instinct is to power up the computer and start surfing Google, there are a

Much, although not all, research can be done using online databases. Get to know the databases and other resources that your school provides for you.

© Sarah Kravits

think
CRITICALLY

Examine Your Response to Internet Research

The World Wide Web has been compared to a "kitchen junk drawer," a disorganized jumble of things both useful and not so useful.[3] What is your reaction to the process of Internet research—excitement, fear, frustration? In a journal entry, respond to this question and analyze why you react this way. If your reaction is negative, analyze the benefit of becoming more comfortable with Internet research. If your reaction is positive, analyze how well you balance Internet research with other sources.

myriad of research resources at your fingertips—whether hard copy or electronic. Many of the materials you'll find in a library have been evaluated by librarians and researchers and are likely to be reliable—a definite time-saver when compared to the number of both credible and less-than-credible sources available online.

Map Out the Possibilities

To select the most helpful information for your research, you need to first know what is available to you. Sign up for a library orientation session. Familiarize yourself with the library resources shown in Key 5.4.

For a key advantage in any search for information, get to know a librarian. Librarians can assist you in locating unfamiliar or hard-to-find sources, navigating catalogs and databases, uncovering research shortcuts, and dealing with pesky equipment. Know what you want to accomplish before asking a question. At many schools, you can query a librarian via cell phone, e-mail, or instant messaging.

Conduct an Information Search

To avoid becoming buried in the sheer magnitude of resources available, use a practical, step-by-step search method. Key 5.5 shows how you start wide and then move in for a closer look at specific sources

When using virtual or online catalogs, you will need to adjust your research methods. Searching library databases requires that you use a *keyword search*—an exploration that uses a topic-related natural language word or phrase as a point of reference to locate other information. To narrow your topic and reduce the number of "hits" (resources pulled up by your search), add more keywords. For example, instead of searching through the broad category "art," focus on "French art" or more specifically, "19th century French art." Key 5.6 shows how to use the keyword system to narrow searches with what is called *Boolean logic*.

Be a Critical Internet Searcher

The *Internet*, a worldwide computer network, can connect you to billions of information sources. Unlike

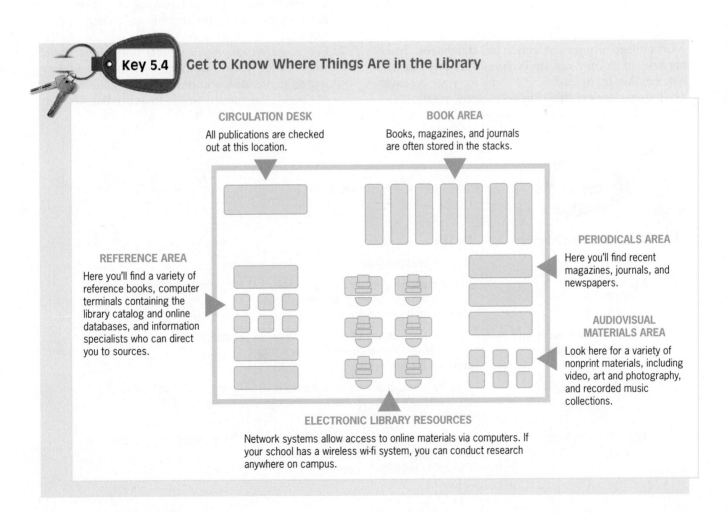

Key 5.4 Get to Know Where Things Are in the Library

CIRCULATION DESK
All publications are checked out at this location.

BOOK AREA
Books, magazines, and journals are often stored in the stacks.

REFERENCE AREA
Here you'll find a variety of reference books, computer terminals containing the library catalog and online databases, and information specialists who can direct you to sources.

PERIODICALS AREA
Here you'll find recent magazines, journals, and newspapers.

AUDIOVISUAL MATERIALS AREA
Look here for a variety of nonprint materials, including video, art and photography, and recorded music collections.

ELECTRONIC LIBRARY RESOURCES
Network systems allow access to online materials via computers. If your school has a wireless wi-fi system, you can conduct research anywhere on campus.

Key 5.5 Use a Step-by-Step Search Method

START WITH GENERAL REFERENCE WORKS

such as encyclopedias, almanacs, dictionaries, biographical references

MOVE TO SPECIALIZED REFERENCE WORKS

such as encyclopedias and dictionaries that focus on a narrow field

USE THE ELECTRONIC CATALOG TO LOCATE MATERIALS

Search the library catalog by author, title, or subject to learn where to locate specific books, periodicals, and journals. Most library catalogs are virtual and can be accessed by computers throughout the library. Ask a librarian for assistance, if needed.

BROWSE THROUGH RELEVANT BOOKS AND ARTICLES

Using your results from the catalog search, dive in deeper by finding and accessing helpful information in books and articles related to your topic.

your college library collection or databases, Internet resources may not be evaluated by anyone who vouches for their quality. As a result, your research depends on critical thinking and asking questions.

Start with Search Engines

Among the most popular and effective search engines are Google (www.google.com) and Yahoo! (www.yahoo.com). Search engines aimed at academic audiences include the Librarian's Index to the Internet (www.lii.org) and INFOMINE (www.infomine.com). At these academic directories, someone has screened the sites and listed only those sources that have been determined to be reputable and regularly updated.

Additionally, your school may include access to certain nonpublic academic search engines in the cost of your tuition. Sites like LexusNexus, InfoTrac, GaleGroup, and OneFile are known for their credibility in the academic world as well as their vast amounts of information. Check with your school's library to see how to access these sites.

Search Strategically

Without a librarian for guidance, you need to master a practical Internet search strategy.

1. *Use natural language phrases or keywords to identify what you are looking for.* Come up with a group of terms or phrases to use in your search.
2. *Use a search engine to isolate potentially useful sites.* Enter your questions, phrases, and keywords in various combinations to generate lists of "hits." Vary word order to see what you can

Key 5.6 Perform an Effective Keyword Search

If You Are Searching For . . .	Do This	Example
A word	Type the word normally.	Aid
A phrase	Type the phrase in its normal word order (use regular word spacing) or surround the phrase with quotation marks.	financial aid or "financial aid"
Two or more keywords without regard to word order	Type the words in any order, surrounding the words with quotation marks. Use *and* to separate the words.	"financial aid" and "scholarships"
Topic A or topic B	Type the words in any order, surrounding the words with quotation marks. Use *or* to separate the words.	"financial aid" or "scholarships"
Topic A but not topic B	Type topic A first within quotation marks, and then topic B within quotation marks. Use *not* to separate the words.	"financial aid" not "scholarships"

think CREATIVELY

Broaden Your Searching

Different search phrases yield different results. Knowing how to phrase your search to get the information you need can make your Internet research more effective. To practice this skill, first think of a topic you will need to research for an upcoming project. Next, brainstorm as many search phrases regarding the topic as you can, listing and thinking of synonyms and related topics. When you have ten different phrases, try them out in two different search engines. Which phrases yielded helpful information? Which ones didn't? Keep a list of helpful phrases and search terms for future reference.

generate. If you get too many hits, try using fewer or more specific keywords.

3. *Skim sites to evaluate what seems most useful.* Check the synopsis of the site's contents, the content providers, and the purpose of the site. Does the site seem relevant, reputable, or biased in favor of a particular point of view? A site owned by a company will want to promote its new product rather than provide unbiased consumer information. Consider the purpose—a blog is apt to focus on opinion in contrast to an article in a scholarly journal, which is likely to focus on facts and research findings.

4. *Save, or bookmark, the sites you want to focus on.* Make sure you can access them again. You may want to copy URLs and paste them into a separate document.

5. *When you think you are done, start over.* Choose another search engine and search again. Different systems access different sites.

The limitations of Internet-only research make it smart to combine Internet and library research. Search engines can't find everything, in part because not all sources are in digital format. The Internet also priori-tizes current information. Furthermore, some digital sources that are not part of your library's subscription offerings cost money. Finally, Internet searches require electricity or battery power and an online connection. Consider printing out Internet materials that you know you will need to reference over and over again.

Evaluate Every Source

Evidence examination is important for all reading materials, but especially when you research on the Internet, because online resources vary widely in reliability. This is where SQ3R can come in. Asking questions about sources is pivotal in determining their validity. Revisit Key 5.1 on page 64 to review effective questioning techniques.

Additionally, Robert Harris, professor and Web expert, has developed an easy-to-remember system for evaluating Internet information called the CARS test for information quality (Credibility, Accuracy, Reasonableness, Support).[4] Use the information in Key 5.7 to question any source you find as you conduct research. You can also use it to test the reliability of non-Internet sources.

Reading is the tool you will use over and over again to acquire information in school, on the job, and in life (your 401(k) retirement plan, local and world news, the fine print in a cell phone contract). Develop the ability to read with focus, purpose, and follow-through, and you will never stop enjoying the benefits.

Credibility	Accuracy	Reasonableness	Support
Examine whether a source is believable and trustworthy.	Examine whether information is correct—that is, factual, comprehensive, detailed, and up to date (if necessary).	Examine whether material is fair, objective, moderate, and consistent.	Examine whether a source is adequately supported with citations.
What are the author's credentials?	*Is it up to date, and is that important?*	*Does the source seem fair?*	*Where does the information come from?*
Look for education and experience, title or position of employment, membership in any known and respected organization, reliable contact information, biographical information, and reputation.	If you are searching for a work of literature, such as Shakespeare's play *Macbeth,* there is no "updated" version. However, you may want reviews of its latest productions. For most scientific research, you will need to rely on the most updated information you can find.	Look for a balanced argument, accurate claims, and a reasoned tone that does not appeal primarily to your emotions.	Look at the site, the sources used by the person or group who compiled the information, and the contact information. Make sure that the cited sources seem reliable and that statistics are documented.
Is there quality control?	*Is it comprehensive?*	*Does the source seem objective?*	*Is the information corroborated?*
Look for ways in which the source may have been screened. For example, materials on an organization's website have most likely been approved by several members; information coming from an academic journal has to be screened by several people before it is published.	Does the material leave out any important facts or information? Does it neglect to consider alternative views or crucial consequences? Although no one source can contain all of the available information on a topic, it should still be as comprehensive as possible within its scope.	While there is a range of objectivity in writing, you want to favor authors and organizations who can control their bias. An author with a strong political or religious agenda or an intent to sell a product may not be a source of the most truthful material.	Test information by looking for other sources that confirm the facts in this information—or, if the information is opinion, sources that share that opinion and back it up with their own citations. One good strategy is to find at least three sources that corroborate each other.

quick! SKILL BUILDING

Think Back

Solidify your knowledge and prepare for tests with this review. Answer the following questions on a separate sheet of paper or electronic file.

▶ Revisit the chapter-opening questions on page 61. Scan the chapter and write a short answer for each.

▶ Pick one section of this chapter and read it using SQ3R. First, develop Q questions. Next, survey the information and read. Then review—answer your Q questions in writing, and create one or more flash cards of key terms.

Credibility	Accuracy	Reasonableness	Support
Is there any posted summary or evaluation of the source?	*For whom is the source written and for what purpose?*	*Does the source seem moderate?*	*Is the source externally consistent?*
You may find abstracts of sources (summary) or a recommendation, rating, or review from a person or organization (evaluation). Either of these—or, ideally, both—can give you an idea of credibility before you decide to examine a source in depth.	Looking at what the author wants to accomplish will help you assess any bias. Sometimes biased information will not be useful for your purpose; sometimes your research will require that you note and evaluate bias (such as if you were to compare Civil War diaries from Union soldiers with those from Confederate soldiers).	Do claims seem possible, or does the information seem hard to believe? Does what you read make sense compared to what you already know? While wild claims may turn out to be truthful, you are safest to check everything out.	Most material is a mix of both current and old information. External consistency refers to whether the old information agrees with what you already know. If a source contradicts something you know to be true, chances are higher that the information new to you may be inconsistent as well.
Signs of a potential lack of credibility:	*Signals of a potential lack of accuracy:*	*Signals of a potential lack of reasonableness:*	*Signals of a potential lack of support:*
Anonymous materials, negative evaluations, little or no evidence of quality control, bad grammar or misspelled words	Lack of date or old date, generalizations, one-sided views that do not acknowledge opposing arguments	Extreme or emotional language, sweeping statements, conflict of interest, inconsistencies or contradictions	Statistics without sources, lack of documentation, lack of corroboration using other reliable sources

Source: Robert Harris, "Evaluating Internet Research Sources," June 15, 2007, VirtualSalt (www.virtualsalt/evalu8it.htm).

Analyze, Create, Practice

Put Reading Skills to Work

At this point in the term you undoubtedly have some reading to do. Using what you've learned in this chapter, choose a page from a textbook you are using this term (or a whole chapter if you really want to get some reading out of the way) to complete the following questions.

Analyze. First, gather information by skimming the excerpt. Identify the headings on the page and the relationships among them. Mark primary-level headings with a #1, secondary headings with a #2, and third-level headings with a #3.

Then evaluate: What do the headings tell you about the content?

....
....
....
....
....
....
....
....

Create. Identify two key concepts and then create a study question for each that will help you learn it.

1. ....

2. ....

Refer back to the multiple intelligence strategies table on page 41 to create a reading plan that works best for you. Identify two elements of that strategy here:

1. ....

2. ....

Practice. Use a marker pen to highlight phrases and sentences. Write marginal notes for later review. Identify where you might write "e.g." to flag an example. After reading the page thoroughly, summarize it here:

....

....

....

....

....

....

....

....

Multiple Intelligences *in action*

List three intelligences in the left-hand column—two that are highly developed for you and one you would like to build. Then in the right-hand column brainstorm one to three strategies for reading and studying that relate to each intelligence.

Intelligence	**Use MI Strategies to Come Up with Solutions**
Example: Bodily-Kinesthetic	*Pace as you review what you've read, and act out central concepts.*
....	....
	....
....	....
	....
....	....

chapter

6

Listening and Note Taking

Taking In and Recording Information

In every classroom, study group, tutoring session, and club meeting, you will encounter information that you may later need. This chapter will help you develop the listening and note-taking skills you need to retain that information. It will also focus on how you engage your critical, creative, and practical abilities while in a classroom setting.

In this chapter, you'll explore answers to the following questions:

How can you become a better listener?

p. 78

How can you improve your note-taking skills?

p. 81

What note-taking systems can you use?

p. 84

How Developed Are Your Listening and Note-Taking Skills?

For each statement, circle the number that best describes how true the statement is for you, from 1 for "not at all true for me" to 5 for "very true for me."

▶ I attend every one of my classes, except when I'm sick or have an emergency.   1 2 3 4 5

▶ I make it my business to arrive a few minutes early for every class.   1 2 3 4 5

▶ I try to stay focused from the beginning to the end of every class on what the instructor and classmates say about the material.   1 2 3 4 5

▶ I have a plan for "capturing" tough ideas I didn't entirely grasp during class.   1 2 3 4 5

▶ I don't let my feelings about my instructors get in the way of listening to their message.   1 2 3 4 5

▶ I try to minimize internal and external distractions when I'm in the classroom.   1 2 3 4 5

▶ I am open to learning about different note-taking systems.   1 2 3 4 5

▶ I prepare to take notes by completing all my assignments before the class.   1 2 3 4 5

▶ I use different note-taking strategies in class depending on the situation.   1 2 3 4 5

▶ I review and revise my notes on the same day I take them.   1 2 3 4 5

If your total ranges from 41–50, you consider your listening and note-taking skills to be fairly well developed.
If your total ranges from 24–40, you consider your listening and note-taking skills to be somewhat developed.
If your total is less than 24, you consider your listening and note-taking skills to be underdeveloped.

Now total your scores.

REMEMBER No matter how developed your listening and note-taking skills, you can improve them with effort. Read the chapter to learn new ways to build these skills, and practice by doing the activities.

How

CAN YOU BECOME A BETTER LISTENER?

The act of *hearing* is not the same as the act of *listening*. You can hear all kinds of things and not understand or remember any of them. Listening is a process that starts with hearing but also includes focused thinking about what you hear. Listening is a learnable skill that engages your critical, cre-ative, and practical thinking abilities and extends far beyond the classroom, enhancing your ability to relate with others in any situation.

Sitting in your classes, you probably have noticed a variety of not-so-academic activities that interfere with listening. Some people may be texting or surfing the Internet, some may be talking or sleeping, and some might just be daydreaming. In all of these cases the students are probably not absorbing much—or any—information from the instructor, and may be distracting you from listening as well. Read on to see how to address these issues, and others, on your path to becoming a better listener.

Issue 1: Distractions That Divide Your Attention

The common distractions that interfere with listening can be divided into *internal distractions* (worry, illness, fatigue, hunger, feeling too hot or too cold) and *external distractions* (chatting, computer use, any kind of movement or noise). Distractions like these nip away at your ability to pay attention.

Fix 1: Focus, focus, focus.

First of all, tell yourself you're in the class to learn and that you *really need* to know the material. You may even want to remind yourself of what you're paying to sit in this class. Find practical ways to minimize distractions.

- Sit near the front of the room.
- Move away from talkative classmates.
- Turn off your cell phone or put it on silent mode when in class.
- Get enough sleep to stay alert.
- Eat enough so you're not hungry—or bring small snacks if allowed.
- Try to put your worries aside during class.

Although you may think that you can handle distractions because you are used to multitasking, understand that multitasking—although often necessary—doesn't create the best possible setup for retention. Although your brain has the capacity to switch back and forth between routine tasks, it overloads when the tasks become harder or too numerous.[1] Even when it is hard, try to keep your focus on one thing at a time.

Issue 2: Listening Lapses

Even the most fantastic instructor can't make you listen. You and you alone can do that. If you decide that a subject is too difficult or uninteresting, you may tune out and miss what comes next. You may also focus on specific points and shut out everything else. Either way, you run the risk of not being prepared later and, in the long run, not making the most of your time.

Fix 2: An I-can-do-it attitude.

- *Start with a productive mindset.* If the class is hard, that's all the more reason to pay attention. Instructors are generally more sympathetic to, and

Listening to other students can be as important as listening to instructors. These students may learn something useful from their fellow student's presentation.

© iStockPhoto

eager to help, students who've obviously been trying even when it's tough.

- *Concentrate.* Work to take in the whole message so you will be able to read notes later, combine your class and text notes, and think critically about what is important. Making connections between ideas can ease the difficulty of the material (or alleviate boredom if you're familiar with the concepts).

- *Refocus.* If you experience a listening lapse, try to get back into the lecture quickly instead of worrying about what you missed. After class, look at a classmate's notes to fill in the gaps.

- *Be aware.* Pay attention to *verbal signposts*—words or phrases that call attention to what comes next—to help organize information, connect ideas, and indicate what is important and what is not. See Key 6.1 for examples.

Issue 3: Rushing to Judgment

It's common to stop listening when you hear something you don't like or don't agree with. You react, and then your emotions take focus. Unfortunately, you can spend valuable class time thinking of all the reasons your instructor is wrong and miss everything else. The situation might not seem particularly bad that day, but when the test comes around, you may feel differently about having missed material.

Judgments also involve reactions to speakers themselves. If you do not like your instructors or have preconceived notions about their race, ethnicity,

Key 6.1 | **Pay Attention to Verbal Signposts**

Signals Pointing to Key Concepts	Signals of Support
A key point to remember . . .	A perfect example . . .
Point 1, point 2, etc.	Specifically, . . .
Signals Pointing to Differences	**Signals That Summarize**
On the contrary, . . .	From this you have learned . . .
On the other hand, . . .	In conclusion, . . .

gender, physical characteristics, or disability, you may dismiss their ideas—and miss out on your opportunity to learn.

Fix 3: Recognize and correct your patterns.

Although it can be human nature to stop listening when you react to a speaker or message, it can make listening a lot harder. College is about broadening your horizons and looking for what different people can teach you, even though they and their beliefs may differ from you and yours. So what do you do?

- Recognize your pattern so you can change it. When you feel yourself reacting to something said in a lecture, stop and take a moment to breathe. Count to ten. Take one more breath and see how you feel.
- Know that you can't hear—and therefore can't learn anything from—others if you are filled with preconceived notions about them and their ideas. Put yourself in their shoes. Would you want them to stop listening to you if they disagreed or would you want to be heard completely?
- Stop it. It's as simple as that. Listen with an open mind even when you disagree or have a negative reaction to an instructor. Being open to the new and different, even when it makes you a bit uncomfortable, is part of what education is about.

Issue 4: Partial Hearing Loss and Learning Disabilities

If you have a hearing loss or a learning disability, listening effectively in class may prove challenging. Learning disabilities can come in a variety of forms affecting different parts of cognition (see Chapter 3, p. 32).

Fix 4: Get help.

If you have a hearing loss, find out about available equipment. For example, listening to a taped lecture at a higher-than-normal volume can help you hear things you missed. Ask instructors if digitalized recordings are available for download to a computer or iPod. Meeting with your instructor outside of class to clarify your notes may also help, as will sitting near the front of the room.

If you have, or think you have, a learning disability, learn what services are available. Talk to your advisor and instructor about your problem, seek out a tutor, visit academic centers that can help (such as the writing center if you have a writing issue), scan the college website, or connect to the office for students with disabilities. Know that you can succeed and that people are there to help you.

Issue 5: Comprehension Difficulties for Speakers of Other Languages

If English isn't your first language, listening and understanding material in the classroom can be challenging, requiring concentration, dedication, and patience. Specialized vocabulary, informal language, and the rate of speech can add to the challenge.

Fix 5: Take a proactive approach to understanding.

Talk to your instructor as soon as possible about your situation. Recognizing a need early and meeting to discuss it keeps your instructor informed and shows your dedication. In some cases, your professor will give you a list of key terms to review before class. During class, keep a list of unfamiliar words and phrases to look up later, but whenever possible don't let these terms prevent you from understanding the main ideas. Focus on the main points of the lecture and plan to meet with classmates after class to fill gaps in your understanding. If, after several weeks, you're still having difficulties, consider enrolling in an English refresher course, getting a tutor, or visit-

think CRITICALLY

Take an Active Listening Challenge

In a journal entry, recall a time when an instructor said something you found upsetting, boring, too easy, or too hard. Analyze your reaction using the following questions:

- What feeling did the situation evoke in you?
- What was the result? Were you more engaged or less engaged? Defensive? Inquisitive?
- What did you do to handle the feeling? How did it affect the rest of your experience?
- Identify which of this chapter's "Issue and Fix" scenarios your situation fits into best and consider the fixes. Analyze which one would suit this situation best and why.

ing the campus advising center for more assistance. Be proactive about your education.

Listening isn't always easy and it isn't always comfortable. As poet Robert Frost once said, "Education is the ability to listen to almost anything without losing your temper or your self-confidence." Keeping an open, engaged mind takes practice, but when excellent listening becomes second nature, you'll thank yourself for the work it took.

How CAN YOU IMPROVE YOUR NOTE-TAKING SKILLS?

You get to class early, open your notebook to a fresh page, and do finger calisthenics to prepare for a writing marathon. You're ready to take notes for the next hour, or at least that's what you think. Today, this particular instructor will make your task a lot harder. Instead of a clear, organized lecture, you are hit with some well-thought-out ideas with a beginning, middle, and end, and other ideas that seem like stream-of-consciousness musings. What can you do?

When taking notes, your goal is to record the important points made during class. This requires that you develop strong note-taking habits and find the right note-taking system, one that is comfortable for you and right for the class, the course content, and the instructor. This section will discuss both needs in depth.

When you become accustomed to taking notes, you'll be able to focus more on the information and less on how you are arranging it on the page. Following the three steps outlined next can help you develop your skills.

Step 1: Prepare

Showing up for class on time is just the start. Here's more about preparing to take notes:

- *Preview your reading material.* Reading assigned materials before class will give you the background to take effective notes. Check your class syllabi daily for assignment due dates and plan your reading time with these deadlines in mind.
- *Review what you know.* Taking 15 minutes before class to review your notes from the previous class and your reading assignment notes for that day will enable you follow the lecture from the start. Without this preparation, you may find yourself flipping back in your notebook instead of listening to new information.
- *Set up your environment.* Find a comfortable seat, away from friends if sitting with them distracts you. Use a separate notebook for each course, and start a new page for each class. If you use a laptop, open the file containing your class notes right away. Be ready to write (or type) as soon as the instructor begins speaking.
- *Gather support.* In each class, set up a support system with one or two students so you can look at their notes after an absence.

- *Choose the best note-taking system.* Take these factors into account to select a system that works best in each class:

  1. *The instructor's style* (which will be clear after a few classes). In the same term, you may have an instructor who is organized and speaks slowly, another who jumps around and talks rapidly, and a third who goes off topic in response to questions. Be flexible as you adapt.
  2. *The course material.* You may decide that an informal outline works best for a highly structured lecture and that a think link (discussed later in the chapter) is right for a looser presentation. Try one note-taking system for several classes and then adjust if necessary.
  3. *Your learning style.* Choose strategies that make the most of your strengths and compensate for weaknesses.

Examples of various note-taking systems, and a more thorough discussion, appear later in the chapter.

Step 2: Record Information During Class

The following practical suggestions will help you record what is important in a format that you can review later:

- *Start a new page or section for each new topic* if your instructor jumps from topic to topic during a single class.

- *Record whatever your instructor emphasizes* by paying attention to verbal and nonverbal cues.
- *Write down all key terms and definitions* so that you can refer back to them easily.
- *Note relevant examples, applications, and links to other material* when you encounter difficult concepts.
- *Ask questions.* If your instructor allows questions during class, ask them. Chances are several other students have similar queries. If your instructor prefers to answer questions at the end of class, keep a separate sheet of paper to jot down questions as you think of them.
- *Write down every question your instructor raises.* These questions may be on a test.
- *Be as organized as you can.* Remember that you can always improve your notes later.
- *Leave blank spaces between points* to make it easy see where one topic ends and another begins. (This suggestion does not apply if you are using a think link.)
- *Draw pictures and diagrams* to illustrate ideas.
- *Be consistent.* Use the same system to show importance—such as indenting, spacing, or underlining—on each page.
- *Record as much as you can* if you have trouble understanding a concept. Then leave space for an explanation and flag the margin with a large question mark. After class, try to clarify your questions by reading the text or ask a classmate or your instructor for help.

think

CREATIVELY

Bring Something New to Note Taking

According to Eastern Illinois University, studies show that people who don't take notes may forget up to 50 percent of a lecture in 24 hours, 80 percent within 2 weeks, and 95 percent within a month.[2]

Avoid being one of those people. Come up with two creative ways to make note taking more interesting. What might help—using a favorite pen, trying a new note-taking system, sitting in a different place? Go against convention. Try out your ideas to see what happens.

- *Consider that your class notes are part, but not all, of what you need to learn.* You will learn best when you combine your text and class notes.
- *Go beyond the PowerPoint.* Increasingly, instructors are using computer software to present lectures in the classroom. Although it may be tempting to simply copy down what's written on the slide, realize that instructors usually show the main points, not the details that may be tested later. Take notes on what your instructor says about each main idea highlighted on a PowerPoint slide.

Finally, don't stop taking notes when your class engages in a discussion. Even though it isn't part of the instructor's planned presentation, important information often surfaces. Key 6.2 has suggestions for how to take notes during class discussions.

Good listening powers note taking. When taking notes in class, stop to listen to the information before deciding what to write down.

© iStockPhoto

Use Shorthand to Save Time When Taking Notes

When you are trying to keep your note taking up to speed with what is going on in class, using shorthand and short phrases instead of full sentences can help. You can also use instant and text messaging symbols. To avoid forgetting what your shorthand means, review your notes while your symbols are fresh. If you tend to forget shorthand symbols, either jot down a key or write the complete word as you review your notes. The following chart shows some popular shorthand notations; you can find more on the Internet.

w/, w/o	with, without		Cf	compare, in comparison to
ur	you are		Ff	following
→	means; resulting in		Q	question
←	as a result of		gr8	great
↑	increasing		Pov	point of view
↓	decreasing		>	more than
b/c	because		=	equals
≈	approximately		b&f	back and forth
+ *or* &	and		Δ	change
Y	why		2	to; two; too
no. *or* #	number		Afap	as far as possible
i.e.	that is,		e.g.	for example
cos	change of subject		c/o	care of
Ng	no good		lb	pound
POTUS	President of the United States		hx	history

Key 6.2 Improve Your Notes During Class Discussions

- Listen to everyone; you never know when something important will be said.

- Listen for threads that weave through comments. They may signal an important point.

- Listen for ideas the instructor likes and for encouraging comments, such as "You make a great point" or "I like your idea."

- Take notes when the instructor rephrases and clarifies a point.

Step 3: Review and Revise Your Notes

By their very nature, class notes require revision. They may be incomplete in some places, confusing in others, and illegible in still others. That is why *it is critical to review and revise your notes as soon as possible after class.* This will enable you to fill in gaps while the material is fresh, to clarify sloppy handwriting, or to raise questions.

NOTE-TAKING SYSTEMS CAN YOU USE?

Now that you have gathered some useful note-taking strategies, take a look at different approaches to note taking. As you read about each system, keep some questions in mind:

- What class or type of instruction would this system be best suited for? Why?
- How could I make use of this system?
- Which system seems most comfortable to me?
- What system might be most compatible with my learning style strengths? Why?

Outlines

Many students use informal outlines for in-class note taking. Key 6.3 shows how the structure of an informal outline helps a student take notes on the topic of tropical rain forests.

Key 6.3 Create an Informal Outline

Tropical Rain Forests

What are tropical rain forests?

—Areas in South America and Africa, along the equator

—Average temperatures between 25° and 30°C (77°–86°F)

—Average annual rainfalls range between 250 to 400 centimeters (100 to 160 inches)

—Conditions combine to create the earth's richest, most biodiverse ecosystem.

  –A biodiverse ecosystem has a great number of organisms coexisting within a defined area.

  –Examples of rain forest biodiversity

    –2½ acres in the Amazon rain forest has 283 species of trees

    –A 3-square-mile section of a Peruvian rain forest has more than 1,300 butterfly species and 600 bird species

    –Compare this biodiversity to what is found in the entire U.S.—only 400 butterfly species and 700 bird species

Source: Teresa Audesirk, Gerald Audesirk, and Bruce E. Byers, Life on Earth, 2nd ed. Upper Saddle River, NJ: Prentice Hall, 2000, pp. 660–661.

Cornell T-Note System

The *Cornell note-taking system,* also known as the *T-note system,* consists of three sections on ordinary notepaper.[3]

• *Notes,* the largest section, is on the right. Skip lines between topics so you can see where sections begin and end.

• *Cue column* goes to the left of your notes. Leave it blank while you take notes, and fill it in later as you review. You might insert keywords or comments to highlight ideas or clarify meaning. You might add examples or diagrams. You might raise questions to answer as you study.

• *Summary* goes at the page bottom. Use this section to summarize critical points in your own words.

Key 6.4 shows how the Cornell system is used in a business course.

Key 6.4 **The Cornell System Has Space for Notes, Comments, and a Summary**

October 3, 2010, p. 1

Understanding Employee Motivation

Purpose of motivational theories
- To explain role of human relations in motivating employee performance
- Theories translate into how managers actually treat workers

2 specific theories
- <u>Human resources model</u>, developed by Douglas McGregor, shows that managers have radically different beliefs about motivation.
  - Theory X holds that people are naturally irresponsible and uncooperative
  - Theory Y holds that people are naturally responsible and self-motivated
- <u>Maslow's Hierarchy of Needs</u> says that people have needs in 5 different areas, which they attempt to satisfy in their work.
  - Physiological need: need for survival, including food and shelter
  - Security need: need for stability and protection
  - Social need: need for friendship and companionship
  - Esteem need: need for status and recognition
  - Self-actualization need: need for self-fulfillment

Needs at lower levels must be met before a person tries to satisfy needs at higher levels.
- Developed by psychologist Abraham Maslow

Cue column:

Why do some workers have a better attitude toward their work than others?

Some managers view workers as lazy; others view them as motivated and productive.

Maslow's Hierarchy

self-actualization needs (challenging job)
esteem needs (job title)
social needs (friends at work)
security needs (health plan)
physiological needs (pay)

Summary: Two motivational theories try to explain worker motivation. The human resources model includes Theory X and Theory Y. Maslow's Hierarchy of Needs suggests that people have needs in 5 different areas: physiological, security, social, esteem, and self-actualization.

Think Links

A *think link,* also referred to as a *mind map* or *word web,* uses shapes and lines to link ideas to supporting details. The visual design makes the connections easy to see, and shapes and pictures extend the material beyond words. This can help illustrate ideas, concepts, and relationships as you take notes.

To create a think link, start by circling or boxing your topic in the middle of the paper. Next, draw a line from the topic and write the name of one major idea at the end of the line. Circle that idea. Then jot down specific facts related to the idea, linking them to the idea with lines. Continue the process, connecting thoughts to one another with circles, lines, and words. Key 6.5, a think link on the sociological concept "stratification," follows this structure.

Charting Method

Sometimes instructors deliver information in such quantities and at such speeds that taking detailed notes becomes nearly impossible. In such situations when there is a lot of material coming at you very quickly, the *charting method* might prove quite useful. It is also excellent for classes presented chronologically or sequentially.

To create charting notes, determine the topics of the day's lecture by looking ahead in your syllabus or contacting your instructor. Then separate your paper into distinct columns such as definitions, important phrases, and key themes. As you listen to the lecture, this will help you track dialogues that can be easy to lose and provide quick memorization tools by splitting material into relevant categories. Key 6.6 shows a partial set of charting notes for a history class.

Other Visual Strategies

Visual strategies work best in small doses to augment other note-taking techniques. Use them when taking text notes or combining class and text notes for review.

- *Pictures and diagrams.* The act of converting material into a visual display will activate both

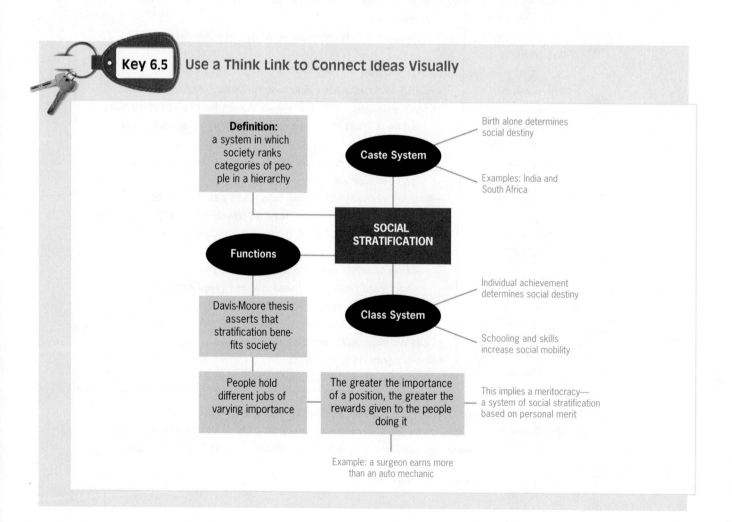

Key 6.5 **Use a Think Link to Connect Ideas Visually**

Definition: a system in which society ranks categories of people in a hierarchy

Caste System
- Birth alone determines social destiny
- Examples: India and South Africa

SOCIAL STRATIFICATION

Functions

Davis-Moore thesis asserts that stratification benefits society

People hold different jobs of varying importance

The greater the importance of a position, the greater the rewards given to the people doing it

Example: a surgeon earns more than an auto mechanic

Class System
- Individual achievement determines social destiny
- Schooling and skills increase social mobility

This implies a meritocracy—a system of social stratification based on personal merit

Key 6.6 | Use a Chart to Take Notes

Time Period	Important People	Events	Importance
1969–1974	Richard Nixon	Watergate, Vietnam War	Ended Vietnam War, opened relations with China, first president to resign

your bodily-kinesthetic attributes as well as your visual intelligence.

- *Timelines.* Use a timeline to organize information into chronological order.
- *Tables.* Use the columns and rows of a table to organize information as you condense and summarize your notes.
- *Hierarchy charts.* Charts showing an information hierarchy can help you visualize how pieces fit together in terms of categories or levels of classification.

Note taking is a very personal skill. It takes time and experience to learn which method is most effective for you. Try out different methods in different situations to discover which works best. Remember, your ability to take your education forward often relies on your ability to capture information in the moment.

PRACTICALLY

Try a New Note-Taking System

Identify a class for which you regularly take notes. ....

Name the note-taking method you generally use in this class. If you don't use a method that has a particular name, describe how you go about taking notes and what they look like.

....

....

When is the next meeting of this class? ....

During that next meeting, choose one note-taking method from this chapter that you have never used or do not regularly use, and take notes using that method. Which method will you use?

....

Finally, after the class period, briefly describe your reaction to the experience. Did it improve your notes, your concentration, your focus? Did it distract you or cause other problems? Would you use it again?

....

....

....

Think Back

Solidify your knowledge and prepare for tests with this review. Answer the following questions on a separate sheet of paper or electronic file.

▶ Revisit the chapter-opening questions on page 77. Scan the chapter and write a short answer for each.

▶ As you review the chapter, take notes on the first section of material using an informal outline. For the second section, use a visual method, such as the mind map or charting method.

Analyze, Create, Practice

Identify Listening and Note-Taking Conditions That Work for You

Put your thinking skills to work to improve your listening and note-taking skills:

Analyze.   Describe a recent class in which you were able to listen effectively and take notes (course title, type of classroom setting, and so forth).

....

....

Describe the instructor's style (lecture, group discussion, Q&A) and any listening barriers.

....

....

Describe your level of preparation and attitude toward the class.

....

....

Describe your note-taking style and the effectiveness of your notes as study tools.

....

....

Now describe a class in which you found it hard to listen and take notes (course title, type of classroom setting, etc.).

....

....

Describe the instructor's style (lecture, group discussion, Q&A) and any listening barriers.

....

....

Describe your level of preparation and attitude toward the class.

....

....

Describe your note-taking style and the effectiveness of your notes as study tools.

....

....

Examine the two situations and identify two conditions that are crucial for you to be able to listen and take notes effectively.

....

....

Create. Brainstorm two ways to improve your listening and note taking in the more difficult situation.

....

....

Practice. Apply your plan this week and see what happens. Make adjustments until you can listen well and take effective notes. Write about your experience here.

....

....

Multiple Intelligences in action

Write three intelligences in the left-hand column—two that are highly developed for you and one you would like to build. Then, in the right-hand column, brainstorm a strategy for listening and/or note taking that relates to each intelligence.

Intelligence	Use MI Strategies to Come Up with Solutions
Example: Naturalistic	*Use the chart method to categorize pieces of information your instructor discusses. Later, identify relationships among the points.*
....	....
	....
....	....
	....
....	....
	....

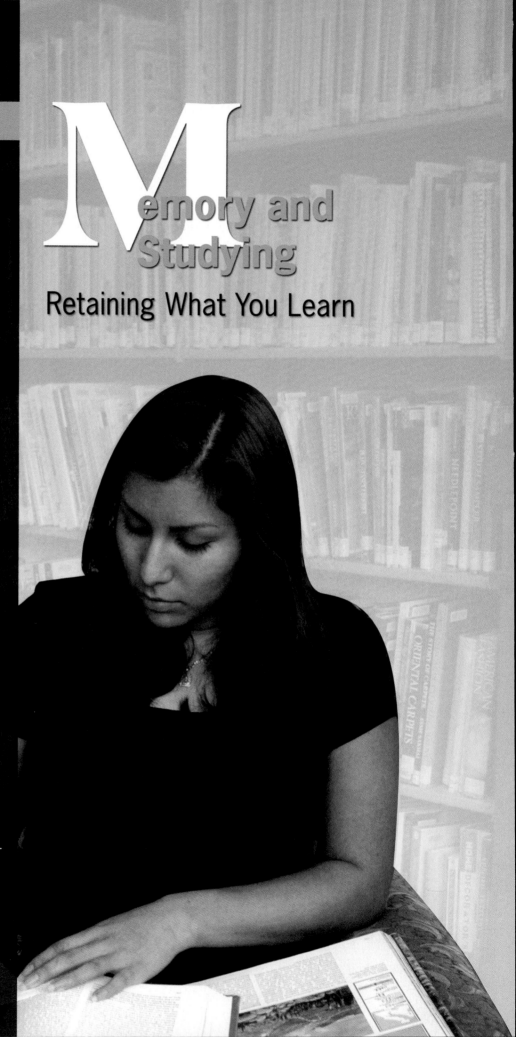

Memory and Studying

Retaining What You Learn

The ability to remember and apply what you learn to a variety of situations will be valuable on test day and, more importantly, throughout your life. As you read this chapter, you will develop your memory and study skills, noting how to maximize your study efforts by using helpful memory strategies and devices.

In this chapter, you'll explore answers to the following questions:

How does memory work?

p. 91

How can you remember what you study?

p. 94

How can mnemonic devices boost recall?

p. 99

Which strategies can make studying for test day a success?

p. 100

quick!
CHECK

How Developed Are Your Memory and Study Skills?

For each statement, circle the number that best describes how true the statement is for you, from 1 for "not at all true for me" to 5 for "very true for me."

▶ I strengthen my ability to remember information by reviewing regularly.	1 2 3 4 5
▶ I use strategies like journalist questions to determine what to study first.	1 2 3 4 5
▶ I seek out study locations that help me focus and learn.	1 2 3 4 5
▶ When studying with others, I employ team strategies to increase the chance of success.	1 2 3 4 5
▶ I believe it is as important to understand *why* information should be learned as it is to learn it.	1 2 3 4 5
▶ I use flash cards and other active memory strategies to remember what I study.	1 2 3 4 5
▶ I create mnemonic devices with vivid images and associations as memory hooks.	1 2 3 4 5
▶ I employ creative techniques like songs, rhymes, and acronyms to help me remember tough material.	1 2 3 4 5
▶ I combine class and text notes together to study from when I have a big test coming up.	1 2 3 4 5
▶ I avoid cramming but understand how to make the most of it if necessary.	1 2 3 4 5

If your total ranges from 41–50, you consider your memory and study skills to be fairly well developed.
If your total ranges from 24–40, you consider your memory and study skills to be somewhat developed.
If your total is less than 24, you consider your memory and study skills to be underdeveloped.

Now total your scores.

REMEMBER No matter how developed your memory and study skills, you can improve them with effort. Read the chapter to learn new ways to build these skills, and practice by doing the activities.

How DOES MEMORY WORK?

Memory anchors all learning and performance on tests as well as at work. The information you remember—concepts, facts, processes, formulas, and more—is the raw material with which you think, write, create, build, and perform your day-to-day actions in school and out. Tasks ranging from high-level chemistry experiments to running a load of laundry through the washing machine all require you to retain and use information in your memory.

Through studying, you build your memory and use it to move toward your goals. This chapter provides a host of memory improvement techniques that you can make your own with a growth mindset and active involvement. The first step is exploring how memory works.

The Information Processing Model of Memory

Memory refers to the way the brain stores and recalls experiences or information acquired through the

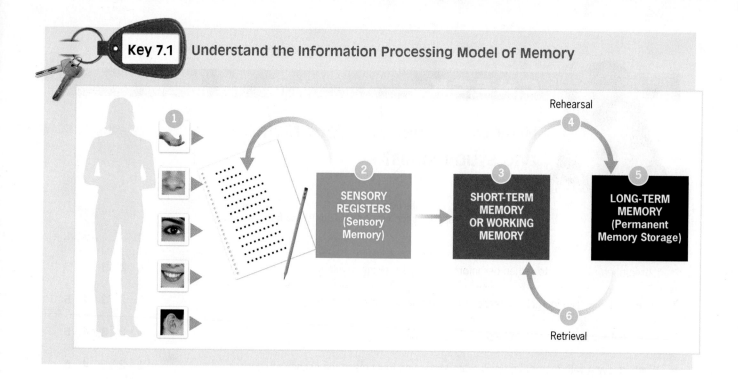

five senses. Unconsciously, your brain sorts through stimuli and stores only what it considers important. The following list describes how the brain forms lasting memories as you read (see Key 7.1 for an illustration).

1. Raw information, gathered through the five senses, reaches the brain (for example, the tune of a song you're learning in your jazz ensemble class).

2. This information enters *sensory registers*—filters that send sensory information to the short-term memory—where it stays for only seconds. (As you play the notes for the first time, the sounds stop in your auditory register.)

3. You then choose to pay attention to some information in the sensory register. When you selectively look, listen, smell, taste, or feel the information, you move it into *short-term memory*, also known as *working memory*, which contains what you are thinking at any moment. (The part of the song that you're responsible for, for example, the clarinet solo, will likely take up residence in your working memory.)

4. Information moves to *long-term memory* through focused, active rehearsal repeated over time. As shown in Key 7.2, long-term memory has three separate storage houses. Long-term memory is the storage house for everything you know from Civil War battle dates to the location of your grade school. There are no limits to how much information long-term memory can hold or how long it can hold it. When you need information from this area, say, for a test, your brain retrieves it and returns it to your short-term memory. (As you practice the song in class and at home, your brain stores the tone, rhythm, and pace in your long-term memory where you will be able to draw on it again.)

The movement of information in your brain, from short-term to long-term memory and then back again, strengthens the connections among neurons (brain cells). As you read in Chapter 1, learning happens and memories are built when neurons grow new dendrites and form new synapses. When you learn an algebra formula, for example, your brain forms new connections. Every time you review it, the connections get stronger.

Why You Forget

Health issues and poor nutrition can cause memory problems. Stress is also a factor; research shows that even short-term stress can interfere with cell communication in the learning and memory regions of the brain.[1] However, *the most common reason that information fails to stay in long-term memory is ineffective studying*—not doing what you need to retain what you learn.

As Key 7.3 shows, retaining information requires continual review. You are still learning information 10 minutes after you hear it the first time. If you review the material over time—after 24 hours, a week, a month, 6 months, and more—you will retain the knowledge. If you do not review, the neural connections will weaken, and eventually you will forget.

LONG-TERM MEMORY

STORAGE OF PROCEDURAL MEMORY

Storage for information about procedures, in other words, how to do things—ride a bike, drive a car, tie your shoes. It can take a while to develop these memories, but they are difficult to lose.

STORAGE OF DECLARATIVE MEMORY

Memories of facts, concepts, formulas, and so on. These are relatively easy to learn, but are easy to forget without continual review.

$$x = \frac{-b \pm \sqrt{b^2 - 4ac}}{2a}$$

STORAGE OF EPISODIC MEMORY

Memories of events linked to personal experiences. To retain an episodic memory, you only need to be exposed to it once.

Key 7.3 Reviewing Is Essential for Maintaining Memories

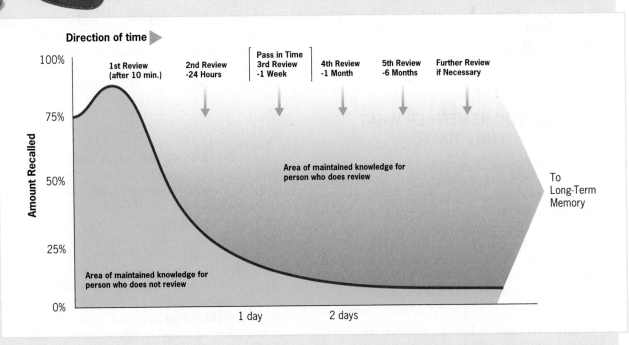

Source: From Use Both Sides of Your Brain *by Tony Buzan, © 1974, 1983 by Tony Buzan. Used by permission of Dutton, a division of Penguin Group (USA) Inc.*

Analyze Your Memory Skills

In a classic study conducted in 1885, researcher Herman Ebbinghaus memorized a list of meaningless three-letter words such as CEF and LAZ. He then examined how quickly he forgot them. Within 1 hour he had forgotten more than 50 percent of what he had learned; after 2 days, he knew fewer than 30 percent of the memorized words.[2] Consider the course(s) in which you have the most difficulty remembering information or procedures. In a journal entry, briefly identify your difficulty and analyze your current study techniques in the course(s), including any steps you have taken to combat the problem. Finally, analyze how your ability to retain information in college may affect your life or work.

If forgetting is so common, why do some people have better memories than others? A few people may have an inborn talent. More often, though, people succeed because they actively and consistently use techniques for improving recall. Those brain-boosting study techniques are available to everyone. Now that you know more about how your memory works, explore ways to retain and retrieve important information.

How CAN YOU REMEMBER WHAT YOU STUDY?

Whatever you study—textbooks, course materials, notes, primary sources—your goal is to anchor important information in long-term memory so that you can use it, for both short-term goals like tests and long-term goals like being an information technology specialist. To remember what you study, you need to carefully figure out and use what works best for you. One great way to do this is to use *journalists' questions*—six questions journalists tend to ask as a writing aid.

1. **When, Where, Who**—determine the times, places, and company (or none) that suit you.
2. **What, Why**—choose what is important to study, and set the rest aside.

3. **How**—find the specific tips and techniques that work best for you.

When, Where, and Who: Choosing Your Best Setting

Figuring out the when, where, and who of studying is all about self-management. You analyze what works best for you, create ideas about how to put that self-knowledge to work, and use practical thinking to implement those ideas as you study.

When

The first part of *When* is "How Much." Having the right amount of time for the job is crucial. One formula for success is a simple calculation: *For every hour you spend in the classroom each week, spend at least 2 to 3 hours preparing for the class.* For example, if you are carrying a course load of 15 credit hours, you should spend 30 hours a week studying outside of class.

The second part of *When* is "What Time." First, determine the time available to you in between classes, work, and other commitments. Then, thinking about when you function best, choose your study times carefully. You may not always have the luxury of being free during your peak energy times—but do the best you can.

The third part of *When* is "How Close to Original Learning." If you can, review notes the same day you

The study location that works for you depends on your individual needs. This student has found he can concentrate best on his physical geology material if he reads it at a table in the library.

© Davis Barber/PhotoEdit

the obvious benefit of greater communication and teamwork skills, group study enhances your ability to remember information by:[3]

- Getting you to say what you know out loud, which solidifies your understanding
- Exposing you to the ideas of others and getting you thinking in different ways
- Increasing the chance that all of the important information will be covered
- Making it more likely that you will study in preparation for a group meeting
- Subjecting you to questions about your knowledge, and maybe even some challenges, that make you clarify and build on your thinking

What and Why: Evaluating Study Materials

Even if you had hours of time and boundless energy, you would be likely to go on overload if you studied every word of information. Before you dive into your books and materials, decide *what* to study by examining *why* you need to know it. Here's how:

- *Choose materials to study.* Within textbooks or other materials, which chapters or sections are important to know for your goal (for example, to study for an upcoming test) and why?
- *Prioritize materials.* Decide which materials demand your best energy, and determine the order for tackling them.
- *Set specific goals.* Looking at what you need to cover and the time available, decide what you will accomplish. Make a list for reference and check things off as you go.
- *Within the sections you study, separate main points from unimportant details.* Ask yourself, "What is the most important information?" Highlight only the key points in your texts, and write notes in the margins about central ideas (see Chapter 5 on reading for more about studying).

took them in class, make an organizer of important information from a text chapter shortly after you read it, and write a summary of a group study session within 24 hours of the meeting.

The final part of *When* is "When to Stop." Take a break when your body is no longer responding. Forcing yourself to study when you're not engaged is not a good use of your time.

Where

Where you study matters. As with time, consider your restrictions first—there may be only so many places available to you, within a reasonable travel distance, and open when you have study time free. Also, were previous study sessions there productive? If you spent too much time trying to block out other distractions, consider another location.

Who

Whom you study with is a personal choice. However, even students who study primarily alone can benefit from working with others from time to time (see Chapter 1 for tips on study group success). Besides

How: Using Study Strategies

After figuring out the *when, where, who, what,* and *why* of studying, focus on the *how*—the strategies that will anchor the information you need in your brain. You may already use several of them. Try as many as you can, and keep what works. Key 7.4 shows them at a glance on the following page.

Purpose, Intention, and Emotional Connection

If you can remember the lyrics to dozens of popular songs but not the functions of the pancreas, perhaps

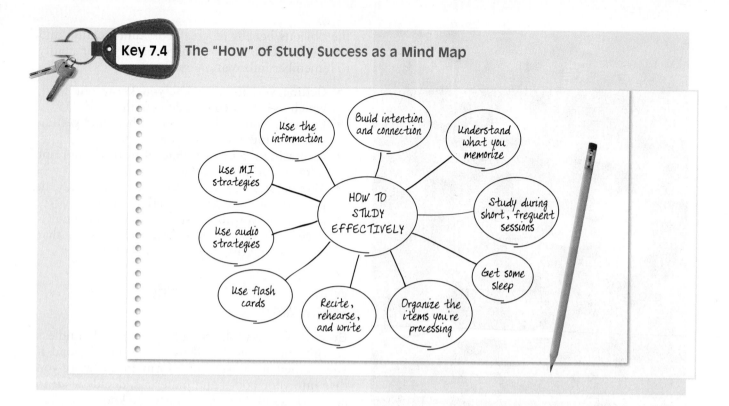

emotion is involved. When you care about something, your brain responds differently, and you learn and remember more easily.

To achieve the same results in school, try to create a purpose and will to remember by finding a kind of emotional involvement with what you study. One way is to think about how learning the material supports your most important reason for succeeding in school—raising a family, achieving a career goal, whatever makes you feel focused and driven.

Cram—Only If You Must

Cramming—studying intensively and around the clock right before an exam—often results in information sinking in temporarily and floating out when the exam is over. *If learning is your goal, cramming is not a good idea.* The reality, however, is that you are likely to cram sometime in college, especially for midterms and finals. When you do, these tips will help:

▶ **Focus on crucial concepts.** Summarize the most important points and try to resist reviewing notes or texts page by page.

▶ **Create a last-minute study sheet to review right before the test.** Write down key facts, definitions, or formulas on a single sheet of paper or on flash cards. If you prefer visual notes, use think links to map out ideas and supporting examples.

▶ **Arrive early.** Review your study aids until you are asked to clear your desk.

▶ **Try to stay calm.** Cramming can jangle your pre-test nerves. Visualize how you want your test day to go, and use any technique that helps you reduce stress during the lead-up time.

Understand What You Memorize

It sounds kind of obvious—but something that has meaning is easier to recall than something that makes little sense. This basic principle applies to everything you study. Figure out logical connections, and use these connections to help you learn.

When you have trouble remembering something new, think about how the new idea fits into what you already know. A simple example: If you can't remember what a word means, look at the word's root, prefix, or suffix. Knowing that the root *bellum* means "war" and the prefix *ante* means "before" will help you recognize that *antebellum* means "before the war."

Study During Short, Frequent Sessions

You can improve your chances of remembering material by learning it more than once. A pattern of short sessions, say three 20-minute study sessions, followed by brief periods of rest is more effective than continual studying with little or no rest. Try studying on your own or with a classmate during breaks in your schedule. Although studying between classes isn't for everyone, you may find that it can help you remember more.

In addition, scheduling regular, frequent review sessions over time will help you retain information more effectively. If you have 2 weeks before a test, set up study sessions three times per week instead of putting the final 2 days aside for hours-long study marathons.[4]

Get Your Body Ready

Even though sleep may take a back seat with all you have to do in crunch times, research indicates that shortchanging your sleep during the week impairs your ability to remember and learn, even if you try to make up for it by sleeping all weekend.[5] Sleep improves your ability to remember what you studied before you went to bed. So does having a good breakfast. Even if you're running late, grab enough food to fill your stomach.

Organize the Items You Are Processing

There are a few ways to do this:

- *Divide longer material into manageable sections.* Master each section, put all the sections together, and then test your memory of all the material.
- *Use the chunking strategy.* Chunking—placing disconnected information into smaller units that are easier to remember—increases memory capacity. For example, though it is hard to remember these ten digits—4808371557—it is easier to remember them in three chunks—480 837 1557. In general, try to limit groups to ten items or fewer.
- *Use organizational tools.* Rely on an outline, a think link, or another organizational tool to record material and the logical connections among the elements (see Chapter 6 for more on note taking).
- *Be careful when studying more than one subject.* When studying for several tests at once, avoid studying two similar subjects back-to-back. Your

think **CREATIVELY**

Focus Despite Frustration

You probably have thought, or heard someone say, "Why do I have to know *this*? I'm never going to use this information again!" Every student experiences the frustration of needing to work hard to remember something that he or she thinks is completely unimportant and irrelevant. How do you handle this, and how *should* you handle it? Apply your creative thinking skills to develop at least five new, innovative ways to approach this common frustration productively. Take some risks, consider other perspectives, and use your imagination.

memory may be more accurate when you study history after biology rather than chemistry after biology.

• *Notice what ends up in the middle—and practice it.* When you are studying, you tend to remember what you study first and last. The weak link is likely to be what you study midway. Knowing this, try to give this material special attention.

Recite, Rehearse, and Write

When you *recite* material, you repeat key concepts aloud, in your own words, to aid memorization. You also summarize these concepts. *Rehearsing* is similar to reciting but is done silently. *Writing* is reciting on paper. Instead of just repeating exactly what you read, use these steps to get the greatest benefit:

• Focus as you read on *main ideas,* which are usually found in the topic sentences of paragraphs. Then recite, rehearse, or write the ideas down.

• Convert each main idea into a keyword, phrase, or visual image—something easy to recall that will set off a chain of memories bringing you back to the original material. Write each keyword or phrase on an index card.

• One by one, look at the keywords on your cards and recite, rehearse, or write all the associated information you can recall. Check your recall against the original material.

These steps are part of the process of consolidating and summarizing lecture and text notes as you study—a key study strategy you will read more about later in this chapter.

Use Flash Cards

Flash cards give you short, repeated review sessions that provide immediate feedback. Use the front of a 3-by-5-inch index card to write a word, idea, or phrase you want to remember. Use the back for a definition, explanation, and other key facts. Carry your cards with you and perform a self-test with them whenever you have a few free moments. Key 7.5 shows two flash cards used to study for a psychology exam.

Use Audio Strategies

Although all students can benefit from audio strategies, they are especially useful if you learn best through hearing.

• *Create audio flash cards.* Record short-answer study questions by leaving 10 to 15 seconds blank after questions, so you can answer out loud. Record the correct answer after the pause to give yourself immediate feedback.

• *Use podcasts.* An increasing amount of information is presented in podcasts—knowledge segments that are downloadable to your computer or MP3 player. Ask your instructors if they intend to make any lectures available in podcast format.

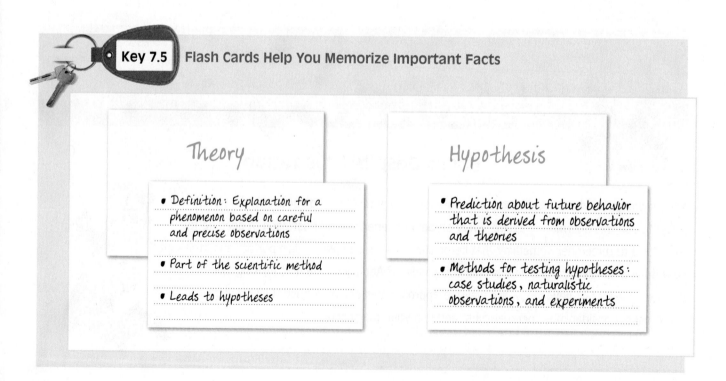

Key 7.5 Flash Cards Help You Memorize Important Facts

Theory
• Definition: Explanation for a phenomenon based on careful and precise observations
• Part of the scientific method
• Leads to hypotheses

Hypothesis
• Prediction about future behavior that is derived from observations and theories
• Methods for testing hypotheses: case studies, naturalistic observations, and experiments

Use Learning Styles Strategies

Look back to your MI and Personality Spectrum assessments in Chapter 3. Identify your strongest areas and locate study techniques applicable for each. For example, if you scored highly in bodily-kinesthetic, try reciting material aloud while standing or walking. Be open to trying something new—even if it sounds a little odd to begin with. Effective studying is about finding what works, often by any means necessary.

Use the Information

In the days after you learn something new, try to use the information in every way you can. Apply it to new situations and link it to problems. Explain the material to a classmate. Test your knowledge to make sure the material is in long-term memory. However, be sure you practice *applying* the knowledge to real-life situations, not just recalling it. Your success depends on the amount that you *learned*, not the amount you memorized.

How CAN MNEMONIC DEVICES BOOST RECALL?

Certain performers entertain audiences by remembering the names of 100 strangers or flawlessly repeating 30 ten-digit numbers. Although these performers probably have superior memories, they also rely on memory techniques, known as *mnemonic devices* (pronounced neh-MAHN-ick), for assistance. Mnemonic devices use vivid associations and acronyms to link new information to what you already know.

think PRACTICALLY

Plan a Study Session

Map out a session that will take place within the next 7 days. Decide how you will learn something important to know for one of your current courses. Answer the questions below to create your session:

When will you study, and for how long?

....

Where will you study?

....

Whom will you study with, if anyone?

....

What will you study?

....

Why is this material important to know?

....

How will you study it—what strategy (or strategies) do you plan to use?

....

....

The final step is putting this plan to work. Date you will use it: ....

Instead of learning new facts by *rote* (repetitive practice), associations give you a "hook" on which to hang these facts and retrieve them later. Mnemonics make information unforgettable through unusual mental associations and visual pictures.

Mnemonics take time and effort to create, and you'll have to be motivated to remember them. Because of this, use them only when necessary—for instance, to clarify confusing concepts. Also know that no matter how clever they are and how easy they are to remember, mnemonics usually do not contribute to understanding. Their sole objective is to help you memorize.

Create Visual Images and Associations

To remember that the Spanish artist Picasso painted *The Three Women*, you might imagine the women in a circle dancing to a Spanish song with a pig and a donkey (*pig-asso*). The most effective images involve bright colors, three dimensions, action scenes, inanimate objects with human traits, and humor.

As another example, say you are trying to learn some Spanish vocabulary, including the words *carta*, *libro*, and *dinero*. Instead of relying on rote learning, you might come up with mental images such as in Key 7.6.

Make Acronyms

An *acronym* is a word (or nonsense word) formed from the first letters of a series of words created to help you remember the series. In history class, you can remember the Allies during World War II— Britain, America, and Russia—with the acronym BAR. This is an example of a *word acronym*, because the first letters of the items you want to remember spell a word.

Other acronyms take the form of an entire sentence in which the first letter of each word stands for the first letter of the memorized term. This is called a *list order acronym*. For example, music students use the phrase "Every Good Boy Does Fine" to remember the notes that correspond to the lines on the treble clef (E, G, B, D, and F).

Use Songs or Rhymes

Some of the classic mnemonic devices are rhyming poems that stick in your mind. One you may have heard is the rule about the order of *i* and *e* in spelling:

> Spell *i* before *e*, except after *c*, or when sounded like *a* as in *neighbor* and *weigh*. Four exceptions if you please: *either, neither, seizure, seize.*

Use your creativity to make up your own poems or songs, linking familiar tunes or rhymes with information you want to remember.

Improving your memory requires energy, time, and work. It also helps to master SQ3R, the textbook study technique introduced in Chapter 5. By going through the steps in SQ3R and using the specific memory techniques described in this chapter, you will be able to learn more in less time—and remember what you learn long after exams are over. These techniques will be equally valuable when you start a career.

Which STRATEGIES CAN MAKE STUDYING FOR TEST DAY A SUCCESS?

Especially in the later stages of review, strategies that help you combine and condense information are crucial. Such strategies help you relate information to what you know, connect information in new ways, and boost your ability to use it to think critically— especially important for essay exams.

Key 7.6 | **Visual Images Aid Recall**

Spanish Word	Definition	Mental Image
carta	letter	A person pushing a shopping cart filled with letters into a post office.
dinero	money	A man eating lasagna at a diner. The lasagna is made of layers of money.
libro	book	A pile of books on a table at a library.

Create a Summary of Reading Material

When you summarize main ideas in your own words, you engage critical thinking, considering what is important to include as well as how to organize and link it together. To construct a summary, focus on the main ideas and examples that support them. Don't include your own ideas or evaluations at this point. Your summary should simply condense the material, making it easier to focus on concepts and interrelationships when you review.

Here are suggestions for creating effective summaries:

- Organize your summary by subject or topic—a textbook chapter, for example, or an article.
- Try to use your own words whenever possible.
- Make your notes simple, clear, and brief, eliminating less important details.
- Consider outlining the text so you can see how ideas relate to one another.
- Identify the main idea of a passage before you write.
- Take notes on tables, charts, photographs, and captions.
- Learn shorthand symbols to write quickly (see Chapter 6).
- Create notes in visual form using charts, tables, or diagrams.
- Use a color-coding system or different-colored pens.

Combine Class and Reading Notes into a Master Set

Studying from either text or class notes alone is not enough; your instructor may present material in class that is not in your text or may gloss over topics that your text covers in depth. The process of combining class and text notes enables you to see patterns and relationships among ideas, find examples for difficult concepts, and much more.

Follow these steps to combine your class and text notes into a master note set:

- *Step 1: Act quickly.* Combine your class and reading notes into a logical, comprehensive presentation while the material is fresh in your mind.
- *Step 2: Condense to the essence.* Reduce your combined notes so they

When you study for a test with a classmate, you can help each other understand difficult concepts as well as fill in the holes in each other's notes.

© Shutterstock

contain only key terms and concepts. Tightening and summarizing forces you to critically evaluate which ideas are most important and to rewrite your notes with only this material. See Key 7.7 for a comprehensive outline and a reduced key term outline of the same material.

- *Step 3: Recite what you know.* As you approach exam time, use the terms in your bare-bones notes as cues for reciting what you know about a topic. Recite out loud during study sessions, writing your responses on paper, making flash cards, or working with a partner—anything to make the process more active.
- *Step 4: Use critical thinking.* Now toss around ideas as you reflect on your combined notes—both the comprehensive and reduced sets. For example, brainstorm examples that illustrate themes, write down new questions, or apply what you've learned to real-world problems.
- *Step 5: Review and review again.* Try to vary your review methods, focusing on active involvement. Recite the material to yourself, have a question-and-answer session with a study partner, or take a practice test. Another helpful technique is to summarize your notes in writing from memory after you review them. This summary will tell you whether you'll be able to recall the information on a test. You may even want to summarize as you read, then summarize from memory, and compare the two summaries.

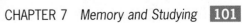

Different Views of Freedom and Equality in the American Democracy

I. U.S. democracy based on 5 core values: freedom and equality, order and stability, majority rule, protection of minority rights, and participation.

   A. U.S. would be a "perfect democracy" if it always upheld these values.

   B. U.S. is less than perfect, so it is called an "approaching democracy."

II. Freedom and Equality

   A. Historian Isaiah Berlin defines freedom as either positive or negative.

      1. Positive freedoms allow us to exercise rights under the Constitution, including right to vote.

      2. Negative freedoms safeguard us from government actions that restrict certain rights, such as the right to assemble. The 1st Amendment restricts government action by declaring that "Congress shall make no law . . ."

   B. The value of equality suggests that all people be treated equally, regardless of circumstance. Different views on what equality means and the implications for society.

      1. Equality of opportunity implies that everyone has the same chance to develop inborn talents.

         a. But life's circumstances — affected by factors like race and income — differ. This means that people start at different points and have different results.

            E.g., a poor, inner-city student will be less prepared for college than an affluent, suburban student.

         b. It is impossible to equalize opportunity for all Americans.

      2. Equality of result seeks to eliminate all forms of inequality, including economic differences, through wealth redistribution.

   C. Freedom and equality are in conflict, say text authors Berman and Murphy: "If your view of freedom is freedom from government intervention, then equality of any kind will be difficult to achieve. If government stays out of all citizen affairs, some people will become extremely wealthy, others will fall through the cracks, and economic inequality will multiply. On the other hand, if you wish to promote equality of result, then you will have to restrict some people's freedoms — the freedom to earn and retain an unlimited amount of money, for example."*

Key Term Outline of the Same Material

Different Views of Freedom and Equality in the American Democracy

I. America's 5 core values: freedom and equality, order and stability, majority rule, protection of minority rights, and participation.

   A. "Perfect democracy"

   B. "Approaching democracy"

II. Value #1 — Freedom and equality

   A. Positive freedoms and negative freedoms

   B. Different views of equality: equality of opportunity versus equality of result

   C. Conflict between freedom and equality centers on differing views of government's role

*Larry Berman and Bruce Allen Murphy, Approaching Democracy: Portfolio Edition, Upper Saddle River, NJ: Prentice Hall, 2005, pp. 6–8.

Think Back

Solidify your knowledge and prepare for tests with this review. Answer the following questions on a separate sheet of paper or electronic file.

▶ Revisit the chapter-opening questions on page 90. Scan the chapter and write a short answer for each.

▶ List what to you are the three most important concepts and three most important strategies in the chapter. Create a mnemonic device, of any type you choose, for each.

Analyze, Create, Practice

Explore Three Types of Memory

As you learned in the chapter, there are different classifications of information in long-term memory. Understanding each can help you use them more effectively when you study.

Analyze.   Describe how you have experienced them.

Episodic memory (events). Example: I remember the first time I conducted an experiment in chemistry class.

....
....
....

Declarative memory (facts). Example: I know that the electoral college must vote before a new U.S. president is officially elected.

....
....
....

Procedural memory (motion). Example: I know how to type without looking at the keyboard.

....
....
....

Now analyze your experience: Which type of information (events, facts, motion) is easiest for you to remember? Why?

....
....
....
....
....

Which type of information is hardest for you to remember? Why?

....
....
....
....

Create. Reflecting on the type of memory that is most difficult for you, brainstorm actions that might help. Try creating a link like this one.

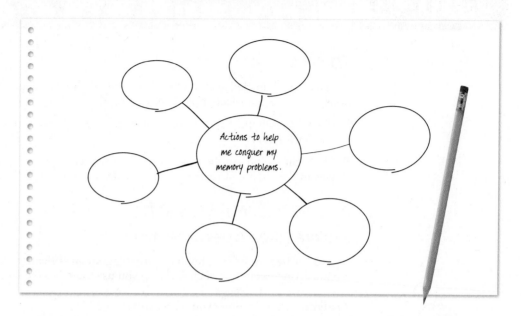

Actions to help me conquer my memory problems.

Practice. Set a goal to try each studying technique in the next couple of weeks. After you've tried all five, write the one that worked best here:

....

Multiple Intelligences in action

List three intelligences in the left-hand column—two that are highly developed for you and one you would like to build. Then in the right-hand column brainstorm a strategy for memory that relates to each intelligence.

Intelligence	Use MI Strategies to Come Up with Solutions
Example: Bodily-Kinesthetic	*Record information on an MP3 player and listen to it as you walk between classes or work out*
....	....
	....
....	....
	....
....	....

8

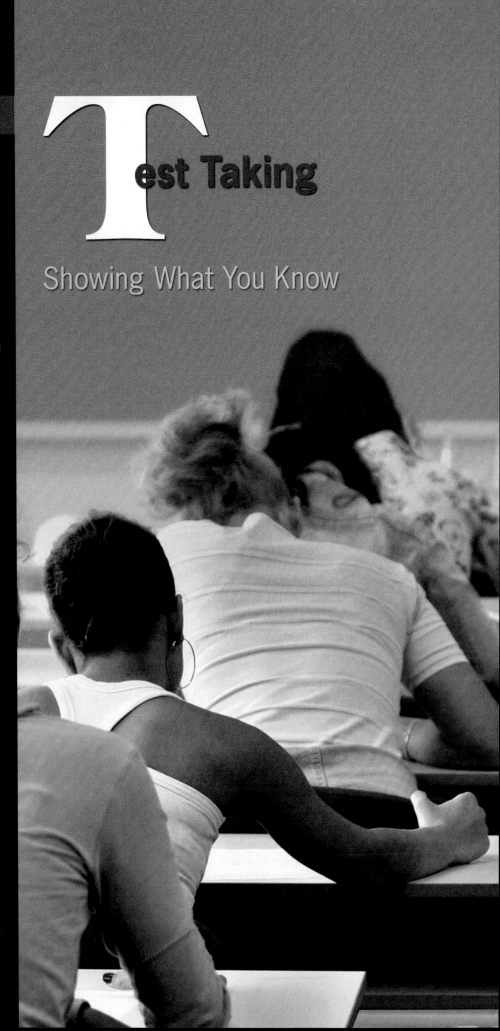

Test Taking

Showing What You Know

Smart test preparation results in real learning that you take from course to course and into your career and life. In this chapter, you will explore ways to build your test preparation and test-taking skills. Key strategies include how to deal with test anxiety, recognizing and adapting your studying to the type of test, and learning from mistakes on tests.

In this chapter, you'll explore answers to the following questions:

How can preparation improve test performance?

p. 106

How can you work through test anxiety?

p. 109

What general strategies can help you succeed on tests?

p. 110

How can you master different types of test questions?

p. 111

What can you learn from test mistakes?

p. 115

How Developed Are Your Test-Taking Skills?

For each statement, circle the number that best describes how true the statement is for you, from 1 for "not at all true for me" to 5 for "very true for me."

▶ I believe preparation is a major key to my success on exams.		1 2 3 4 5
▶ I use strategies to help me predict what will be on tests.		1 2 3 4 5
▶ I find that creating a study schedule helps me stay in control of upcoming exams.		1 2 3 4 5
▶ When I recognize signs of test anxiety, I use relaxation methods to calm down.		1 2 3 4 5
▶ I read test directions before beginning an exam.		1 2 3 4 5
▶ I use certain strategies to answer questions I'm unsure of.		1 2 3 4 5
▶ I don't think cheating on exams is ever worth it.		1 2 3 4 5
▶ I know the difference between objective and subjective questions and how to answer each.		1 2 3 4 5
▶ I know which strategies to use to answer tough essay questions.		1 2 3 4 5
▶ I learn from my testing mistakes.		1 2 3 4 5

If your total ranges from 41–50, you consider your test-taking skills to be fairly well developed.
If your total ranges from 24–40, you consider your test-taking skills to be somewhat developed.
If your total is below 24, you consider your test-taking skills to be underdeveloped.

Now total your scores.

REMEMBER No matter how developed your test preparation and test-taking skills, you can improve them with effort. Read the chapter to learn new ways to build these skills, and practice by doing the activities.

_____

How CAN PREPARATION IMPROVE TEST PERFORMANCE?

Although you may dread taking tests and exams, consider this: *The goal of a test is to see what you have learned.* Every day that you are learning—by attending class, staying on top of assignments, completing readings and projects, and participating in class discussions—you are preparing for tests. The following measures will help you prepare as exams approach.

Identify Test Type and What You Will Be Expected to Know

As soon as you learn about an upcoming test and before you start studying, find out as much as you can, including the following:

- *Topics that will be covered.* Will the test cover everything since the term began or will it be more limited?
- *Material you will be tested on.* Will the test cover only what you learned in class and in the text or will it also include outside readings?

Part of successful test preparation is knowing when to stop. To avoid overload, study in shorter segments over a period of time, and get the sleep you need before test day.

© Alvis Upitis/Image Bank/Getty Images

- *Types of questions.* Will the questions be objective (multiple choice with only one correct answer, multiple choice with more than one correct answer, true–false, sentence completion), subjective (essay), or a combination?
- *Supplemental information you may be able to have.* Is the test open book (meaning you can use your class text)? Open note (meaning you can use any notes you've taken)? Both? Or neither? Are you able to work with a partner on any part of it? Is it a take-home exam? Will you be expected to complete part or all of it online?

Instructors routinely answer questions like these. If you are unsure, ask for clarification. Chances are, some other students are wondering the same thing.

As you begin thinking about any test, remember that *not all tests are created equal*—a quiz is not as important as a midterm or final, for example, although accumulated grades on small quizzes add up and can make a difference in your final grade. Plan and prioritize your study time and energy according to the value of the quiz or test.

Determine Where and How the Test Will Be Given

Where you take a test can affect your performance. For instance, a take-home exam may sound like an easy A, but distractions like children and TV can threaten your focus. Similarly, if you miss a test date and need to make it up, you may find yourself taking an exam in a testing center. Being prepared for the stresses of your environment will help you manage test time.

Online tests, like open book tests, may seem easier than tests in the classroom. In reality, due to the wide amount of information available at your fingertips, online tests are generally more challenging and require strong critical thinking skills. You may be able to Google factual information about a topic, but test questions will probably ask you to analyze and evaluate situations related to that information.

Create a Study Schedule and Checklist

If you establish a plan ahead of time and write it down, you will be more likely to follow it. Use journalists' questions to map out a study plan.

- Ask *what* and *why* to decide what you will study. Go through your notes, texts, related primary sources, and handouts, and set aside materials you don't need. Then prioritize the remaining materials to focus on the information most likely to be on the exam.
- Ask *when*, *where*, and *who*—and use the time management and goal-setting skills from Chapter 2—to prepare a schedule. Consider all of the relevant factors—your study materials, whom you will study with, the number of days until the test, and the time and place you can study each day. Note study sessions in your planner ahead of time.
- Ask *how* to figure out what strategies you will use.

A comprehensive *checklist* will help you organize and stay on track as you prepare. Use the organizer in the Think Practically exercise on pages 116–117.

Review Reading and Study Strategies

Put what you learned about thinking, reading, memory, and studying in Chapters 4, 5, and 6 into action to give yourself the best shot at remembering material.

- *Think critically.* College exams often ask you to analyze and apply material in more depth than you experienced in high school. For example, your history instructor may ask you to place a primary source in its historical context. Prepare for these challenges as you study by continually asking critical thinking questions.

• *Use SQ3R.* This reading method provides an excellent structure for reviewing your reading materials.

• *Employ strategies from* how *questions.* Use flash cards, audio strategies, chunking, or anything else that suits you and the material you are studying.

• *Review and apply mnemonic devices.* Memory strategies help make what you review stick.

• *Actively review your combined class and text notes.* Create summaries and master sets of combined text and class notes to give yourself comprehensive study tools.

Make and Take a Pretest

Use end-of-chapter text questions to create your own pretest. If your course doesn't have an assigned text, develop questions from notes and assigned readings. Old homework problems will also help target areas that need work. Some texts also provide online activities and pretests designed to help you review material. Keep in mind that the same test preparation skills you learn in college will help you do well on standardized tests for graduate school.

Answer your questions under test-like conditions—in a quiet place, with no books or notes (unless the exam is open book), where you can see a clock to tell you when to quit.

Prepare for Final Exams

Studying for final exams, which usually take place the last week of the term, is a major commitment that requires careful time management. Your college may schedule study days (also called a *reading period*) between the end of classes and the beginning of finals. Lasting from a day or two to several weeks, this period gives you time to prepare for exams and finish papers.

End-of-year studying requires flexibility. Libraries are often packed, and students may need to find alternative locations. Consider outdoor settings (if weather permits), smaller libraries (many departments have their own libraries), and empty classrooms. Set up times and places that will provide the atmosphere you need.[1]

Prepare Physically

Most tests ask you to work at your best under pressure, so try to get a good night's sleep before the exam. Sleep improves your ability to remember what you studied before you went to bed.

Eating a light, well-balanced meal that is high in protein (eggs, milk, yogurt, meat and fish, nuts, and peanut butter) will keep you full longer than carbohydrates (breads, candy, and pastries). When time is short, don't skip breakfast—grab a quick meal such as a few tablespoons of peanut butter, a banana, or a high-protein granola bar.

think CRITICALLY

Analyze Test Anxiety

According to a recent study by researchers at the Institute of HeartMath, "Students with high levels of test anxiety scored 15 points lower in both math and English than those with low test anxiety."[2] In a journal entry, identify and analyze your specific test-taking fears. What factors cause anxiety for you—the material, the type of test, the environment, or something else? What lies behind your fear? Make your anxiety more manageable by using critical thinking to take it apart.

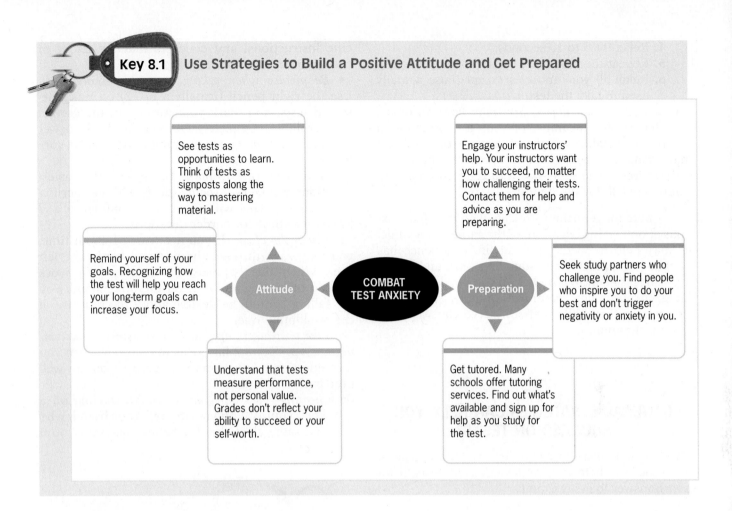

Key 8.1 Use Strategies to Build a Positive Attitude and Get Prepared

See tests as opportunities to learn. Think of tests as signposts along the way to mastering material.

Engage your instructors' help. Your instructors want you to succeed, no matter how challenging their tests. Contact them for help and advice as you are preparing.

Remind yourself of your goals. Recognizing how the test will help you reach your long-term goals can increase your focus.

Attitude

COMBAT TEST ANXIETY

Preparation

Seek study partners who challenge you. Find people who inspire you to do your best and don't trigger negativity or anxiety in you.

Understand that tests measure performance, not personal value. Grades don't reflect your ability to succeed or your self-worth.

Get tutored. Many schools offer tutoring services. Find out what's available and sign up for help as you study for the test.

How CAN YOU WORK THROUGH TEST ANXIETY?

A certain amount of stress can be a good thing. You are alert, ready to act, and geared up to do your best. Some students, however, experience incapacitating stress before and during exams, especially midterms and finals. Test anxiety can cause sweating, nausea, dizziness, headaches, and fatigue. It can reduce concentration and cause you to forget everything you learned. Sufferers may get lower grades because their performance does not reflect what they know.

Prepare Well and Have a Positive Attitude

Being prepared—both by reviewing material and following a detailed study plan—is the most essential way to ready yourself for an academic showdown. Only by knowing the material as best you can will you have reason to believe in your ability to pass the test. The other key tool is a positive attitude that says, "I know this material and I'm ready to show it." Use the strategies in Key 8.1 to be both prepared and positive.

Test Time Strategies

When test time comes, several strategies may help you manage and calm test anxiety.

- *Manage your environment.* Make a conscious effort to sit away from students who might distract you. If it helps, listen to relaxing music on an MP3 player while waiting for class to begin.
- *Use positive self-talk.* Tell yourself that you can do well and that it is normal to feel anxious, particularly before an important exam.
- *Practice relaxation.* Close your eyes, breathe deeply and slowly, and visualize positive mental images like getting a good grade. Or try a more physical tensing-and-relaxing method:[3]
  1. Put your feet flat on the floor.
  2. With your hands, grab underneath the chair.
  3. Push down with your feet and pull up on your chair at the same time for about 5 seconds.

4. Relax for 5 to 10 seconds.

5. Repeat the procedure two or three times.

6. Relax all your muscles except those actually used to take the test.

• *Bring a special object.* You may have an object that has special meaning for you—a photograph, a stone or crystal, a wristband, a piece of jewelry, a hat. Bring it along and see if it provides comfort or inspiration at test time. Use it to get focused and to calm yourself during the test.

A note for returning students who may feel anxious about having been "out of the game" for a while: It may help to focus on what life experience has taught you. For instance, handling work and family pressures is likely to have helped you build important time management, planning, organizational, and communication skills that will serve you well in a testing situation.

What GENERAL STRATEGIES CAN HELP YOU SUCCEED ON TESTS?

Even though every test is different, certain general strategies will help you handle almost all tests, from short-answer to essay exams.

• *Choose the right seat.* Your goal is to choose a seat that will put you in the right frame of mind and minimize distractions. Find a seat near a window, next to a wall, or in the front row so you can look into the distance. Know yourself: For many students, it's smart to avoid sitting near friends.

• *Write down key facts.* Before you even look at the test, write down key information, including formulas, rules, and definitions, that you don't want to forget. (Use the back of the question sheet so your instructor knows that you made these notes after the test began.)

• *Start with the big picture.* Spend a few minutes at the start gathering information about the questions— how many of which types are in each section, along with their point values. Use this information to schedule your time.

• *Directions count, so read them.* Reading test directions carefully can save you trouble. For example, you may be required to answer only one of three essay questions, or you may be penalized for incorrect responses to short-answer questions.

• *Mark up the questions.* Mark up instructions and keywords to avoid careless errors. Circle qualifiers—words and phrases that can alter a sentence's meaning, such as *always, never, all, none, sometimes,* and *every;* verbs that communicate spe-

cific instructions; and concepts that are tricky or need special attention.

• *Be precise when taking a machine-scored test.* Use the right pencil (usually a no. 2) on machine-scored tests, and mark your answer in the correct space, filling it completely. Periodically check answer numbers against question numbers to make sure they match.

• *Work from easy to hard.* Begin with the easiest questions and answer them quickly without sacrificing accuracy. This will boost your confidence and leave more time for harder questions.

• *Watch the clock.* If you are worried about time, you may rush through the test and have time left over. When this happens, check over your work instead of leaving early. If, on the other hand, you are falling behind, be flexible about the best use of the remaining time.

• *Take a strategic approach to questions you cannot answer.* Key 8.2 has ideas to consider when you face questions that stump you, even if you are well prepared.

• *Cheating—just don't do it.* You're starting on a test when your cell phone vibrates. Your friend, who has this same class the day before, has sent you a

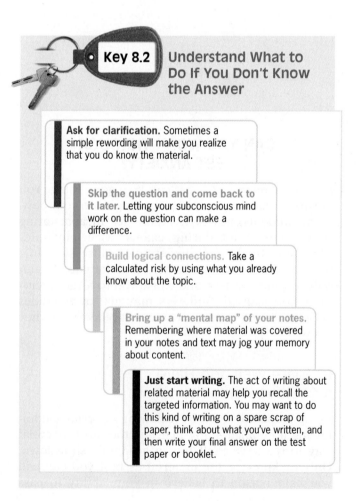

Key 8.2   Understand What to Do If You Don't Know the Answer

Ask for clarification. Sometimes a simple rewording will make you realize that you do know the material.

Skip the question and come back to it later. Letting your subconscious mind work on the question can make a difference.

Build logical connections. Take a calculated risk by using what you already know about the topic.

Bring up a "mental map" of your notes. Remembering where material was covered in your notes and text may jog your memory about content.

Just start writing. The act of writing about related material may help you recall the targeted information. You may want to do this kind of writing on a spare scrap of paper, think about what you've written, and then write your final answer on the test paper or booklet.

What to Do When a Multiple-Choice Question Has You Stumped

If you have read a multiple-choice question carefully and you are sure that you don't know the answer, don't give up yet. Several strategies will help you narrow down your choices and give you a better chance of choosing the right one.

▶ **Are there any choices you know are wrong?** If so, eliminate them first.

▶ **Is the choice relevant?** An answer may be accurate, but unrelated to the question. Eliminate any irrelevant choices.

▶ **Is the choice accurate on its own terms?** If there's an error in the choice—for example, a term that is incorrectly defined—eliminate it.

▶ **Does the choice contain a qualifier?** Absolute qualifiers like *always*, *never*, *all*, *none*, and *every* often make a choice incorrect. Conservative qualifiers like *often*, *most*, *rarely*, and *sometimes* can make a choice correct.

▶ **Are two choices similar?** Chances are that if two out of four choices closely resemble each other, one of them is right.

▶ **Watch out for "all/none of the above."** If you know that one or more answers are not correct, avoid "all of the above." If you are fairly certain that at least one answer is correct, avoid "none of the above."

---

text with answers to the multiple-choice sections. Although cheating has the immediate gain of possibly passing a test or getting a few free answers, its long-term consequences aren't so beneficial. If you cheat, you run the risk of being caught and subsequently disciplined (which can include expulsion), not to mention that you probably will not actually learn the material. Think carefully about whether the risks of cheating outweigh the benefits.

How CAN YOU MASTER DIFFERENT TYPES OF TEST QUESTIONS?

Every type of test question is a different way of finding out how much you know. Questions fall into two general categories.

• *Objective questions.* You generally choose or write a short answer, often selecting from a limited number of choices, for objective questions. They can include multiple-choice, fill-in-the-blank, matching, and true-or-false questions.

• *Subjective questions.* Demanding the same information recall as objective responses, subjective questions also require you to plan, organize, draft, and refine a response. All essay questions are subjective.

This section will discuss various question types within these two categories. For each, you will find suggestions on how to approach them and what to watch out for. Key 8.3 shows samples of real test questions from Western civilization and macroeconomics college texts published by Pearson Education. Included are multiple-choice, true–false, fill-in-the-blank, and essay questions. Analyzing the types, formats, and complexities of these questions will help you gauge what to expect when you take exams.

Objective Questions

Multiple-Choice Questions

Use these tips to tackle multiple-choice questions:

• *Read the directions carefully and try to think of the answer before looking at the choices.* Then read the choices and make your selection.

• *Underline keywords and phrases.* If the question is complicated, try to break it down into small sections that are easy to understand.

• *Make sure you read every word of every answer.* Focus especially on qualifying words such as *always*, *never*, *tend to*, *most*, *often*, and *frequently*. Look also for negatives in a question ("Which of the following is *not* . . .").

• *When questions are linked to a reading passage, read the questions first.* This will help you focus

From Chapter 29, "The End of Imperialism," in *Western Civilization: A Social and Cultural History*, 2nd edition

Multiple-Choice Question

India's first leader after independence was:

A. Gandhi   B. Bose   C. Nehru   D. Sukharno   *(answer: C)*

Fill-in-the-Blank Question

East Pakistan became the country of _____ in 1971.

A. Burma   B. East India   C. Sukharno   D Bangladesh   *(answer: D)*

True–False Question

The United States initially supported Vietnamese independence.   T   F   *(answer: false)*

Essay Question

Answer one of the following:

1. What led to Irish independence? What conflicts continued to exist after independence?

2. How did Gandhi work to rid India of British control? What methods did he use?

From Chapter 6, "Unemployment and Inflation," in *Macroeconomics: Principles and Tools*, 3rd edition

Multiple-Choice Question

If the labor force is 250,000 and the total population 16 years of age or older is 300,000, the labor-force participation rate is

A. 79.5%   B. 83.3%   C. 75.6%   D. 80.9%   *(answer: B)*

Fill-in-the-Blank Question

Mike has just graduated from college and is now looking for a job, but has not yet found one. This causes the employment rate to _____ and the labor-force participation rate to _____.

A. increase; decrease   C. stay the same; stay the same

B. increase; increase   D. increase; stay the same   *(answer: C)*

True–False Question

The Consumer Price Index somewhat overstates changes in the cost of living because it does not allow for substitutions that consumers might make in response to price changes.   T   F   *(answer: true)*

Essay Question

During a press conference, the Secretary of Employment notes that the unemployment rate is 7.0%. As a political opponent, how might you criticize this figure as an underestimate? In rebuttal, how might the secretary argue that the reported rate is an overestimate of unemployment?

(Possible answer: The unemployment rate given by the secretary might be considered an underestimate because discouraged workers, who have given up the job search in frustration, are not counted as unemployed. In addition, full-time workers may have been forced to work part-time. In rebuttal, the secretary might note that a portion of the unemployed have voluntarily left their jobs. Most workers are unemployed only briefly and leave the ranks of the unemployed by gaining better jobs than they had previously held.)

Sources: [Western Civilization test items] Margaret L. King, Western Civilization: A Social and Cultural History, 2nd ed., Upper Saddle River, NJ: Pearson Education, Inc., 2003. Questions from Instructor's Manual and Test Item File by Dolores Davison Peterson. Used with permission. [Macroeconomics test items] Arthur O'Sullivan and Steven M. Sheffrin, Macroeconomics: Principles and Tools, 3rd ed., Upper Saddle River, NJ: Pearson Education, Inc., 2003. Questions from Test Item File 2 by Linda Ghent. Used with permission.

on the information you need to answer the questions.

True-or-False Questions

Look for absolute qualifiers (such as *all, only,* and *always*), which often make an otherwise true statement false and conservative qualifiers (*generally, often, usually,* and *sometimes*), which often make an otherwise false statement true. Be sure to read *every* word to avoid jumping to an incorrect conclusion. Common problems in reading too quickly include missing negatives (*not, no*) that would change your response.

Matching Questions

Matching questions ask you to match terms in one list with the terms in another list.

- *Make sure you understand the directions.* The directions tell you whether each answer can be used only once (common practice) or more than once.
- *Start with the matches you know.* On your first run-through, pencil in these matches. When you can use an answer only once, you may have to adjust if you rethink a choice.
- *Finally, tackle the matches you're not sure of.* Think back to your class lectures, text notes, and study sessions as you try to visualize the correct response.

Fill-in-the-Blank Questions

Fill-in-the-blank questions ask you to supply one or more words or phrases to complete the sentence.

- *Be logical.* Insert your answer; then reread the sentence from beginning to end to be sure it makes sense and is factually and grammatically correct.
- *Note the length and number of the blanks.* If two blanks appear right after one another, the instructor is probably looking for a two-word answer. If a blank is longer than usual, the correct response may require additional space.
- *If you are uncertain, guess.* Have faith that after hours of studying, the correct answer is somewhere in your subconscious mind and that your guess is not completely random.

Subjective Questions

Essay Questions

Essay questions ask you to organize your ideas and write well under time pressure. The following steps will help improve your responses.

1. *Read every question.* Decide which to tackle (if there's a choice). Use critical thinking to identify exactly what the question is asking.

2. *Map out your time.* Schedule how long to allot for each answer, remembering that things don't always go as planned. Above all, be flexible.

think CREATIVELY

Create Your Own Test

Think about an upcoming test in a course you are taking now. Use the tips in this chapter to predict the material that will be covered, the types of questions that will be asked (multiple choice, essay, etc.), and the nature of the questions (a broad overview or specific details).

Then create a test to study from. Your goal is to write questions that your instructor is likely to ask and that make you think about the material in different ways.

1. Write the questions you come up with on a separate sheet of paper.

2. Take your created pretest and see how you do.

ANALYZE—Break into parts and discuss each part separately.

COMPARE—Explain similarities and differences.

CONTRAST—Distinguish between items being compared by focusing on differences.

CRITICIZE—Evaluate the issue, focusing on its problems or deficiencies.

DEFINE—State the essential quality or meaning.

DESCRIBE—Paint a complete picture; provide the details of a story or the main characteristics of a situation.

DIAGRAM—Present a drawing, chart, or other visual.

DISCUSS—Examine completely, using evidence and often presenting both sides of an issue.

ELABORATE ON—Start with information presented in the question, and then add new material.

ENUMERATE/LIST/IDENTIFY—Specify items in the form of a list.

EVALUATE—Give your opinion about the value or worth of a topic and justify your conclusion.

EXPLAIN—Make the meaning clear, often by discussing causes and consequences.

ILLUSTRATE—Supply examples.

INTERPRET—Explain your personal views and judgments.

JUSTIFY—Discuss the reasons for your conclusions or for the question's premise.

OUTLINE—Organize and present main and subordinate points.

PROVE—Use evidence and logic to show that a statement is true.

REFUTE—Use evidence and logic to show that a statement is not true or tell how you disagree with it.

RELATE—Connect items mentioned in the question, showing, for example, how one item influenced another.

REVIEW—Provide an overview of ideas and establish their merits and features.

STATE—Explain clearly, simply, and concisely.

SUMMARIZE—Give the important ideas in brief, without comments.

TRACE—Present a history of a situation's development, often by showing cause and effect.

---

3. *Focus on action verbs.* Key 8.4 shows verbs that tell you what to do to answer the question. Underline action verbs and use them to guide your writing.

4. *Plan.* Think about what the question is asking and what you know. On scrap paper, map your ideas and supporting evidence. Then develop a thesis statement. Don't skimp on planning. Not only does planning result in a better essay, but it also reduces stress.

5. *Draft.* Use the following guidelines as you draft your answer:

- State your thesis, and then get right to the evidence that backs it up.
- Structure your essay so that each paragraph presents an idea that supports the thesis.

- Use clear language and tight logic to link ideas to your thesis and to create transitions between paragraphs.
- Look back at your planning notes periodically to make sure you cover everything.
- Wrap it up with a short, to-the-point conclusion.

6. *Revise.* Although you may not have the time to rewrite your entire answer, you can improve it with minor changes. If you notice anything missing, use editing marks to neatly insert it into the text. When you're done, make sure it's the best possible representation of your ideas.

As you check over your essay, ask yourself questions about it:

- Have I answered the question?
- Does my essay begin with a clear thesis statement, and does each paragraph start with a strong topic sentence that supports the thesis?
- Have I provided the support necessary in the form of examples, statistics, and relevant facts to prove my argument, organized with tight logic?
- Is my conclusion an effective wrap-up?

7. *Edit.* Check for mistakes in grammar, spelling, punctuation, and usage. Correct language—and neat, legible handwriting—reduces problems that may lower your grade.

The purpose of a test is to see how much you know, not merely to get a grade. Embrace this attitude to learn from your mistakes.

Evaluating their test results will help these students understand their performance as well as learn from their mistakes.

© Sarah Kravits

What CAN YOU LEARN FROM TEST MISTAKES?

Congratulations! You've finished the exam, handed it in, gone home to a well-deserved night of sleep. At the next class meeting you've returned refreshed, rejuvenated, and ready to accept a high score. As you receive the test back from your instructor, you look wide-eyed at your grade. *How could that be?*

No one aces every test. And no one understands every piece of the material perfectly. Making mistakes on tests and learning from them is as much a part of your academic experience as studying, taking notes, working with others, and yes, even getting good grades. After all, if you never made any mistakes, what would you have to learn from?

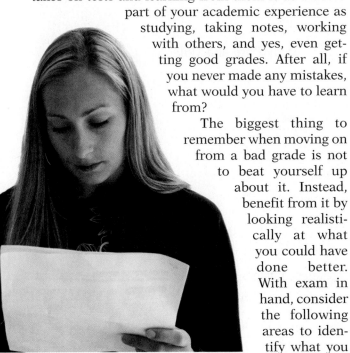

The biggest thing to remember when moving on from a bad grade is not to beat yourself up about it. Instead, benefit from it by looking realistically at what you could have done better. With exam in hand, consider the following areas to identify what you

can correct—and perhaps change the way you study for, or take, your next exam.

- *Rework the questions you got wrong.* Try to rewrite an essay, recalculate a math problem from the original question, or redo questions following a reading selection.
- *After reviewing your mistakes, fill in your knowledge gaps.* If you didn't understand important concepts, develop a plan to learn the material.
- *Talk to your instructor.* Focus on specific mistakes on objective questions or a weak essay. If you are not sure why you were marked down on an essay, ask what you could have done better. If you feel that an essay was unfairly graded, ask for a rereading.
- *Rethink the way you studied.* The earlier in the term you make positive adjustments the better, so make a special effort to analyze and learn from early test mistakes.
- *If you fail a test, don't throw it away.* Use it to review troublesome material, especially if you will be tested on it again.

Finally, if you can see test taking for what it is—a way to make sure that you are retaining what you learn—you will be more able to separate your value as a student and a person from your test grades. Using what you've read about skills and techniques will help you manage fears, anxieties, and habits regarding exams so you can focus on your most important job—learning.

PRACTICALLY

Create and Use an Organized Study Plan[4]

Organizing and defining your study goals will help you make the most of your time. Use this form as a guide to note important information for your next exam. Make a copy or recreate it on an electronic file. Get in the habit of using it to organize your time and materials for any important exam.

Course: .... *Instructor:* ....

Date, time, and place of test: ....

Type of test (midterm, quiz, other): ....

Test information (question types, length, effect on final grade, etc.): ....

....

....

Topics to be covered, in order of importance:

1. ....

2. ....

3. ....

4. ....

5. ....

Study schedule, including study materials (texts, class notes, homework problems, etc.) and the dates and times you plan to complete each:

Material   **Study Date and Time**

1. ....

2. ....

3. ....

4. ....

5. ....

Materials to bring to the test (textbook, sourcebook, calculator, computer):

....

....

Special study arrangements (study group meetings, instructor conference, tutoring), including scheduled times:

....

....

Study routine adjustments to maximize your strongest intelligences (for example, interpersonal learners study with others, musical learners create learning tunes):

....

....

Life-management issues (such as rearranging work hours to study with a classmate):

....

....

quick! SKILL BUILDING

Think Back

Solidify your knowledge and prepare for tests with this review. Answer the following questions on a separate sheet of paper or electronic file.

▶ Revisit the chapter-opening questions on page 105. Scan the chapter and write a short answer for each.

▶ As you review the chapter, find a section of important information that is not directly addressed in the chapter-opening questions. Create one short-answer question and one essay question on this information, and write out the answers.

Analyze, Create, Practice

Prepare for Test Success

Using a test from this term on which you wish you had performed better, answer the following questions regarding your preparation, success, and thoughts on future adjustments.

Analyze. Look at the problems listed below. Circle one or more that affected your test grade. If you had a problem that didn't appear here, write it in the empty space.

- Incomplete preparation
- Fatigue
- Feeling rushed during the test
- Shaky understanding of concepts

- Confusion about directions
- Test anxiety
- Poor essay organization or writing
- ....

Analyze your most significant problem (or only problem). What do you think caused this problem?

....

....

....

....

....

How did this problem directly affect your performance on the test? Be specific.

....

....

What techniques did you use to prepare for this test, and how much time did you spend?

....

....

Create. If you had absolutely no restrictions on time or other obstacles to good studying, how would you have prepared for this test? Describe what you would have done.

....

....

Practice. Thinking about how your ideal test prep differs from your actual preparation, describe how you will adjust your plan the next time you face a similar test.

Actions I took this time, but *won't* next time:

....

....

....

Actions I did *not* take this time, but *will* next time:

....

....

....

Multiple Intelligences in action

List three intelligences in the left-hand column—two that are highly developed for you and one you would like to build. Then in the right-hand column brainstorm a strategy for test taking that relates to each intelligence.

Intelligence	**Use MI Strategies to Come Up with Solutions**
Example: Musical	*Replace the words of "Happy Birthday" with a series of terms you're having trouble remembering.*
....	....
	....
....	....
	....
....	....
	....

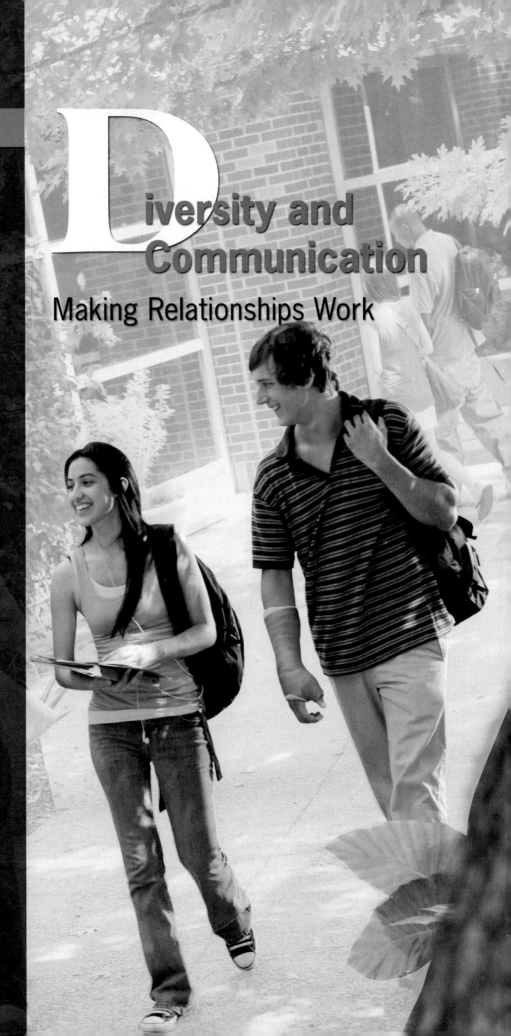

chapter

9

College brings exposure to new and diverse values, lifestyles, backgrounds, and people. Being open to these experiences and interactions will help you relate and work more effectively in college and beyond. This chapter will help you build cultural competency and communication skills, two building blocks for collaborative relationships.

In this chapter, you'll explore answers to the following questions:

How can you develop cultural competence?

p. 120

How can you communicate effectively?

p. 124

How do you make the most of personal relationships?

p. 128

Diversity and Communication
Making Relationships Work

How Developed Are Your Cultural Competence, Communication, and Relationship Skills?

For each statement, circle the number that best describes how true the statement is for you, from 1 for "not at all true for me" to 5 for "very true for me."

▶ I understand that some kinds of diversity are visible and others aren't.	1 2 3 4 5
▶ I try not to let prejudices and stereotypes affect my judgment of any individual.	1 2 3 4 5
▶ When I see discrimination, I speak up even if it doesn't involve me.	1 2 3 4 5
▶ I try to get to know other cultures through friendships, travel, reading, and generally being open-minded.	1 2 3 4 5
▶ I try to give and receive criticism constructively.	1 2 3 4 5
▶ In my relationships, I try to be assertive rather than aggressive or passive.	1 2 3 4 5
▶ When I communicate, I try to regulate my feelings without letting my anger show.	1 2 3 4 5
▶ I seek and maintain friendships with positive people.	1 2 3 4 5
▶ I use different communication tools, but I don't let technology get in the way of person-to-person relationships.	1 2 3 4 5
▶ I do my best to get out of destructive relationships as quickly as possible.	1 2 3 4 5

If your total ranges from 41–50, you consider your cultural competence, communication, and relationship skills to be fairly well developed.

If your total ranges from 24–40, you consider your cultural competence, communication, and relationship skills to be somewhat developed.

If your total is less than 24, you consider your cultural competence, communication, and relationship skills to be underdeveloped.

Now total your scores.

_____

REMEMBER No matter how developed your cultural competence, communication, and relationship skills, you can improve them with effort. Read the chapter to learn new ways to build these skills, and practice by doing the activities.

How CAN YOU DEVELOP CULTURAL COMPETENCE?

Diversity exists within each person and among all people. You may work with people from different backgrounds or hear and see different people as you buy groceries, swim at a pool, or go out with friends. You may experience diversity within your family—often the kind of diversity that is not visible. Even if friends or family members share your racial and ethnic background, they may differ in how they learn, the way they communicate, or their sexual orientation.

Interacting successfully with all kinds of people is the goal of *cultural competence,* which refers to

When you share a goal with someone, personal differences may fade into the background. This teacher and student share a goal of repairing an internal computer component.

© David Barber/PhotoEdit

the ability to understand and appreciate differences among people and adjust behavior in ways that enhance relationships and communication. According to the National Center for Cultural Competence, developing cultural competence is based on five actions:[1]

1. Valuing diversity
2. Identifying and evaluating personal perceptions and attitudes
3. Being aware of what happens when different cultures interact
4. Building knowledge about other cultures
5. Using what you learn to adapt to diverse cultures as you encounter them

As you develop cultural competence, you heighten your ability to analyze how people relate to one another. Most important, you develop practical skills that enable you to bridge the gap between yourself and others.[2]

Cultural competence is about more than just passive tolerance of the world around you. It moves further than that, toward *acceptance*. When you practice tolerance only, you may not actively dislike people from different cultures or treat them rudely or with prejudice. You are simply indifferent. You don't actively seek confrontation but you don't seek out harmony either.

Acceptance is the practice of acknowledging other cultures and actively working toward teamwork and friendship. Acceptance requires you to not only recognize the differences between cultures but to celebrate them as an enriching part of life. Moving from passive tolerance to active acceptance is part of developing cultural competence.

Action 1: Value Diversity

Every time you meet someone new, you have a choice about how to interact. You won't like everyone you meet, but if you value diversity, you will choose to treat people with tolerance and respect, avoiding assumptions about them and granting them the right to think and believe without being judged.

Action 2: Identify and Evaluate Personal Perceptions and Attitudes

Whereas people may value the *concept* of diversity, they may have a hard time sticking to their principles when they confront the *reality* of diversity in their own lives. This disconnect is often linked to prejudices and stereotypes.

Prejudice

To be prejudiced means to prejudge others, usually on the basis of gender, race, sexual orientation, disability, religion, age, or other characteristics. Prejudice may even occur without a person's awareness because of factors like the following that can operate below the surface.

- *Influence of family and culture.* Children learn attitudes—including intolerance, superiority, and hate—from their parents, peers, and community.
- *Fear of differences.* It is human to fear the unfamiliar and to make assumptions about it.
- *Experience.* One bad experience with a person of a particular age, race, or religion may lead someone to condemn all people with the same characteristic.

Stereotypes

Prejudice is usually based on stereotypes—assumptions made, without proof or critical thinking, about the characteristics of a person or group, based on human and cultural factors such as the following:

- *Desire for patterns and logic.* People often try to make sense of the world by using the labels, categories, and generalizations that stereotypes provide.
- *Media influences.* The more people see stereotypical images—the airhead beautiful blonde, the jolly fat man—the easier it is to believe that stereotypes are universal.
- *Laziness.* Labeling group members according to a characteristic they seem to have in common takes less energy than asking questions that illuminate the qualities of individuals.

Stereotypes derail personal connections and block effective communication; pasting a label on a person makes it hard to see the real person underneath. Even stereotypes that seem "positive" may be untrue and get in the way of perceiving uniqueness. Key 9.1 lists some of the "positive" and "negative" stereotypes often heard in media or in conversations.

Action 3: Be Aware of What Happens When Cultures Interact

Interaction among people from different cultures can promote learning, build mutual respect, and broaden perspectives. However, as history shows, such interaction can also produce problems. At their mildest, these problems create roadblocks that obstruct relationships and communication. At their worst, they set the stage for acts of *discrimination* or, when prejudice turns violent, even *hate crimes*—crimes motivated by a hatred of specific characteristics ascribed to the victim, usually directed at people based on their race, ethnicity, or religious or sexual orientation.

Federal law says that you cannot be denied basic opportunities and rights because of your race, creed, color, age, gender, national or ethnic origin, religion, marital status, potential or actual pregnancy, or potential or actual illness or disability (unless the illness or disability prevents you from performing required tasks and unless accommodations are not possible). Despite these legal protections, discrimination is common and often appears on college campuses. Students may not want to work with students of other races, members of campus clubs may reject prospective members because of religious differences, and so on.

Action 4: Build Cultural Knowledge

Focusing on the positive aspects of intercultural interaction prepares you to push past negative possibilities and open your mind to positive ideas. You have a personal responsibility to learn about people who are different from you, including those you are likely to meet on campus. What are some practical ways to begin?

- *Read* newspapers, books, magazines, and websites that expose you to different perspectives.
- *Ask questions* of all kinds of people, about themselves and their traditions.

| **Key 9.1** | Both Positive and Negative Stereotypes Mask Uniqueness |

Positive Stereotype	Negative Stereotype
Women are nurturing.	Women are too emotional for business.
African Americans are great athletes.	African Americans struggle in school.
Hispanic Americans are family oriented.	Hispanic Americans have too many kids.
White people are successful in business.	White people are cold and power hungry.
Gay men have a great sense of style.	Gay men are overly effeminate.
People with disabilities have strength of will.	People with disabilities are bitter.
Older people are wise.	Older people are set in their ways.
Asian Americans are good at math and science.	Asian Americans are poor leaders.

Analyze the Effects of Diversity

With Native Americans along with immigrants from over 40 countries, the U.S. population has always featured a mix of races, religious orientations, ethnicities, languages, and much more.[3] In a journal entry, analyze the positive and negative effects when many different people coexist. Examine what happens when different types of people come together to live or work in a shared space, using your college campus as an example.

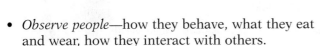

- *Observe people*—how they behave, what they eat and wear, how they interact with others.
- *Travel internationally and locally* where you can experience different ways of living.
- *Build friendships* with fellow students or co-workers you would not ordinarily approach.

Building knowledge also means exploring yourself. Talk with family, read, and seek experiences that educate you about your own cultural heritage. Then share what you know with others.

Action 5: Adapt to Diverse Cultures

Here's where you take everything you have gathered—your value of diversity, your self-knowledge, your understanding of how cultures interact, your information about different cultures—and put it to work with practical actions. Let the following suggestions inspire your own creative ideas about improving how you relate to others.

- *Look past external characteristics.* If you meet a woman with a disability, get to know her. She may be an accounting major and love baseball. These characteristics—not just her physical person—describe who she is.
- *Put yourself in other people's shoes.* Ask questions about what other people feel, especially if there's a conflict. Offer friendship to someone new in class.
- *Adjust to cultural differences.* When you understand someone's way of being and put it into practice, you show respect and encourage communication. For example, if a study group member takes offense

at a particular kind of language, avoid it when you meet.

- *Stand up against prejudice, discrimination, and hate.* When you hear a prejudiced remark or notice discrimination taking place, you may choose to

Communication with others is essential to every school and work goal, from team projects to study groups to on-the-job collaborations.

© Shutterstock

Discover Hidden Diversity

Being able to respond to people as individuals requires that you become aware of the diversity that is not always on the surface. This exercise will help you dig deeper.

- Start by examining your own uniqueness. Brainstorm ten characteristics that describe you. Keep references to your ethnicity or appearance (brunette, Cuban American, and so on) to a minimum, and fill the list with traits that aren't obvious (laid-back, only child, 24 years old, drummer, gay, intrapersonal learner, and so on).

- Next, pair up with a classmate whom you do not know well. On a separate paper, list what you know about the person; chances are most of them will be visible.

- Then talk together, aiming to learn more about each other. With what you discover while talking, add to and adjust your lists.

- Finally, answer these questions: What did you learn about your classmate that you would never have suspected on first meeting? What did your classmate learn about you? What does this tell you about the need to delve beneath the surface to find out what really makes people tick?

---

make a comment or to approach an authority such as an instructor or dean. Sound the alarm on hate crimes—let authorities know if you suspect that a crime is about to occur, and support organizations that encourage tolerance.

- *Recognize that people everywhere have the same basic needs.* Everyone loves, thinks, hurts, hopes, fears, and plans. When you are trying to find common ground with diverse people, remember that you are united first through your essential humanity.

Just as there is diversity in skin color and ethnicity, there is diversity in the way people communicate. Effective communication enables people of all cultures to connect.

How CAN YOU COMMUNICATE EFFECTIVELY?

Spoken communication that is clear promotes success at school and work as well as in personal rela-

tionships. Successfully intelligent communicators analyze and adjust to communication styles, learn to give and receive criticism, and work through communication problems.

Adjust to Communication Styles

When you speak, your goal is for listeners to receive the message as you intended. Problems arise when one person has trouble "translating" a message coming from someone using a different communication style. Multiple intelligences provide clues about communication style and can give you different strategies for reaching the other person.

For example, generations come with personal and lifestyle characteristics that can affect intergenerational communication. Because much of communication is simply trying to understand where the other person is coming from, being able to recognize and adapt to differences caused by generation gaps can help you communicate successfully. Key 9.2

Generation	Communication Style	Communication Challenges	Tips for Communicating
Baby Boomers (1946–1964)	Focus on personal growth and achievement Politically correct Inclined to use both face-to-face and electronic communication	Can easily misunderstand instant electronic communication (texts, IMs, blogs, etc.) Uncomfortable with conflict Judgmental	Be open and direct (Boomers are the "show me" generation) Use face-to-face or electronic communication Provide details
Generation X (1965–1980)	Casual Pragmatic Skeptical Unimpressed by authority Use e-mail	Impatient Cynical Communication can be limited to e-mail or other noninteractive forms of communication	Use e-mail as primary communication Ask for feedback Keep it short to hold attention Use an informational style
Generation Y or Millennials (1980–1994)	Value self-expression over self-control Respect must be earned Comfortable with online communication Spend a lot of time online	Overly focused on accessing information electronically Teaching older generations to use technology erodes sense of respect for elders Inexperience dealing with people	Use e-mail, voicemail, and texts Communicate with visuals Use humor Respect their knowledge Encourage them to break rules when thinking

Note: The majority of people from all generations prefer face-to-face communication to written or electronic communication.

Source: Some information from a table on different generations by Greg Hammil, "Mixing and Managing Four Generations of Employees." FDU Magazine, Winter/Spring 2005 (www.fdu.edu/newspubs/magazine/05ws/generations.htm).

offers some helpful communication tips for interacting with various generations.

Although adjusting to communication styles helps you speak and listen more effectively, you also need to understand and learn how to effectively give and receive criticism.

Know How to Give and Take Criticism

Criticism can be either constructive or unconstructive. Constructive criticism is a practical problem-solving strategy, focusing on improving a situation. Unconstructive criticism, conversely, focuses on what went wrong and is often delivered negatively, creating bad feelings.

When offered constructively, criticism can help bring about important changes. Consider a case in which someone has continually been late to study group sessions. The group leader can comment in one of two ways. Which comment would encourage you to change your behavior?

- *Constructive.* The group leader talks privately with the student: "I've noticed that you've been late a lot. We count on you to contribute. Is there a problem that is keeping you from being on time? Can we help?"
- *Unconstructive.* The leader watches the student arrive late and says, in front of everyone, "If you can't start getting here on time, there's really no point in your coming."

Constructive comments can help you learn and improve. Be open to what you hear, and remember that most people want you to succeed.

Offering Constructive Criticism

When offering constructive criticism, use the following strategies to increase its effectiveness:

- *Criticize the behavior, not the person.* Avoid personal attacks. "You've been late to five group meetings" is preferable to "You're lazy."

- *Define the specific problem.* Try to focus on the facts, backing them up with specific examples and minimizing emotions.
- *Suggest new approaches and offer help.* Talk about practical ways to handle the situation. Brainstorm creative options. Help the person feel supported.
- *Use a positive approach and hopeful language.* Express your belief that the person can turn the situation around.

Receiving Criticism

When you find yourself on criticism's receiving end, use the following techniques:

- *Analyze the comments.* Listen carefully and then evaluate what you hear. What does it mean? What is the intent? Try to let unconstructive comments go without responding.

- *Ask for suggestions on how to change your behavior.* Be open to what others say.
- *Summarize the criticism and your response to it.* The goal is for everyone to understand the situation.
- *Use a specific strategy.* Apply problem-solving skills to analyze the problem, brainstorm ways to change, choose a strategy, and take practical action to make it happen.

One of the biggest barriers to successful communication is conflict, which can result in anger and even violence. With effort, you can manage conflict and stay away from those who cannot.

Manage Conflict

Conflicts, both large and small, arise over a clash of ideas or interests. You may have small conflicts with a housemate over a door left unlocked. You

Reading Body Language

Body language has an extraordinary capacity to express people's real feelings through gestures, eye movements, facial expressions, body positioning and posture, touching behaviors, vocal tone, and use of personal space. Why is it important to know how to analyze body language?

▶ **Nonverbal cues shade meaning.** What you say can mean different things depending on body positioning or vocal tone.

▶ **Culture influences how body language is interpreted.** For example, in the United States, looking away may be a sign of anger or distress; in Japan, it is usually a sign of respect.

▶ **Nonverbal communication influences first impressions.** Nonverbal elements, including tone of voice, posture, and eye contact, usually come across first and strongest.

Although reading body language is not an exact science, the following practical strategies will help you use it to improve communication.

▶ **Engage your emotional intelligence.** Understanding body language is part of the data you can use to figure out what people are feeling. It will also help you make effective decisions about how to use your own body language.

▶ **Pay attention to what is said through nonverbal cues.** For others as well as yourself, focus on tone, body position, and whether cues reinforce or contradict spoken words.

▶ **Adjust behavior based on cultural differences.** In cross-cultural conversation, discover what seems appropriate by paying attention to what others do and by noting how others react to what you do. Then, consider making changes based on your observations.

▶ **Adjust to the person or situation.** What body language might you use when making a presentation in class? Meeting with your advisor? Confronting an angry co-worker? Use your physicality to communicate effectively.

may have major conflicts with an instructor about a failing grade. Conflict, as unpleasant as it can be, is a natural part of human interaction and can lead to greater understanding if the people who conflict communicate effectively as they try to resolve their differences. To prevent or resolve conflict, you can choose from several strategies.

Conflict Prevention Strategies

Some strategies can help you prevent conflict from starting in the first place.

- *Send "I" messages.* "I" messages communicate your needs rather than attacking someone else. Creating these messages involves some simple rephrasing: "You didn't lock the door!" becomes "I was worried when I came home and found the door unlocked." "I" statements soften the conflict by highlighting the effects that the other person's actions have on you, rather than focusing on the person or the actions themselves. These statements help the receiver feel more willing to respond, perhaps offering help and even admitting mistakes.
- *Be assertive.* Most people tend to express themselves in one of three ways—aggressively, assertively, or passively. *Aggressive* communicators focus primarily on their own needs and can become impatient when needs are not satisfied. *Passive* communicators focus primarily on the needs of others and often deny themselves power, causing frustration. *Assertive* communicators are able to declare and affirm their opinions while respecting the rights of others to do the same. Assertive behavior strikes a balance between aggression and passivity and promotes the most productive communication. Key 9.3 contrasts these three communication styles.

What can aggressive and passive communicators do to move toward a more assertive style? Aggressive communicators might take time before speaking, use "I" statements, listen to others, and avoid giving orders. Passive communicators might acknowledge anger, express opinions, exercise the right to make requests, and know that their ideas and feelings are important.

Conflict Resolution

All too often, people deal with conflict by avoiding it altogether (a passive tactic that shuts down communication) or escalating the intensity (an aggressive tactic that often leads to fighting). Conflict resolution demands calm communication, motivation, and careful thinking. Use critical, creative, and practical thinking skills to apply the problem-solving plan from Chapter 4.

Trying to calm anger is an important part of resolving conflict. All people get angry at times—at people, events, and themselves. However, excessive anger can contaminate relationships, stifle communication, and turn friends and family away.

Manage Anger

Psychologists report that angry outbursts may actually make things worse. When you feel yourself losing control, try some of these practical anger management techniques.

- *Relax.* Breathe deeply. Slowly repeat a calming phrase like "Take it easy" or "Relax."
- *Change your environment.* Take a break from what's upsetting you. Take a walk, go to the gym, see

Key 9.3	Assertiveness Fosters Successful Communication	
Aggressive	**Assertive**	**Passive**
Blaming, name-calling, and verbal insults: "You created this mess!"	Expressing oneself and letting others do the same: "I have thoughts about this—first, what is your opinion?"	Feeling that one has no right to express anger: "No, I'm fine."
Escalating arguments: "You'll do it my way, no matter what it takes."	Using "I" statements to defuse arguments: "I am uncomfortable with that choice and want to discuss it."	Avoiding arguments: "Whatever you want to do is fine."
Being demanding: "Do this."	Asking and giving reasons: "Please consider doing it this way, and here's why . . ."	Being noncommittal: "I'm not sure what the best way to handle this is."

Manage Technology Use

List some positive and negative effects that technology has had on your relationships and communication.

....

....

Next, list three ways that you can minimize any negative effects technology may have on you.

1. ....

2. ....

3. ....

Now, take action: Choose two of your ideas, use them for a week, and evaluate the results.
If either or both work for you, stick with them.

---

a movie. Come up with a creative idea that will help you calm down.

• *Think before you speak.* When angry, most people tend to say the first thing that comes to mind, even if it's hurtful. Instead, wait until you are in control before you say something.

• *Do your best, but remember that not all problems have solutions.* Instead of blowing up, analyze a challenging situation, make a plan, and begin. If you fall short, you will know you made an effort and be less likely to turn your frustration into anger.

• *Get help if you can't keep your anger in check.* If you consistently lash out, you may need the help of a counselor. Many schools have mental health professionals available to students.

Your ability to communicate and manage conflict has a major impact on your relationships. Successful relationships are built on self-knowledge, good communication, and hard work.

How DO YOU MAKE THE MOST OF PERSONAL RELATIONSHIPS?

Personal relationships with friends, classmates, spouses and partners, and parents can be sources of great satisfaction and inner peace. Good relation-ships can motivate you to do your best at school, on the job, and in life. When relationships fall apart, however, nothing may seem right.

Use Positive Relationship Strategies

Apply strategies to improve personal relationships.

• *Prioritize personal relationships.* When you devote time and energy to education, work, and activities you enjoy, you get positive results. Do the same for your relationships.

• *If you want a friend, be a friend.* If you treat others with the kind of loyalty and support that you appreciate, you will be likely to receive the same in return.

• *Work through tensions.* Negative feelings can grow and cause problems when left unspoken.

• *Take risks.* If you open yourself up, you stand to gain the incredible benefits of companionship.

• *If a relationship fails, find ways to cope.* When an important relationship becomes strained or breaks up, analyze the situation and choose practical strategies to move on. Some people need time alone; others need to be with friends and family. Some need a change of scene; some need to let off steam with exercise or other activities. Whatever you do, believe that in time you will emerge from the experience stronger.

Plug into Communication Technology Without Losing Touch

Modern technology has revolutionized the way people communicate. Not even 30 years ago, the telephone, mail, and telegrams were the only alternatives to speaking in person. Today, you can call or text on a mobile phone; you can write a note via e-mail, instant message, or Twitter; you can communicate through blogs and chat rooms; and you can learn about one another on social networking sites such as Facebook.

However, despite allowing you to communicate faster, more frequently, and with more people at one time than ever before, communication technologies do have drawbacks.

- It is easy to misunderstand the tone or meaning of IMs, e-mail, and text messages.
- Communication technologies can devour hours of time.
- Prioritizing electronic communication over real-time connections can derail relationships.
- Revealing too much about yourself on social networking sites may cause trouble, because many employers check these sites for information about prospective job candidates.[4]

Ultimately, you will develop your own personal communication "recipe," consisting of how much you want to communicate and what methods you want to use. Keep everything in moderation, and let technology enhance in-person interaction rather than replace it.

Avoid Destructive Relationships

On the far end of the spectrum are relationships that turn destructive. The more you are informed, the less likely you are to be involved.

Sexual Harassment

Both men and women can be victims, although the most common targets are women. If you feel degraded by anything that goes on at school or work, address the person whom you believe is harassing you, or speak to a dean or supervisor. Harassment often takes the form of sexually degrading comments that demean and embarrass the victim. College administrators will enforce rules against sexual harassment but they first have to know that an incident took place.

Violent Relationships

Violent relationships among students are increasing.[5] One in five students has experienced and reported at least one violent incident while dating, from being slapped to more serious violence. Although relationship violence can happen to anyone at any age, women in their teens and twenties are more likely to be victims than older women. One theory is that they are more uneasy about leaving destructive relationships and often believe that violence is normal.

Analyze the situation and use problem-solving skills to come up with practical options. If you see warning signs such as controlling behavior, unpredictable mood swings, personality changes associated with alcohol and drugs, and outbursts of anger, consider ending the relationship. If you are being abused, call a shelter or abuse hotline or seek counseling. If you need medical attention, go to a clinic or hospital emergency room.

Rape and Date Rape

Any intercourse or anal or oral penetration by a person against another person's will is defined as rape. Rape is primarily an act of rage and control, not sex. Acquaintance rape, or *date rape*, refers to sexual activity during an arranged social encounter that is against one partner's will, including situations where one partner is too drunk or drugged to give consent. Date rapists sometimes sedate victims with odorless, tasteless drugs like rohypnol, GHB, or ketamine, which are difficult to detect in a drink.

Prevention is the first line of defense. Communicate—clearly and early—what you want and don't want. Keep a cell phone handy. Avoid alcohol or drugs that might hamper awareness. Maintain control of your drink at all times (avoid open-source containers like punch bowls).

If you are raped, whether by an acquaintance or a stranger, seek medical attention immediately. Talk to a friend or counselor. Consider reporting the incident to the police or to campus officials. And continue to get help through counseling, a rape survivor group, or a hotline.

Communicating effectively is a skill that takes a lifetime to perfect. However, learning the skills now is the first step toward developing fulfilling, lasting relationships later.

Think Back

Solidify your knowledge and prepare for tests with this review. Answer the following questions on a separate sheet of paper or electronic file.

▶ Revisit the chapter-opening questions on page 119. Scan the chapter and write a short answer for each.

▶ Go back to the Quick Check self-assessment. From the list, choose one item that you want to develop further. Set a specific goal based on what you read in the chapter. Describe your goal and plan in a short paragraph, including a time frame and specific steps.

Analyze, Create, Practice

Offer Constructive Criticism

Analyze.   Think of a relationship that could be improved if you were able to offer constructive criticism to a friend or family member. Describe what you're facing.

....

....

....

....

....

Create.   Now imagine that you have a chance to speak to this person. First describe the setting—time, place, atmosphere—where you think you would be most successful.

....

....

....

....

....

Develop your "script," keeping in mind what you know about constructive criticism. Write down your key points, keeping in mind the goal you want to achieve.

....

....

....

....

....

Practice.   Now put your plan into action and discuss the issue with the person. Did you make the progress you had hoped for? Write down what happened. Even if the relationship still has problems, were your efforts worth it? Would you try to use constructive criticism again—with the same person or another person?

....

....

....

....

....

Multiple Intelligences in action

List three intelligences in the left-hand column—two that are highly developed for you and one you would like to build. Then in the right-hand column brainstorm a strategy for communicating that relates to each intelligence.

Intelligence

Example: Interpersonal

Use MI Strategies to Come Up with Solutions

Discuss problems in groups.

....

....

....

....

....

....

....

....

....

chapter

10

How well you do in school is directly related to your physical and mental health. In this chapter you will explore ways to handle academic and life stress, avoid illness and emotional strain, and make effective decisions about substances and sex.

In this chapter, you'll explore answers to the following questions:

How can you manage stress?
p. 133

How can you make effective decisions about substances?
p. 139

How can you make smart decisions about sex?
p. 140

Wellness and Stress Management

Staying Healthy in Mind and Body

How Developed Are Your Stress Management and Wellness Skills?

For each statement, circle the number that best describes how true the statement is for you, from 1 for "not at all true for me" to 5 for "very true for me."

▶ I can recognize when stress is harming my health.   **1 2 3 4 5**

▶ I try not to take on too many commitments at once—especially if I know that I won't be able to meet deadlines.   **1 2 3 4 5**

▶ I eat healthfully, even when I am stressed.   **1 2 3 4 5**

▶ I make time to exercise regularly, especially when I'm under stress.   **1 2 3 4 5**

▶ I get an adequate amount of sleep on a regular basis.   **1 2 3 4 5**

▶ I know how to prevent mental health problems such as depression, anxiety, and eating disorders.   **1 2 3 4 5**

▶ I avoid taking addictive substances that will undermine my health, including drugs, tobacco, and excessive alcohol.   **1 2 3 4 5**

▶ I admire people who face their mental health and substance abuse problems and seek help.   **1 2 3 4 5**

▶ I think critically about sexual decisions and take responsibility for them.   **1 2 3 4 5**

▶ I know that there is no cure for HIV-AIDS and that it can be transmitted through sex.   **1 2 3 4 5**

If your total ranges from 41–50, you consider your stress management and wellness skills to be fairly well developed.
If your total ranges from 24–40, you consider your stress management and wellness skills to be somewhat developed.
If your total is less than 24, you consider your stress management and wellness skills to be underdeveloped.

Now total your scores.

REMEMBER No matter how developed your stress management and wellness skills, you can improve them with effort. Read the chapter to learn new ways to build these skills, and practice by doing the activities.

How CAN YOU MANAGE STRESS?

Going to school, working full- or part-time, raising children, participating in activities, doing an internship, volunteering—it can add up to a lot of time and stress. If you're feeling high levels of *stress*—the physical or mental strain that occurs when your body reacts to pressure—you're not alone. Stress levels among college students have increased dramatically in recent years.[1]

Dealing with stress can be an everyday challenge. The greater your stress, the greater the toll it may take on your health and on your ability to achieve your goals. However, this doesn't mean that you should try to get rid of *all* stress; moderate stress is actually good for you. It motivates you to do well on tests, finish assignments on time, and prepare for presentations.

Psychologists T. H. Holmes and R. H. Rahe found that stress is linked to both positive *and* negative changes.[2] Key 10.1 is an adaptation of their stress-rating scale, designed for college students. Based on events you've encountered within the last year, it delivers a "stress score" that indicates your likelihood of having or developing a stress-related health problem. Knowing the factors that create stress can help you learn to handle demands and ongoing pressures.

Manage Stress by Managing Time

Every time management strategy you learned in Chapter 2 is also a stress management strategy. Here are some reminders about how effective time management can help you cope:

• *Be realistic about commitments.* Students who combine work and school may become overloaded and fall behind, increasing the risk of dropping out. Set up a schedule you can realistically meet. You may need more than 4 years to graduate but taking extra time is better than not graduating at all.

• *Focus on one goal at a time.* Stress can be exhausting when you have five pressing assignments in five different classes all due in the next week. Focus on one at a time, completing it to the best of your ability, before moving to the next and the next until you're through.

• *Check things off.* When you complete to-do list items, you reduce pressure. Less pressure, less stress. Use a physical action when you complete a task—delete it from your list, crumple up a reminder note—to reinforce the reality that you are making progress.

• *Reach out to others.* Trying to do it all on your own may not be possible and can actually make things worse. Call on family and friends to take the

Key 10.1 Use This Assessment to Determine Your "Stress Score"

Add up the number of points corresponding to the events you have experienced in the past 12 months.

1. Death of a close family member	100	16. Increase in work load at school	37
2. Death of a close friend	73	17. Outstanding personal achievement	36
3. Divorce (self or parents)	65	18. First quarter/semester in college	36
4. Jail term	63	19. Change in living conditions	31
5. Major personal injury or illness	63	20. Serious argument with an instructor	30
6. Marriage	58	21. Lower grades than expected	29
7. Firing from a job	50	22. Change in sleeping habits	29
8. Failing an important course	47	23. Change in social activities	29
9. Change in health of a family member	45	24. Change in eating habits	28
10. Sex problem	44	25. Chronic car trouble	26
11. Serious argument with close friend	40	26. Change in the number of family gatherings	26
12. Change in financial status	39	27. Too many missed classes	25
13. Change in major	39	28. Change of college	24
14. Trouble with parents	39	29. Dropping more than one class	23
15. New girlfriend or boyfriend	37	30. Minor traffic violations	20

Total: _____

If your score is 300 or higher you are at high risk for developing a health problem. If your score is between 150 and 300 you have a 50 percent chance of experiencing a serious health change within two years. If you score is below 150 you have up to a 30 percent chance of a serious health change.

Source: Paul Insel and Walton Roth, Core Concepts in Health, *4th ed., Palo Alto, CA: Mayfield Publishing Company, 1985, p. 29.*

pressure off. Switch shifts at work to free up study time or ask a friend to take your kids the day before a test.

If you are in good physical and mental health, stress will be less likely to stop you in your tracks.

Eat Right

Eating well and getting exercise can be tough for students. The food environment in college is often filled with unhealthy choices, and students tend to sit a lot, eat on the run, and get too busy to exercise. Healthy eating requires *balance* (varying your diet) and *moderation* (eating reasonable amounts). Key 10.2 presents some ways to incorporate both into your life.

The Centers for Disease Control has information about weight ranges. Try the calculator for body mass index (BMI) at www.cdc.gov/healthyweight/ assessing/bmi/index.html. If you want to lose weight,

set a reasonable goal and work toward it at a pace of approximately one to two pounds a week. Losing weight and keeping it off take time and patience.

Get Exercise

Being physically fit enhances your general health, increases your energy, helps you cope with stress, and keeps you focused on your goals. Here are some ways to make exercise a part of your life:

- Walk or cycle to classes and meetings. When you reach your building, use the stairs.
- Use your school's fitness facilities in between classes.
- Play team recreational sports at school or in your community.
- Find activities you can do on your own time, such as running or lifting weights.
- Work out with friends or family to combine socializing and exercise.

Key 10.2 Create Positive Food Habits

- Vary what you eat, focusing on fruits and vegetables
- Choose foods with limited fat, cholesterol, and trans fats
- Replace sugary snacks with fresh or dried fruit
- Keep healthy snacks within reach
- Limit calorie-heavy alcoholic drinks and sugar-heavy soda
- Notice and reduce portion sizes
- Plan meals and minimize late-night eating sprees
- Substitute other activities for stress-related eating
- Get help from weight-loss organizations and on-campus support

If you overload on caffeine, it can become less effective and may disrupt your sleep patterns. Choose your coffee breaks carefully and try to avoid drinking caffeine late at night.

© Shutterstock

Remember that your health is your responsibility. Your parents can encourage you to eat right, your doctor can prescribe medications when you're sick, but only you can prioritize exercise and fitness. Think preventatively about your well-being and take charge of your choices.

Get Enough Sleep

College students are often sleep deprived. Research indicates that students need 8 to 9 hours of sleep a night to function well, but students average 6 to 7 hours—and often get much less.[3] Inadequate sleep hinders your ability to concentrate, raises stress levels, and makes auto accidents more likely. It also reduces your ability to remember what you studied.

Students, overwhelmed with responsibilities, often feel that they have no choice but to prioritize schoolwork over sleep. Some stay up regularly until the wee hours of the morning to study. Others pull "all-nighters" from time to time to get through a tough project or paper.

For the sake of your health and your GPA, find a way to get enough sleep. Look for such tell-tale symptoms of sleep deprivation as being groggy in the morning, dozing off during the day, or needing caffeine to make it through the day. Sleep expert Gregg D. Jacobs has the following practical suggestions for improving sleep habits:[4]

- *Reduce consumption of alcohol and caffeine.* Caffeine may keep you awake, especially if you drink it late. Alcohol causes you to sleep lightly, making you feel less rested when you awaken.
- *Exercise regularly.* Regular exercise, especially in the afternoon or early evening, promotes sleep.
- *Take naps.* Taking short afternoon naps can reduce the effects of sleep deprivation.
- *Be consistent.* Try to establish somewhat regular times to wake up and go to bed.
- *Manage your environment.* Wear something comfortable, turn down the lights, and keep the room cool. Use earplugs, soft music, or white noise if you're dealing with outside distractions.

Address Mental Health Issues

Although feeling anxious is normal at times, especially when you are have a lot to do, some people react to high levels of stress in more serious ways. Mental health disorders interfere with your ability to reach your goals, and they can be caused or worsened by problematic health decisions.

Of these disorders, depressive disorder (clinical depression) has become fairly common on college campuses, due in part to the wide range of stressors that students experience. At its worst, depression can lead to suicidal thoughts and attempts. Recent research reports that nearly half of surveyed students reported feelings of depression at some point, with over 30 percent saying that the level of depression made it difficult to function at times.[5]

Key 10.3 shows possible causes of depression with some typical symptoms and offers helpful coping strategies.

Eating Disorders

Millions of people develop serious and sometimes life-threatening *eating disorders* every year, including anorexia nervosa, bulimia, and binge eating disorder. Negative effects of these disorders range from fertility and obesity issues to digestive tract and other

think
CRITICALLY

Analyze Your Sleep Habits

In a survey of nearly 10,000 students at the University of Minnesota, students who reported getting adequate sleep had a higher average GPA than those who reported sleep difficulties.[6]

In a journal entry, analyze your sleep needs by answering these three questions: Do you get enough sleep, and why or why not? What signals indicate that you need more sleep? What effects do your sleep habits have on your daily life?

Key 10.3 **Know the Causes and Symptoms of Depression**

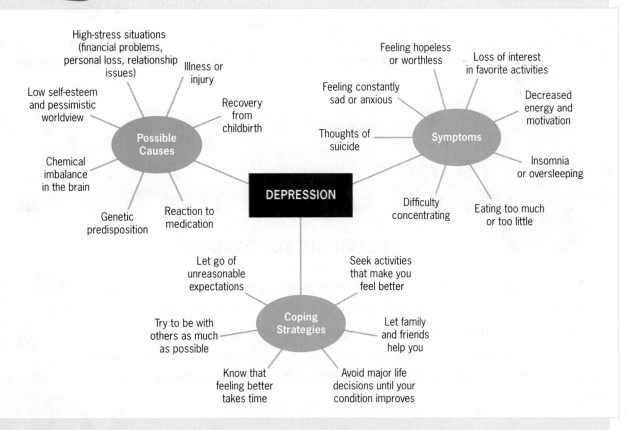

DEPRESSION

Possible Causes
- High-stress situations (financial problems, personal loss, relationship issues)
- Illness or injury
- Recovery from childbirth
- Low self-esteem and pessimistic worldview
- Chemical imbalance in the brain
- Genetic predisposition
- Reaction to medication

Symptoms
- Feeling hopeless or worthless
- Loss of interest in favorite activities
- Feeling constantly sad or anxious
- Decreased energy and motivation
- Thoughts of suicide
- Insomnia or oversleeping
- Difficulty concentrating
- Eating too much or too little

Coping Strategies
- Let go of unreasonable expectations
- Seek activities that make you feel better
- Try to be with others as much as possible
- Let family and friends help you
- Know that feeling better takes time
- Avoid major life decisions until your condition improves

Source: Depression, National Institutes of Health publication 02-3561, National Institutes of Health, 2002.

▶ Students say that their top stressors are schoolwork (74%), grades (71%), and financial worries (62%).

▶ 62% of graduating seniors are worried about finding a full-time job after graduation.

▶ Students say that stress interferes with motivation (63%), makes it tough to work (63%), and makes them not want to participate in social activities (55%).

▶ 34% said they have felt depressed at some point in the last 3 months.

▶ 70% reported that they have never considered reaching out to a trained professional for help with stress or anxiety.

organ damage, heart failure, and even death. There are three basic types of eating disorders:[8]

• *Anorexia nervosa.* People with anorexia nervosa restrict their eating and become dangerously underweight. They may also engage in overexercising, vomiting, and abuse of diuretics and laxatives. Anorexia nervosa is often linked to excessive anxiety and perfectionism.

• *Bulimia nervosa.* People with bulimia engage in "binge episodes," which involve eating excessive amounts of foods and feeling out of control. Following the binge, the person feels remorseful and attempts to purge the calories through self-induced vomiting, laxative abuse, excessive exercise, or fasting.

• *Binge eating disorder.* Binge eating disorder is the most common eating disorder. People with this condition eat large amounts of food and feel out of control, similar to those with bulimia, but they do not purge after a binge episode. They also tend to eat unusually fast, eat in secret, eat until they feel uncomfortably full, and feel ashamed of their eating behavior.

If you recognize yourself in any of these descriptions, contact your student health center or cam-

think CREATIVELY

Reach Out for Support

Consider what areas of your physical or mental health interfere with goal achievement. Would you be willing to reach out to people who can help you make positive changes? Name an area of concern and brainstorm three different resources that could help you. Consider resources at your school that support student health—medical/counseling clinic, exercise facilities, support groups, and so on—as well as online sources and outside groups. Of the resources, identify two that you plan to follow up on.

pus counseling center for help. For general advice about mental health issues, see Campus Mental Health: Know Your Rights! at www.bazelon.org/121/rightsguide.htm. The right help can change—or, in some cases, even save—your life.

CAN YOU MAKE *How* EFFECTIVE DECISIONS ABOUT SUBSTANCES?

The stresses of college lead some students to experiment with alcohol, tobacco, and other potentially addictive substances. Although these substances may alleviate stress temporarily, they have potentially serious consequences and often derail you from your goals.

You are responsible for analyzing the potential consequences of what you introduce into your body. Asking critical thinking questions can help you identify the underlying reasons for your choice and help you look further down a path you may not want to take.

- Why do I want to do this?
- Am I doing this to escape from other problems?
- What positive and negative effects might my behavior have?
- Why do others want me to do this? What do I really think of these people?
- How would my actions affect my family?

Analyze your situation with care. Then make choices that are in your best interest.

Alcohol

Alcohol is a depressant and the most frequently abused drug on campus. Even a few drinks affect thinking and muscle coordination. Prolonged use can also lead to addiction.

According to the Centers for Disease Control (CDC), your tolerance and reaction to alcohol can depend on a variety of factors including but not limited to age, gender, race or ethnicity, physical condition, the amount of food consumed before drinking, how quickly alcohol is consumed, use of drugs or prescription medications, and family history.[9] Key 10.4 shows the varying levels of drinking behaviors defined by the CDC.

Binge drinking is a serious problem on campus. Students who binge drink are more likely to miss classes, perform poorly, experience physical problems (memory loss, headache, stomach issues), become depressed, and engage in unplanned or unsafe sex.[10] If you drink, think carefully about

When you can take a break, try out different ways to have fun. These students escape to some open space for a picnic.

© Jeff Greenberg/Photo Researchers

the effects on your health, safety, and academic performance.

Drugs

College students may use drugs to relieve stress, be accepted by peers, or just to try something new. In most cases, the negative consequences of drug use outweigh any temporary high. Drug use violates federal, state, and local laws, and you may be arrested, tried, and imprisoned for possessing even a small amount of drugs. You can jeopardize your health, your reputation, your student status, and your ability to get a job if you are caught using drugs. Key 10.5 on page 141 shows details about several drugs, both legal and illegal, that show up on college campuses.

Tobacco

The 2007 National Survey on Drug Use and Health found that nearly 25.6 percent of full-time college students reported smoking at least once in the month before they were surveyed, and 41.2 percent of students attending less than full time had smoked at least once within the previous month.[11]

Many students use tobacco as a stress reliever and then become hooked on nicotine, a highly addictive drug found in all tobacco products. Nicotine's immediate effects may include an increase in blood pressure and heart rate, sweating, and throat irritation. Long-term effects may include high blood pressure, bronchitis and emphysema, stomach ulcers, heart disease, and cancer.

	Men	Women
MODERATE DRINKING		
Lower risk drinking pattern equaling "having no more than 1 drink per day for women and no more than 2 drinks per day for men."	per day	per day
HEAVY DRINKING		
For men, heavy drinking is typically defined as consuming an average of more than 2 drinks per day. For women, heavy drinking is typically defined as consuming an average of more than 1 drink per day.	+ per day	+ per day
BINGE DRINKING		
"A pattern of alcohol consumption that brings the blood alcohol concentration (BAC) level to 0.08% or above . . . usually corresponds to 5 or more drinks on a single occasion for men or 4 or more drinks on a single occasion for women, generally within about 2 hours."	in 2 hrs.	in 2 hrs.

If you smoke regularly, you can quit by being motivated, persevering, and seeking help. The positive effects of quitting—increased life expectancy, lung capacity, and energy, as well as significant financial savings—may inspire any smoker to make a lifestyle change. If you're interested in quitting, the Centers for Disease Control provides a website with quitting resources at www.cdc.gov/tobacco/quit_smoking/how_to_quit/index.htm.

Facing Addiction

If you think you may be addicted to alcohol or drugs, seek help through counseling and medical centers, detoxification centers, and support groups. Because substances often cause physical and chemical changes and psychological dependence, habits are tough to break and quitting may involve a painful withdrawal. Asking for help isn't an admission of failure but a courageous move to reclaim your life.

Working through substance abuse problems can lead to restored health and self-respect. Helpful resources can help you generate options and develop practical plans for recovery:

- *Counseling and medical care.* You can find help from school-based, private, government-sponsored, or workplace-sponsored resources. Ask your school's counseling or health center, your personal physician, or a local hospital for a referral.

- *Detoxification ("detox") centers.* If you have a severe addiction, you may need a controlled environment where you can separate yourself completely from drugs or alcohol.

- *Support groups.* Alcoholics Anonymous (AA) has led to other support groups for addicts such as Overeaters Anonymous (OA) and Narcotics Anonymous (NA).

How CAN YOU MAKE SMART DECISIONS ABOUT SEX?

What sexuality means to you and the role it plays in your life are personal choices. However, the physical act of sex can go beyond the private realm. Individual sexual conduct can result in an unexpected pregnancy and passing on *sexually transmitted diseases or infections* (STDs or STIs). These consequences affect everyone involved in the sexual act and, often, their families.

Part of being physically and mentally healthy involves thinking through sexual decisions and being aware of sexually transmitted infections that can derail your plans. Just as your success in school depends on your ability to manage time, your success in school can also depend on making choices that maintain health and safety—yours as well as those of the person with whom you are involved. Analyze

Drug	Drug Category	User Effects	Potential Physical Effects, Short-Term and Long-Term	Danger of Dependence
Cocaine (also called *coke, blow, snow*) and crack cocaine (also called *crack* or *rock*)	Stimulant	Alert, stimulated, excited, energetic, confident	Nervousness, mood swings, sexual problems, stroke or convulsions, psychoses, paranoia, coma at large doses	Strong
Marijuana and hashish (also called *pot, weed, herb*)	Cannabinol	Euphoric, mellow, little sensation of time, paranoid	Impaired judgment and coordination, bronchitis and asthma, lung and throat cancers, anxiety, lack of motivation, fertility problems	Moderate
Heroin (also called *smack, dope, horse*) and codeine	Opiates	Warm, relaxed, without pain, without anxiety	Infection of organs, inflammation of the heart, convulsions, abscesses, risk of needle-transmitted diseases	Strong, with heavy use
Glue, aerosols (also called *whippets, poppers, rush*)	Inhalants	Giddy, lightheaded, dizzy, excited	Damage to brain, liver, lungs, and kidneys; suffocation; heart failure	Insubstantial
Ecstasy (also called *X, XTC, vitamin E*)	Stimulant	Heightened sensual perception, relaxed, clear, fearless	Fatigue, anxiety, depression, heart arrhythmia, hyperthermia from overexertion and lack of fluid intake during use	Insubstantial
Ephedrine (also called *chi powder, zest*)	Stimulant	Energetic	Anxiety, elevated blood pressure, heart palpitations, memory loss, stroke, psychosis, insomnia	Strong
Gamma hydroxyl butyrate (GHB) (also called *G, liquid ecstasy, goop*)	Depressant	Uninhibited, relaxed, euphoric	Anxiety, vertigo, increased heart rate, delirium, agitation	Strong
Ketamine (also called *K, Special K, vitamin K*)	Anesthetic	Dreamy, floating, having an "out of body" sensation, numb	Neuroses, disruptions in consciousness, reduced ability to move	Strong
OxyContin (also called *Oxy, OC, legal heroin*)	Analgesic (containing opiate)	Relaxed, detached, without pain or anxiety	Overdose death can result when users ingest or inhale crushed time-release pills or take them in conjunction with alcohol or narcotics	Moderate, with long-term use
Anabolic steroids (also called *roids, juice, hype*)	Steroid	Increased muscle strength and physical performance, energetic	Stunted growth, mood swings, male-pattern baldness, breast development (in men) or body hair development (in women), mood swings, liver damage, insomnia, aggression, irritability	Insubstantial
Methamphetamine (also called *meth, speed, crank*)	Stimulant	Euphoric, confident, alert, energetic	Seizures, heart attack, strokes, vein damage (if injected), sleeplessness, hallucinations, high blood pressure, paranoia, psychoses, depression, anxiety, loss of appetite	Strong, especially if taken by smoking

Source: Drug Policy Alliance, www.drugpolicy.org/drugbydrug/.

PRACTICALLY

Evaluate Your Substance Use

Think you may have a problem with drugs or alcohol? The following survey will help you identify possible areas of need. Keep in mind that one Yes answer may indicate a need to look carefully at your habits. Three or more Yes answers indicate that you may have a problem and that you should speak with a counselor.

Within the Last Year

Ⓨ Ⓝ **1.** Have you tried to stop drinking or taking drugs but found that you couldn't do so for long?

Ⓨ Ⓝ **2.** Do you get tired of people telling you they're concerned about your drinking or drug use?

Ⓨ Ⓝ **3.** Have you felt guilty about your drinking or drug use?

Ⓨ Ⓝ **4.** Have you felt that you needed a drink or drugs in the morning—as an "eye-opener"—to cope with a hangover?

Ⓨ Ⓝ **5.** Do you drink or use drugs alone?

Ⓨ Ⓝ **6.** Do you drink or use drugs every day?

Ⓨ Ⓝ **7.** Have you found yourself regularly thinking or saying "I need" a drink or any type of drug?

Ⓨ Ⓝ **8.** Have you lied about or concealed your drinking or drug use?

Ⓨ Ⓝ **9.** Do you drink or use drugs to escape worries, problems, mistakes, or shyness?

Ⓨ Ⓝ **10.** Do you find you need increasingly larger amounts of drugs or alcohol in order to achieve a desired effect?

Ⓨ Ⓝ **11.** Have you forgotten what happened while drinking or using drugs because you had a blackout?

Ⓨ Ⓝ **12.** Have you spent a lot of time, energy, or money getting alcohol or drugs?

Ⓨ Ⓝ **13.** Has your drinking or drug use caused you to neglect friends, your partner, your children, or other family members, or caused other problems at home?

Ⓨ Ⓝ **14.** Have you gotten into an argument or a fight that was alcohol or drug related?

Ⓨ Ⓝ **15.** Has your drinking or drug use caused you to miss class, fail a test, or ignore schoolwork?

Ⓨ Ⓝ **16.** Have you been choosing to drink or use drugs instead of attending social events or performing hobbies you used to enjoy?

Ⓨ Ⓝ **17.** Has your drinking or drug use affected your efficiency on the job or caused you to fail to show up at work?

Ⓨ Ⓝ **18.** Have you continued to drink or use drugs despite any physical problems or health risks that your use has caused or made worse?

Ⓨ Ⓝ **19.** Have you driven a car or performed any other potentially dangerous tasks while under the influence of alcohol or drugs?

Ⓨ Ⓝ **20.** Have you had a drug- or alcohol-related legal problem or arrest (possession, use, disorderly conduct, driving while intoxicated, etc.)?

When You're Finished   Write an action plan based on your results. Include at least three steps you will take to address the results of your survey. If you answered No to every question, create an action plan to keep you on track.

Source: Adapted from the Criteria for Substance Dependence and Criteria for Substance Abuse in the *Diagnostic and Statistical Manual of Mental Disorders,* Fourth Edition, published by the American Psychiatric Association, Washington, D.C., and from materials entitled "Are You An Alcoholic?" developed by Johns Hopkins University.

Disease	Symptoms	Health Problems If Untreated	Treatments
Chlamydia	Discharge, painful urination, swollen or painful joints, change in menstrual periods for women	Can cause pelvic inflammatory disease (PID) in women, which can lead to sterility or ectopic pregnancies; infection; miscarriage or premature birth.	Curable with full course of antibiotics; avoid sex until treatment is complete.
Gonorrhea	Discharge, burning while urinating	Can cause PID, swelling of testicles and penis, arthritis, skin problems, infections.	Usually curable with antibiotics; however, certain strains are becoming resistant to medication.
Genital herpes	Blister-like itchy sores in the genital area, headache, fever, chills	Symptoms may subside and then reoccur, often in response to high stress levels; carriers can transmit the virus even when it is dormant.	No cure; some medications, such as Acyclovir, reduce and help heal the sores and may shorten recurring outbreaks.
Syphilis	A genital sore lasting one to five weeks, followed by a rash, fatigue, fever, sore throat, headaches, swollen glands	If it lasts over four years, it can cause blindness, destruction of bone, mental illness, or heart failure; in the case of birth, can cause death or deformity.	Curable with full course of antibiotics.
Human papilloma virus (HPV, or genital warts)	Genital itching and irritation, small clusters of warts	Can increase risk of cervical cancer in women; virus may remain in body and cause recurrences even when warts are removed.	Treatable with drugs applied to warts or various kinds of wart removal surgery. Vaccine (Gardasil) newly available; most effective when given to women before exposure to HPV.
Hepatitis B	Fatigue, poor appetite, vomiting, jaundice, hives	Some carriers will have few symptoms; others may develop chronic liver disease that may lead to other diseases of the liver.	No cure; some will recover, some will not. Bed rest may help ease symptoms. Vaccine is available.

sexual issues carefully, weighing the positive and negative effects of your choices.

Birth Control

Birth control can be defined as "the use of any practices, methods or devices to prevent pregnancy from occurring."[12] The choice to use birth control is a private one. If you choose to make use of a birth control method, evaluate the pros and cons of each option for yourself and your partner. As you learn about the options, consider cost, ease of use, reliability, comfort, and protection against STIs. Talk with your partner and together make a choice that is comfortable for both of you. For more information, check your library, the Internet, or a bookstore;

talk to your doctor; or ask a counselor at the student health center.

STIs spread through sexual contact (intercourse or other sexual activity that involves contact with the genitals). All are highly contagious. The only birth control methods that offer some degree of protection are male and female condoms (latex or polyurethane only), which prevent skin-to-skin contact. Have a doctor examine any irregularity or discomfort as soon as you detect it. Key 10.6 describes common STIs.

AIDS and HIV

The most serious STI is AIDS (acquired immune deficiency syndrome), which is caused by the human immunodeficiency virus (HIV). AIDS has no cure and can result in death. Medical science continues to develop drugs to combat AIDS and its related illnesses. Although the drugs can slow the progression of the infection and extend life expectancy, there is currently no known cure.

People acquire HIV through sexual relations, by sharing hypodermic needles for drug use, and by receiving infected blood transfusions. You cannot become infected unless one of those fluids is involved. Therefore, it is unlikely you can contract HIV from toilet seats, hugging, kissing, or sharing a glass. Other than not having sex at all, a latex condom, used properly, is the best defense against AIDS.

To be safe, have an HIV test done at your doctor's office or at a government-sponsored clinic. Your school's health department may also administer HIV tests, and home HIV tests are available over the counter. Consider requiring that any sexual partner be tested as well. If you are infected, inform all sexual partners and seek medical assistance. If you're interested in contacting support organizations in your area, call the National AIDS Hotline at 1-800-342-AIDS.

The life of a college student always has been—and will continue to be—filled with stresses and pressures. Understanding the nature of those stressors and creating ways to deal with them successfully can eliminate unnecessary worries from your already packed schedule. Being aware of yourself and your needs is a positive step toward owning your place in the world.

quick! SKILL BUILDING

Think Back

Solidify your knowledge and prepare for tests with this review. Answer the following questions on a separate sheet of paper or electronic file.

▶ Revisit the chapter-opening questions on page 132. Scan the chapter and write a short answer for each.

▶ Review the chapter and identify ten important statistics. Create a think link (mind map or visual organizer) that incorporates them and shows what categories they are in (physical health, mental health, substance management, and so on).

Analyze, Create, Practice

Improve Your Physical Health

Make a change that will benefit you.

Analyze. Pick a topic—eating, drinking, sleeping, sexual activity—that you would like to handle more effectively. To examine why it is a problem, ask yourself what behaviors and attitudes affect this action? What are the positive and negative side effects of each?

Example:	*Issue:*	binge drinking
	Behavior:	I binge drink probably three times a week.
	Attitude:	I don't think it's any big deal. I like using it to escape.
	Positive effects:	I have fun with my friends. I feel confident, accepted, social.
	Negative effects:	I feel hung over and foggy the next day. I miss class.

Your turn:	*Issue:*	....
	Behavior:	....
	Attitude:	....
	Positive effects:	....

Negative effects: ....

Question to think about: Is it worth it?

Create. First think about what you want to change and why. Then explore options to come up with a plan. For example, the binge drinker might consider cutting back or trying a social activity that does not involve drinking.

How you might change your behavior: ....

....

How you might change your attitude: ....

....

Positive effects you think these changes would have: ....

....

Practice. Put a health improvement plan into action. Choose two actions—one to improve your attitude and the other to improve your behavior—that you think would have positive effects. Commit to these actions with specific plans and watch the positive change happen.

Attitude improvement plan: ....

....

Behavior improvement plan: ....

....

Multiple **Intelligences** *in action*

List three intelligences in the left-hand column—two that are highly developed for you and one you would like to build. Then in the right-hand column brainstorm a strategy for maintaining wellness and managing stress that relates to each intelligence.

Intelligence	**Use MI Strategies to Come Up with Solutions**
Example: Intrapersonal	*Journal about issues that stress you out and keep you from focusing.*
....	....
	....
....	....
	....
....	....
	....

chapter

11

Managing Money

Living Within Your Means

Knowing how to deal with money should be a top priority for nearly every college student. This chapter provides information that will help you to make more effective decisions about credit cards, budgets, and money management.

In this chapter, you'll explore answers to the following questions:

quick!

CHECK

How Developed Are Your Money Management Skills?

For each statement, circle the number that best describes how true the statement is for you, from 1 for "not at all true for me" to 5 for "very true for me."

▶ I separate my money from my self-worth. What I earn doesn't define who I am.   **1 2 3 4 5**

▶ I understand how I tend to perceive, and use, money.   **1 2 3 4 5**

▶ I create a monthly budget and stick to it as much as possible.   **1 2 3 4 5**

▶ I have a realistic understanding of how much money I can spend.   **1 2 3 4 5**

▶ I rarely spend more money than I have available.   **1 2 3 4 5**

▶ If I work, I try to schedule it so that it doesn't interfere with schoolwork.   **1 2 3 4 5**

▶ I know what financial aid I am eligible for and I apply for it.   **1 2 3 4 5**

▶ I use credit cards for major purchases, not for day-to-day expenses.   **1 2 3 4 5**

▶ I consistently pay credit card and other bills on time.   **1 2 3 4 5**

▶ I try to put away whatever money I can to provide for my future.   **1 2 3 4 5**

If your total ranges from 41–50, you consider your money management skills to be fairly well developed.
If your total ranges from 24–40, you consider your money management skills to be somewhat developed.
If your total is less than 24, you consider your money management skills to be underdeveloped.

Now total your scores.

REMEMBER No matter how developed your money management skills, you can improve them with effort. Read the chapter to learn new ways to build these skills, and practice by doing the activities.

What DOES MONEY MEAN IN YOUR LIFE?

According to the American Psychological Association, nearly three out of four Americans cite money as the number one stressor in their lives.[1] For the majority of college students, the combined costs of tuition, course materials, fees, and living expenses mean that money is tight—for some, it's disturbingly tight. However, keeping your goals in focus and managing your money effectively can greatly reduce financial stress.

How You Perceive and Use Money

Your spending and saving behavior and attitudes about money reflect your values, goals, and self-image. You might spend your money as soon as you earn it, or you might save for the future. You might charge everything, use cash only, or do something in between. You might measure your success based on how much money you have or define your worth in nonmaterial terms. As you analyze who you are as a money manager, consider the influences in Key 11.1.

Money coach Connie Kilmark notes that you cannot change how you handle money until you analyze your attitudes and behaviors. "If managing money was just about math and the numbers, everyone would know how to manage their finances sometime around the fifth grade," she says.[2] When you take an honest look at how you feel about money, you can make more effective financial decisions based on what works best for you.

Needs Versus Wants

When spending money, people often confuse what they *need* with what they *want*. True needs are few and basic: food, water, air, shelter (rent or mortgage as well as home maintenance costs and utilities), family and friends, and some mode of transportation. Everything else is technically a want—something you would like to have but can live without. When people spend money on those wants, they often find that they don't have enough cash available for needs.

Spending $1,000 on a flat-screen may seem like no big deal, but it won't do you much good if you are watching TV in an ice-cold house because of a boiler that needs a $1,000 repair.

Check your spending for purpose. What do you buy with your money? Are the items you purchase necessary? When you do spend on a want rather than a need, are you doing so thoughtfully by planning the added expense into your monthly budget? If you get a clear idea of what you want and what you need, you can think through spending decisions more effectively. This is not to say that you should never spend money on wants. The main goal is to make sure that you satisfy your needs first, and then see how much money is left over for your wants. For college students, money management attitudes and skills play out through budgeting and credit card use.

How CAN YOU CREATE AND USE A BUDGET?

Creating a practical budget that works requires that you use your critical, creative, and practical think-

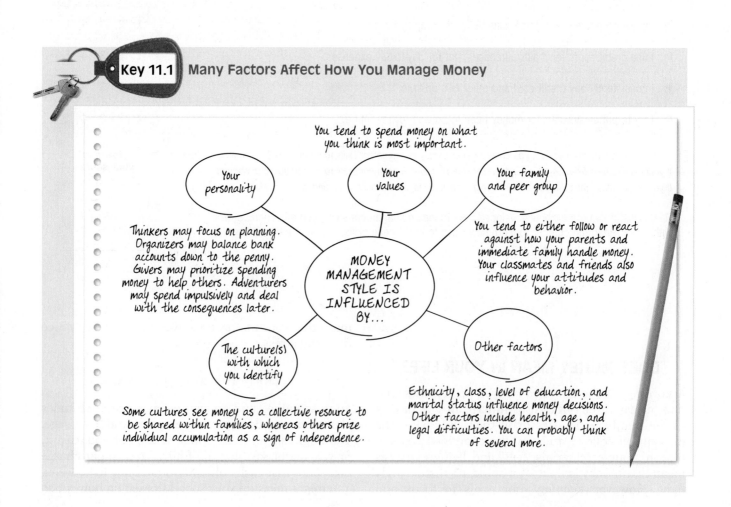

Key 11.1   **Many Factors Affect How You Manage Money**

You tend to spend money on what you think is most important.

Your personality

Your values

Your family and peer group

MONEY MANAGEMENT STYLE IS INFLUENCED BY...

Thinkers may focus on planning. Organizers may balance bank accounts down to the penny. Givers may prioritize spending money to help others. Adventurers may spend impulsively and deal with the consequences later.

You tend to either follow or react against how your parents and immediate family handle money. Your classmates and friends also influence your attitudes and behavior.

The culture(s) with which you identify

Other factors

Some cultures see money as a collective resource to be shared within families, whereas others prize individual accumulation as a sign of independence.

Ethnicity, class, level of education, and marital status influence money decisions. Other factors include health, age, and legal difficulties. You can probably think of several more.

think CRITICALLY

Analyze Your View of Money

Reread the description of each factor in Key 11.1. In a journal entry, analyze how each affects the way in which you view and manage your finances. Include comments on the following:

- Your values
- Your personality
- Your culture
- Your family and peer groups
- Other factors you find relevant

ing abilities. First, *analyze* your resources (money flowing in) and expenditures (money flowing out). Next, *create* new and different ways to make changes, especially if your expenditures exceed your income. Finally, take *practical action* to adjust spending or earning to come out even or ahead. Because many expenses are billed monthly, most people use a month as a unit of time when budgeting.

Budgeting takes effort and time. Find time each week, if you can, to tally receipts and keep track of where your money goes.

© Sarah Kravits

Your biggest expense right now is probably the cost of your education, including tuition and room and board. However, that expense may not hit you fully until after you graduate and begin to pay back your student loans. (Financial aid options will be explored later in the chapter.) For now, include in your budget only the part of the cost of your education you are paying while you are in school.

Figure Out What You Earn

To determine what is available to you on a monthly basis, start with the money you earn in a month's time at any regular job. Then, if you have savings set aside for your education or any other source of income, determine how much of it you can spend each month and add that amount. If you have a grant for the entire year, for example, divide it by 12 (or by how many months you are in school over the course of a year) to see how much you can use each month.

Figure Out What You Spend

First, note regular monthly expenses like rent, phone, and cable (look at past checks and electronic debits to estimate what the month's bills will be). Some expenses, like automobile and health insurance, may be billed once or twice a year. In these cases, divide the yearly cost by 12 to see how much you spend every month. Then, over a month's time, record cash

Common Sources of Income	Common Expenses
• Take-home pay from a full-time or part-time job	• Rent or mortgage
• Take-home pay from summer and holiday employment	• Tuition you are paying now
• Money earned from work-study or paid internship	• Books and other course materials
• Money from parents or other relatives	• Utilities (electric, gas, oil, water)
• Scholarships	• Telephone (cell phone and/or land line)
• Grants	• Food
• Loans	• Clothing, toiletries, household supplies
	• Child care
	• Transportation and auto expenses (gas, maintenance, service)
	• Credit cards and other payments on credit (car payment)
	• Insurance (health, auto, homeowner's or renter's, life)
	• Entertainment (cable TV, movies, eating out, books and magazines, music downloads)
	• Computer-related expenses, including online service costs
	• Miscellaneous expenses

or debit card expenditures in a small notebook—anything over five dollars. Be sure to count smaller purchases if they are frequent (for example, one or two pricey coffees a day add up over time). Added together, your regular expenses and other expenditures will show how much you spend in a month. Key 11.2 lists common sources of income as well as customary expenses for college students.

Use the total of all your monthly expenses as a baseline for other months, realizing that your expenditures will vary depending on what is happening in your life and even the season (for example, the cost to heat your home may be much greater in the winter than in the summer).

Evaluate the Difference

Focusing on the particular month you are examining, subtract your monthly expenses from your monthly income. Ideally, you have money left over—to save or to spend. However, if you are spending more than you take in, ask some focused questions.

- *Examine your expenses.* Did you forget to budget for recurring expenses such as the cost for semi-annual dental visits? Or was your budget derailed by an emergency expense?

- *Examine your spending patterns and priorities.* Did you spend money wisely during the month, or did you overspend on luxuries?
- *Examine your income.* Do you bring in enough money? Do you need another source?

Adjust Expenses or Earnings

If you are spending more than you are earning, you can either earn more or spend less. To increase income, consider taking a part-time job, increasing hours at a current job, or finding scholarships or grants. To decrease spending, reduce or cut purchases you don't need to make.

Rely on your dominant multiple intelligences to plan your budget. For example, whereas logical-mathematical learners may take to a detail-oriented budgeting plan, visual learners may want to create a budget chart on a program like Quicken, or bodily-kinesthetic learners may want to dump receipts into a big jar and tally them at the end of the month.

Juggle Work and School

If the only way to keep your budget balanced is to work while you are in school, know that you are not

Find Ways to Spend Less

Think about all the ways you spend money. Where can you trim a bit? For instance, look for an expense you can reduce or eliminate, find discounts, or barter a product or service for one that a friend can provide.

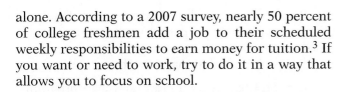

Give yourself a day or two to brainstorm, then write your list on a sheet of paper or record it electronically. Choose three ideas with the best chance of success and try them. As a reality check and an incentive, put cash in a jar daily or weekly in the amounts that these changes save you, and see how much you have by the end of the month.

alone. According to a 2007 survey, nearly 50 percent of college freshmen add a job to their scheduled weekly responsibilities to earn money for tuition.[3] If you want or need to work, try to do it in a way that allows you to focus on school.

Establish Your Needs

Think about what you need from a job. Ask questions like these:

- How much money do I need to make—weekly, per term, for the year?
- What time of day is best for me? Should I consider night or weekend work?
- Can my schedule handle a full-time job, or should I look for part-time work?
- Do I want hands-on experience in a particular field?
- How flexible a job do I need?
- Can I, or should I, find work at my school or as part of a work-study program?

Analyze the Impact

Working while in school has pros and cons:

- *Pros.* General and career-specific experience; developing contacts; possible enhanced school performance (although full-time work can be problematic, working up to 15 hours a week may actually help

you become more efficient about how you schedule your time)
- *Cons.* Time commitment that reduces available study time; reduced opportunity for social and extracurricular activities; having to shift gears mentally from work to classroom; stretching yourself too thin; fatigue

Your goal is to earn the money you need without derailing your education. If you make careful choices about work and about how you schedule your life around it, you can reach that goal.

How CAN YOU MAKE THE MOST OF FINANCIAL AID?

Financing your education—alone or with the help of your family—involves gathering financial information and making decisions about what you can afford and how much help you may need. *Never assume you are not eligible for aid.* Almost all students are eligible for some kind of need-based or merit-based financial assistance.

Know What Aid Is Available

Aid comes in the form of student loans, grants, and scholarships. The federal government administers

Ways to Save Money

With a little effort, you can find ways to trim your spending. Here are a few ideas:

▶ Share living space

▶ Rent movies or borrow them from friends or the library

▶ Eat at home more often

▶ Use grocery and clothing coupons from the paper or online

▶ Take advantage of sales, buy store brands, and buy in bulk

▶ Find play and concert tickets that are discounted for students

▶ Walk or use public transportation

▶ Bring lunch from home

▶ Shop in secondhand or consignment stores or swap clothing with friends

▶ Communicate via e-mail or snail mail

▶ Ask a relative to help with child care, or create a babysitting co-op

▶ Reduce electricity costs by cutting back on air conditioning and switching to compact fluorescent bulbs (CFLs) in your lamps at home

---

the primary loan and grant programs, although many private sources may offer grants and scholarships as well.

• *Scholarships*. Scholarships are awarded to students who show talent or ability in specific areas (academic achievement, sports, the arts, citizenship, or leadership). Scholarships do not require repayment.

• *Grants*. Grants are awarded to students who show financial need. Like scholarships, they do not have to be paid back.

• *Student loans*. As the recipient of a student loan, you are responsible for paying back the amount you borrow, plus interest, according to a predetermined payment schedule that may stretch over years.

Key 11.3 lists federal grant and loan programs. Additional information about each is available in various federal student aid publications, which you can find at your school's financial aid office, request by phone (800-433-3243), or access online at http://studentaid.ed.gov/PORTALSWebApp/students/english/publications.jsp.

 **Key 11.3** Get to Know Your Federal Loan and Grant Programs

Grants

• *Pell* (need based, available to undergraduates with no other degrees)

• *Federal Supplemental Educational Opportunity, or FSEOG* (need based, only available at participating schools)

• *Work-study* (need based, paying an hourly wage for selected jobs)

Loans

• *Perkins* (for those with exceptional financial need)

• *Stafford* (for students enrolled at least half-time)

• *PLUS* (available to students claimed as dependents by their parents)

Source: http://studentaid.ed.gov/PORTALSWebApp/students/english/index.jsp.

Your school can help you wade through paperwork for grants, loans, or scholarships. This student gets help from someone in the financial aid office as she prepares applications.

© Mary Ann Chastain/AP Images

Apply for Aid

The key word for success in this process is *early*. Research early; get forms early; and apply early. The earlier you complete the process, the greater your chances of being considered for aid.

• *For federal aid.* Fill out the Free Application for Federal Student Aid (FAFSA) electronically. The form can be found through your college's financial aid office or website or via the U.S. Department of Education's website (www.ed.gov/finaid.html). You will create a personal portfolio—called "MyFSA"—on the site that will store all the information you enter, including your FAFSA and any other forms. The U.S. Department of Education has an online tool called FAFSA Forecaster you can use to estimate how much aid you qualify for. You need to reapply every year for federal aid. This is a *free* form—if you hear about services charging a fee for completing your FAFSA, avoid them.

• *For private aid.* Thoroughly investigate what you may be eligible for. Visit the financial aid office, search libraries and the Web (including your school's website), and go through books that list scholarships and other aid. Know details that may help you identify sources available to you (you or your family's military status, ethnic background, membership in

organizations, religious affiliation, and so on). Once you have identified possibilities, apply according to the materials and guidelines provided by the organization offering aid.

If you do receive aid from your college or elsewhere, follow all rules and regulations, especially maintaining good academic standing and meeting yearly application deadlines (in most cases, you have to reapply *every year* for aid). Finally, take a new look each year at what's available. You may be eligible for different grants or scholarships than when you first applied.

Think Critically About Aid

The decisions you make now about how to finance your education will affect your future. Ask careful questions about the following:

• *Where you get your money.* Scholarships and grants, if you can get them, are best because you don't have to pay them back. Federal loans are the next best option because they tend to have lower interest rates than private loans.

• *How much money you get.* Financial aid experts recommend that you borrow only what you truly need and no more. Look at the Bureau of Labor Statistics online to see what you might expect to earn when you graduate. One rule says that if your total debt will be more than twice your expected yearly salary, you need to rethink your plan.[4] This may mean changing your career goal, finding a less expensive school, or searching for other sources of aid to supplement smaller loans.

• *The terms of your loan.* Different loans have different terms. Get to know your loan—how long you can wait before starting to pay it, how much you will need to pay per month, how long you have to pay it back, what your interest rate is, and any other important details. Make sure you fulfill all of your obligations set out in the terms.

In part because of rising education costs that don't match increases in wages and salaries, students are borrowing ever-larger amounts of money. Consequently, the number of students *defaulting* on loans—in other words, walking away from them—is on the rise, and even personal bankruptcy won't make student loans go away.[5] The consequences for defaulting on a loan are severe and include credit trouble, inability to apply for further aid, money taken from your salary or Social Security payment, and more. To avoid trouble later, borrow only what you can pay back See www.finaid.org for more helpful information about managing loans and avoiding financial nightmares.

What WILL HELP YOU USE CREDIT CARDS WISELY?

Student loans are one way of borrowing the money you need to live and study. There is a much more expensive form of borrowing—credit cards. A typical college student receives dozens of credit card offers. These offers—and the cards that go along with them—are a double-edged sword: They are a handy alternative to cash and can help build a strong credit history if used appropriately. But they also can plunge you into a hole of debt. Students are acquiring cards in droves—in fact, in 2009, only 2 percent of undergraduates had no credit history.[6]

Credit cards can be a particular danger for students. Credit companies often target students with a positive spin about credit cards, knowing that many lack knowledge about how credit works. Too much focus on what they can purchase with credit cards can lead students into trouble. Recent statistics from a survey of undergraduates illustrate the situation:[7]

- As of 2008, 50 percent of undergraduates reported having four or more credit cards.
- Students who hold credit cards carry an average outstanding balance of $3,173.
- 21 percent of undergraduates have a credit card balance between $3,000 and $7,000.
- Nine out of ten students report paying for direct education expenses, including textbooks and school supplies, with credit cards. Students who use credit cards for educational expenses estimate spending an average of $2,200 on such services alone.
- College-age consumers now have the second-highest rate of bankruptcy, just after those aged 35 to 44.

Many college students charge books and tuition as well as expenses like car repair, food, and clothes. Before they know it, they are deeply in debt. It's hard to notice trouble brewing when you don't see your wallet taking a hit.

How Credit Cards Work

To charge means to create a debt that must be repaid. The credit card issuer earns money by charging interest, often 18 percent or higher, on unpaid balances. Here's an example: Say you have a $3,000 unpaid balance on your card at an annual interest rate of 18 percent. If you make the $60 minimum payment every month, it will take 8 years to pay off your debt, assuming that you make no other purchases. The effect on your wallet is staggering.

Original debt	$3,000
Cost to repay credit card loan at an annual interest rate of 18 percent for 8 years	$5,760
Cost of using credit	**$2,760** ($5,760 – $3,000)

By the time you finish, you will have repaid nearly *twice* your original debt.

Keep in mind that credit card companies are in the business to make money and don't have your financial best interests at heart. Focusing on what's best for your finances is *your* job, and the first step is to know as much as you can about credit cards. Start with the important concepts presented in Key 11.4, and make sure you read the fine print of any card you are considering, so that you know what you are getting into.

Look for Credit Pitfalls

In response to recent economic changes, credit card disclaimers and policies can cause problems unless you stay alert. Here are a few you should note, both when seeking a new card and when looking at existing card statements:

- *New fees.* In addition to annual fees becoming once again common, a card may charge fees for reward programs, paying your bill by phone, or even checking your balance.
- *Shrinking or disappearing grace periods.* In the past, a "grace period" of a few days may have given you a chance to pay late but avoid fees. Now, even slightly late payments will usually result in a fee charged to your card.
- *Reward program changes.* Even with a reward program you've enjoyed for a while, such as airline miles or cash back, keep checking your statements. Cards may charge for reward programs or may change or remove them if you are late with a payment.
- *"Fee harvesting" cards.* Some cards feature low credit limits and come loaded with extra fees. After the fees are tacked onto the low credit limit, very little is left to spend and consumers often end up going over their limit—resulting in more fees.

Manage Credit Card Debt

Prevention is the best line of defense. To avoid excessive debt, ask yourself questions before charging: Would I buy it if I had to pay cash? Can I pay off the balance in

What is this?	**What do you do with it?**
Annual percentage rate (APR) is the amount of interest charged on the money you don't pay off in any given month. The higher your APR, the higher your finance charges.	Shop around for low rates (check www.studentcredit.com). Look for fixed rates. Watch out for low rates that skyrocket to over 20 percent after a few months or a late payment.
Cash advance is an immediate loan, in cash, from the credit card company.	Use a cash advance only in an emergency. Finance charges begin immediately and you may also have to pay a transaction fee.
Credit limit is the maximum amount your card company allows you to charge, including all fees and cash advances.	Card companies generally set low credit limits for students, but your limit may rise if you pay on time. Avoid charging up to the limit, so that you have credit available for emergencies.
Finance charges include interest and fees and are calculated each month.	The only way to avoid a finance charge is to pay your balance in full by the due date.
Minimum payment refers to the amount set by the card company you must pay by the statement due date to avoid penalty, usually very small compared to the amount owed.	Make the minimum payment at the very least—but remember that the more you can pay each month, the less the interest.

full at the end of the billing cycle? If I buy this, what purchases will I have to put off or give up altogether? These strategies will also help you stay in control:

• *Choose your card wisely.* Look for cards with low interest rates, no annual fee, a rewards program, and a grace period (a week or two to pay your bill without having to pay interest).

• *Use reminders.* To pay your bills on time, set up a reminder system that activates a week or so before the due date. You can create an e-mail alert through your card account, make a note in your planner, or set an alarm on your electronic planner.

• *If you get into trouble, call the credit company and ask to set up a payment plan.* Then, going forward, try to avoid the same mistakes. If you still need help, contact organizations such as the National Foundation for Credit Counseling (www.nfcc.org) or American Financial Solutions (1-888-282-5899) for help.

Build a Good Credit Score

Many people go through periods when they have a hard time paying bills. Falling behind on payments, however, could result in a poor *credit score* (also referred to as a *credit rating*) that can make it tough to get a loan or finance a large purchase. Your credit score is a prediction of your ability to pay back debt. If you've ever bought a car, signed up for a credit card, or purchased insurance, the deal you got was related to your credit score. If you're looking to rent an apartment, sign up for a new cell phone plan, connect utilities at your home, or even start a job where you may be required to handle money, someone will be examining your credit score.

Most credit scores are determined from a credit scoring scale that runs from 300 to 850; in general, a higher score will earn you better interest rates. For example, a person with a score of 520 would pay a much higher percentage and monthly bill on a mortgage of $100,000 than a person with a score of 720. If you're trying to keep your score in good shape, or if you need to get your score back on track, look at Key 11.5 (p. 158) to get an idea of what affects your credit.

Building, maintaining, and repairing credit is an ongoing challenge. The three primary credit bureaus—Experian, TransUnion, and Equifax—will provide you a report containing your credit score and other important information about your credit history. Also, a venture called VantageScore can give you a credit score that takes the average of your scores from all three companies and may provide a more accurate and consistent view of your credit. See www.annualcreditreport.com or www.vantagescore.com for more information.

One of the most practical lessons you'll learn is how to manage money. It is a responsibility common to nearly everyone. Learning to manage money in school is one thing that can make the postgraduation transition into the "real world" that much easier.

Map Out Your Budget

Use this exercise to see what you take in and spend and to decide what adjustments you need to make. Consider using an online calculator such as www.calculatorweb.com for this task.

Step 1: Estimate your current expenses in dollars per month, using the accompanying table. This may require tracking expenses for a month if you don't already keep a record of your spending. The grand total is your overall monthly expenses. If any expense comes only once a year, enter it in the "Annual Expenses" column and divide by 12 to get your "Monthly Expenses" figure for that item.

EXPENSES	MONTHLY EXPENSES	ANNUAL EXPENSES
Education		
Books		
Tuition and fees		
Computer, supplies, lab		
Housing		
Dorm, rent, mortgage		
Utilities		
Phone including long distance, cell phone		
Cable TV, Internet		
Electricity, gas		
Water, garbage		
Transportation and Travel		
Car payment		
Auto insurance, maintenance and repairs, registration, emissions inspections		
Gas, public transportation, parking permits, tolls		
Vacation trips, trips home		
Food		
Groceries, cafeteria meal plan, eating out, snacks		
Health		
Health insurance		
Gym, equipment, sports, fitness		
Medical, dental, prescriptions		
Personal		
Entertainment including CDs, socializing		
Laundry		
Clothing		
Household supplies, furnishings		

EXPENSES (Continued)	MONTHLY EXPENSES	ANNUAL EXPENSES
Credit card payments		
Student loan or other loan repayment		
Donations: charity, church, gifts		
Child care		
Other: emergencies, hobbies		
Total Expected Expenses		

Step 2: Calculate your average monthly income. As with income, if any source of income arrives only once a year, enter it in the "Annual" column and divide by 12 to get the monthly figure. For example, if you have a $6,000 scholarship for the year, your monthly income would be $500 ($6,000 divided by 12).

INCOME/RESOURCES	MONTHLY INCOME	ANNUAL INCOME
Employment (assume 28% average income tax)		
Family contribution		
Financial assistance: grants, federal and other loans		
Scholarships		
Interest and dividends		
Other gifts, income, and contributions		
Total Expected Income		

Step 3: Subtract the grand total of your monthly expenses from the grand total of your monthly income:

Income per Month	
Expenses per Month	
Difference (income or expense)	

Step 4: If you have a negative cash flow, what would you change? You can increase income, decrease spending, or both. List two ideas about how to get your cash flow back in the black.

1. ....

2. ....

quick! SKILL BUILDING

Think Back

Solidify your knowledge and prepare for tests with this review. Answer the following questions on a separate sheet of paper or electronic file.

▶ Revisit the chapter-opening questions on page 146. Scan the chapter and write a short answer for each.

▶ Review the section on credit cards. Create an informal outline summarizing the most important points to remember.

35% HOW YOU PAY YOUR BILLS

Remember: Always paying your bills on time is great; always paying them late is bad. Declaring bankruptcy is worse.

30% AMOUNT OF MONEY YOU OWE AND THE AMOUNT OF AVAILABLE CREDIT

Statistically, people who have a lot of credit available tend to use it, which makes them a less attractive credit risk.

15% LENGTH OF CREDIT HISTORY

In general, the longer you've had credit, the more points you get.

10% MIX OF CREDIT

Statistically, people with a variety of credit types usually understand how to use credit better. Thus, having different types of credit—such as credit cards, loans, and mortgages—looks better to creditors.

10% NEW CREDIT APPLICATIONS

Depending on the length and overall health of your credit history, applying for new lines of credit can indicate certain behaviors signaling your reliability to lenders. Usually, multiple applications are less favorable when seen on shorter histories.

Source: QuickenLoans, www.quickenloans.com/home-buying/learn/credit/what-is-a-good-credit-score.

Analyze, Create, Practice

Overcome Financial Anxiety

Start with an honest examination of how you relate to money.

Analyze.   Evaluate your values regarding money. Using the descriptions on page 148 of what influences people's reactions to money, fill in the following blanks regarding your personal beliefs.

What I value spending money on

....

....

....

How I describe my money "personality"

....

....

....

How money is viewed in my culture

....

....

....

How my family and friends tend to handle money

....

....

....

Create. If you had enough money for your expenses and then some, what would you do with the extra? Would you save it, spend it, do a little of both? Imagine and explore what you would do if you had an extra $1,000 to spend this year.

....

....

....

....

Practice. Look for practical ways to move toward the scenario you imagined. Realistically, how can you make the $1,000 happen? You may need to make some sacrifices in the short term. Come up with two specific plans of changes that will move you toward your goal.

1. ....

2. ....

Multiple Intelligences in action

List three intelligences in the left-hand column—two that are highly developed for you and one you would like to build. Then in the right-hand column brainstorm a strategy for money management that relates to each intelligence.

Intelligence	Use MI Strategies to Come Up with Solutions
Example: Visual-Spatial	*Keep a color-coded budget with a color designated for each category of money you spend (food, shopping, bills, etc).*
....	....
	....
....	....
	....
....	....
	....

chapter

12

Careers and More

Building a Successful Future

The skills and attitudes you acquire in school fuel future success. This chapter offers strategies for how to function effectively in the workplace. Finally, it will focus on how what you've learned in this course can help you achieve goals in school, work, and life.

In this chapter, you'll explore answers to the following questions:

How can you prepare for career success?

p. 161

How can you conduct an effective job search?

p. 168

How will your learning in this course bring success?

p. 170

How can you create and live your personal mission?

p. 170

quick!
CHECK

How Ready Are You for Career and Life Success?

For each statement, circle the number that best describes how true the statement is for you, from 1 for "not at all true for me" to 5 for "very true for me."

▶ I am considering my learning style, personality, and experience as I think about potential jobs and careers.   **1 2 3 4 5**

▶ I have thought about possible career paths and what they might mean for my life now and in the future.   **1 2 3 4 5**

▶ I am prepared to adjust to change both in my life and in the workplace.   **1 2 3 4 5**

▶ I know how to find and use career-related resources (offices and people) at my school.   **1 2 3 4 5**

▶ I have a basic resumé written that I can modify and update for job applications.   **1 2 3 4 5**

▶ I intend to continue to learn throughout my life and know that the modern workplace will require it.   **1 2 3 4 5**

▶ I believe that I can grow my intelligence with effort and focus.   **1 2 3 4 5**

▶ I have built skills in the four areas that the Partnership for 21st Century Learning says will be crucial for success in the future.   **1 2 3 4 5**

▶ I have a sense of my personal mission in life—who I am, what I want to do, and the values by which I live.   **1 2 3 4 5**

▶ I use critical, creative, and practical thinking skills to achieve my most important goals.   **1 2 3 4 5**

If your total ranges from 41–50, you consider yourself to be ready for college, work, and life success.
If your total ranges from 24–40, you consider yourself to be somewhat ready for college, work, and life.
If your total is less than 24, you do not yet feel ready to succeed in college, work, and life.

Now total your scores.

REMEMBER No matter how ready you are for success in college, work, and life, you can improve with effort. Read the chapter to learn new ways to prepare for success, and practice by doing the activities.

How CAN YOU PREPARE FOR CAREER SUCCESS?

The earlier in your college education that you consider career goals, the more you can use your time in college to prepare you for work, in both job-specific and general ways. As you read this section, keep in mind that all of the skills you acquire in college—thinking, teamwork, writing, goal setting, and others—prepare you for workplace success, no matter what career is right for you.

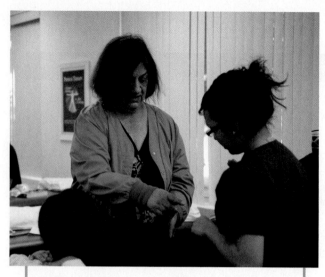

Taking courses in an area of interest can help you see how well a job in this area might suit you. These students get hands-on experience in respiratory therapy as well as advice from an experienced instructor.

© Sarah Kravits

Consider Your Personality and Strengths

Because who you are as a learner relates closely to who you are as a worker, your assessment results from Chapter 3 will give you helpful clues in the search for the right career. The Multiple Intelligences assessment points to information about your natural strengths and challenges, which can lead you to careers that involve these strengths. Look at Key 12.1 to see how intelligences may link up with various careers.

The Personality Spectrum assessment is equally as significant, because it focuses on how you work best with others, and career success depends in large part on your ability to function in a team. Key 12.2 focuses the four dimensions of the Personality Spectrum on career ideas and strategies. Look for your strengths and decide what you may want to keep in mind as you search. Look also at areas of challenge, and try to identify ways to boost your abilities in those areas. Even the most ideal job involves some tasks that are not in your area of comfort.

Finally, one other way to investigate how your personality and learning strengths may inform career choice is to take an inventory based on the Holland Theory. Psychologist John Holland theorized that personality was related to career choice, and he came up with six different types that identify both personality and career area: Realistic, Investigative, Artistic, Social, Enterprising, and Conventional (together known as RIASEC).[1] Holland developed two interest surveys that allow people to identify their order of preference for the six types and help them link their stronger types to career areas. Ask your career center about these surveys—the Vocational Preference Inventory (VPI) and the Self-Directed Search (SDS).

Be Strategic

With awareness of your talents and strengths, focus on making a practical, personal plan to achieve your career goals. First, create a timeline to illustrate the steps of your plan toward a specific career goal. Working with an advisor, career office employee, or mentor, establish a time frame and write your steps by when they should happen. If your plan is five years long, for example, indicate what you plan to do by the fourth, third, and second years, and then the first year, including a six-month goal and a one-month goal for that first year.

After you establish your time frame, focus on details. Make specific plans for pursuing the jobs or careers that have piqued your interest. Set goals that establish whom you will talk to, what courses you will take, what skills you will work on, what jobs or internships you will investigate, and any other research you need to do.

Build Knowledge and Experience

It's hard to choose the right career path without knowledge or experience. Courses, internships, jobs, and volunteering are four great ways to build both.

Courses Take a course or two in your areas of interest to determine whether you like the material and learn it successfully. Find out what courses are required for a major in those areas and decide if you are willing to study this material during college. Check out your school's course catalog for detailed information on the courses involved.

Internships Temporary, usually unpaid work programs, internships are designed to provide supervised practical experience in different professional fields. Your career center may list summer or year-round internship opportunities. For more comprehensive guides, check out reference books such as those published by Vault and Internet sources like www.internships.com and www.princetonreview.com.

Jobs You may discover career opportunities while earning money during a part-time job. Someone

Key 12.1 Multiple Intelligences May Open Doors to Careers

Multiple Intelligence	Look into a career as a . . .	Multiple Intelligence	Look into a career as a . . .
Bodily-Kinesthetic	• Carpenter or draftsperson • Physical therapist • Mechanical engineer • Dancer or actor • Exercise physiologist	Musical	• Singer or voice coach • Music teacher • Record executive • Musician or conductor • Radio DJ or sound engineer
Intrapersonal	• Research scientist • Computer engineer • Psychologist • Economist • Author	Logical-Mathematical	• Doctor or dentist • Accountant • Attorney • Chemist • Investment banker
Interpersonal	• Social worker • PR or HR rep • Sociologist • Teacher • Nurse	Verbal-Linguistic	• Author or journalist • TV/radio producer • Literature or language teacher • Business executive • Copywriter or editor
Naturalistic	• Biochemical engineer • Natural scientist (geologist, ecologist, entymologist) • Paleontologist • Position with environmental group • Farmer or farm management	Visual-Spatial	• Graphic artist or illustrator • Photographer • Architect or interior designer • Art museum curator • Art teacher • Set or retail stylist

who takes a legal proofreading job to make extra cash might discover an interest in law. Someone who answers phones for a newspaper company might be drawn into journalism.

Volunteering Helping others in need can introduce you to careers and increase your experience. Schools often sponsor volunteer groups or establish committees to organize volunteering opportunities. You may even be able to find opportunities that mesh with an area of interest. Many employers look favorably on volunteering.

Service learning The goal of service learning is to provide the community with service and students with knowledge gained from hands-on experience.[2] Students in service learning programs enroll in for-credit courses in which volunteer service and related assignments are required. Talk to your advisor about whether your school offers service learning programs.

Dimension	Strengths on the Job	Challenges on the Job	Look for Jobs/Careers That Feature . . .
Thinker 	Problem solving Development of ideas Keen analysis of situations Fairness to others Efficiency in working through tasks Innovation of plans and systems Ability to look strategically at the future	A need for private time to think and work A need, at times, to move away from established rules A dislike of sameness—systems that don't change, repetitive tasks Not always being open to expressing thoughts and feelings to others	Some level of solo work/think time Problem solving Opportunity for innovation Freedom to think creatively and to bend the rules Technical work Big-picture strategic planning
Organizer 	High level of responsibility Enthusiastic support of social structures Order and reliability Loyalty Ability to follow through on tasks according to requirements Detailed planning skills with competent follow-through Neatness and efficiency	A need for tasks to be clearly, concretely defined A need for structure and stability A preference for less rapid change A need for frequent feedback A need for tangible appreciation Low tolerance for people who don't conform to rules and regulations	Clear, well-laid-out tasks and plans Stable environment with consistent, repeated tasks Organized supervisors Clear structure of how employees interact and report to one another Value of, and reward for, loyalty
Giver 	Honesty and integrity Commitment to putting energy toward close relationships with others Finding ways to bring out the best in self and others Peacemaker and mediator Ability to listen well, respect opinions, and prioritize the needs of co-workers	Difficulty in handling conflict, either personal or between others in the work environment Strong need for appreciation and praise Low tolerance for perceived dishonesty or deception Avoidance of people perceived as hostile, cold, or indifferent	Emphasis on teamwork and relationship building Indications of strong and open lines of communication among workers Encouragement of personal expression in the workplace (arrangement of personal space, tolerance of personal celebrations, and so on)
Adventurer 	Skillfulness in many different areas Willingness to try new things Ability to take action Hands-on problem-solving skills Initiative and energy Ability to negotiate Spontaneity and creativity	Intolerance of being kept waiting Lack of detail focus Impulsiveness Dislike of sameness and authority Need for freedom, continual change, and constant action Tendency not to consider consequences of actions	A spontaneous atmosphere Less structure, more freedom Adventuresome tasks Situations involving change Encouragement of hands-on problem solving Travel and physical activity Support of creative ideas and endeavors

Analyze How Hard Work Relates to Success

Through hard work, everybody can succeed in American society. In a recent survey, nearly four out of five college freshmen agreed with this statement.[3] Think about it, and respond in a journal entry. In your response, consider these questions: What does this statement mean to you? Do you agree or disagree? What facts support it or disprove it?

Investigate Career Paths

Career possibilities extend far beyond what you can imagine. Ask instructors, relatives, mentors, and fellow students about careers. Explore job listings, occupation lists, assessments, and other information about careers and companies at your school's career center. Check your library for books on careers or biographies of people who worked in fields that interest you. Look at Key 12.3 for the kinds of analytical questions that will aid your search. Keep the following in mind as you look.

• *A wide array of job possibilities exists for most career fields.* For example, the medical world consists

of more than doctors and nurses. Administrators run hospitals, researchers test drugs, pharmacists prepare prescriptions, security experts ensure patient and visitor safety, and so on.

• *Within each job, there are a variety of tasks and skills.* For instance, you may know that an instructor teaches, but you may not realize that instructors also write, research, study, design courses, give presentations, and counsel. Take your career exploration beyond first impressions to get an accurate picture of the careers that interest you.

• *A variety of occupations pay well.* Rewarding jobs go beyond law, finance, and medicine. According to data from the U.S. Labor Department, careers with

Key 12.3 Ask Questions Like These to Analyze How a Career Area or Job May Fit You

What personality types are best suited to this kind of work?	Do I respect the company or the industry? The product or service?
What are the prospects for moving up to higher-level positions?	Does this company or industry accommodate special needs (child care, sick days, flex time)?
What are the educational requirements (certificates or degrees, courses)?	Do I need to belong to a union? What does union membership involve?
What can I do in this area that I like and do well?	Are there opportunities near where I live (or want to live)?
What skills are necessary?	What other expectations exist (travel, overtime, etc.)?
What wage or salary and benefits can I expect?	Do I prefer the service or production end of this industry?

comfortable earnings include electricians, aircraft mechanics, and more.[4] Look up the U.S. Bureau of Labor's Occupational Outlook Handbook or see salary.com for information on average salaries in different fields.

Know What Employers Want

When you apply for a job, it is important to realize that prospective employers look for particular skills and qualities that mark you as a promising candidate. Most employers require you to have specific technical skills, but in this rapidly changing workplace, general life skills and emotional intelligence may be even more crucial to your success.

General Skills

In the modern workplace, workers will hold an average of ten jobs through their productive working years.[5] The high rate of job and workplace change means that abilities such as successful thinking and teamwork are crucial to workplace success. Many of these general skills can also be described as *transferable* skills—general skills learned through job or life experience that you can use with (or transfer to) a new and different job or career. Key 12.4 describes transferable skills that employers look for.

Emotional Intelligence

Employers are also drawn to emotionally intelligent job candidates, as you learned in Chapter 1. Your emotional intelligence has an impact on your effectiveness. Consider this scenario: You arrive at work distracted by a personal problem and tired from studying late the night before. Your supervisor is overloaded with a major project due that day. The person you work most closely with is arriving late due to a car problem. In other words, everyone

Key 12.4 **Employers Look for Candidates with These Important Skills**

Skill	Why Is It Useful?
Communication	Good listening, speaking, and writing skills are keys to working with others, as is being able to adjust to different communication styles.
Critical thinking	An employee who can analyze choices and challenges, as well as assess the value of new ideas, stands out.
Creativity	The ability to come up with new concepts, plans, and products helps companies improve and innovate.
Practical thinking	No job gets done without employees who can think through a plan for achieving a goal, put it into action, and complete it successfully.
Teamwork	All workers interact with others on the job. Working well with others is essential for achieving workplace goals.
Goal setting	Teams fail if goals are unclear or unreasonable. Employees and companies benefit from setting realistic, specific goals and achieving them reliably.
Cultural competence	The workplace is increasingly diverse. An employee who can work with, adjust to, and respect people from different backgrounds and cultures is valuable.
Leadership	The ability to influence and motivate others in a positive way earns respect and career advancement.
Positive attitude	Other employees will gladly work with, and often advance, someone who completes tasks with positive, upbeat energy.
Integrity	Acting with integrity at work—communicating promptly, being truthful and honest, following rules, giving proper notice—enhances value.
Flexibility	The most valuable employees understand the constancy of change and have developed the skills to adapt to its challenges.
Continual learning	The most valuable employees take personal responsibility to stay current in their fields.

is strung out. What does an emotionally intelligent person do? Remember the three actions of emotional intelligence:

- *Tune in to everyone's emotions first.* You: Tired and distracted. Your co-worker: Worried about the car and about being late. Your supervisor: Agitated about the project.
- *Understand what the emotions are telling you.* Making the deadline that day might be more challenging than anticipated. Everyone is going to need to set aside distracted, negative thinking and maintain an extra-focused and positive state of mind to get through it.
- *Take action toward positive outcomes.* You come up with several ideas.

1. Prioritize your task list so that you can concentrate on what is most pressing.
2. Put a memo on your supervisor's desk saying that you are available to support her as she nails down the loose ends on her urgent project.
3. Call your co-worker on his cell phone while he settles the car problem and let him know the status at work, preparing him to prioritize and to support the supervisor.
4. Ask another co-worker to bring in a favorite midmorning snack to keep everyone going on what looks to be a long day.

The current emphasis on teamwork has highlighted emotional intelligence in the workplace. The more adept you are at working with others, the more likely you are to succeed.

Expect Change

The working world is always in flux, responding to technological developments, global competition, and other factors. Think about the following as you prepare for your own career.

Growing and declining career areas Rapid workplace change means that a growth area today may be declining tomorrow—witness the sudden drop in Internet company jobs and fortunes in 2001. The U.S. Bureau of Labor keeps updated statistics on the status of various career areas. For example, for the period 2006 to 2016, of the ten fastest-growing occupations identified by the bureau, six are related to health care.[6]

Workplace trends Companies, to save money, are hiring more temporary employees (temps) and fewer full-time employees. Temporary jobs offer flexibility, few obligations, and often more take-home pay, but have limited benefits. Also, in response to changing needs, companies are offering more "quality of life" benefits such as telecommuting, job sharing, and on-site child care. You can track these changes by scanning hard copy or online versions of business-focused publications such as *Fortune, Business Week,* and the *Wall Street Journal.*

think
CREATIVELY

Look at Careers "Out of the Box"

You may be under pressure to choose a career that your family and friends would approve of or that earns a certain amount of money. Ask "what if"—What would you do if these factors didn't exist? Create a list of "dream jobs" you would go for if it didn't matter how much money you made and no one in your life would disapprove of your choice.

Personal change Even difficult personal changes can open doors that you never imagined were there. For example, after being diagnosed with Parkinson's at only 30, actor Michael J. Fox found new passions in life as a best-selling author and advocate for others suffering from the degenerative disease.

With what you know about general workplace success strategies, you can search effectively for a job that works for you.

How CAN YOU CONDUCT AN EFFECTIVE JOB SEARCH?

Whether you are looking for a job now or planning ahead for a search closer to graduation, you have choices about how to proceed. Maximize your success by using the resources available to you, knowing the basics about resumés and interviews, and planning strategically.

Use Available Resources

Use your school's career planning and placement office, your networking skills, classified ads, and online services to help you explore possibilities for career areas or specific jobs.

Your School's Career Planning and Placement Office

Generally, the career planning and placement office deals with postgraduation job opportunities, whereas the student employment office, along with the financial aid office, has information about working during school. At either location you might find job listings, interview sign-up sheets, and company contact information. The career office may hold frequent informational sessions on different topics. Your school may also sponsor job or career fairs that give you a chance to explore job opportunities. Get acquainted with the career office early in your college career.

Networking

The most basic type of networking—talking to people about fields and jobs that interest you—is one of the most important job-hunting strategies. Networking contacts can answer questions regarding job hunting, job responsibilities and challenges, and salary expectations. You can network with friends and family members, instructors, administrators, counselors, alumni, employers, co-workers, people

Take advantage of career fairs sponsored by your school or town. These career fair attendees pick up useful information and applications from different employers.

© Adam Lau/AP Images

you meet through extracurricular activities, and others.

Online social networking can also help you in your job search. Tools like Facebook, Twitter, and LinkedIn allow members to create personalized pages and connect with other individuals through groups, fan pages, and similar interests. During a job search, these sites can be used to meet potential employers through others and showcase portfolio pieces. A word of caution: Your online presence is public. Before you post anything, remember: If you wouldn't want a potential employer (or your parents, instructor, or religious leader) to see it, don't post it.

Online Services and Classified Ads

Although classified ads are still helpful when looking locally, the Internet is capable of storing tons of information without having to spend money on paper and ink. Therefore, more employers post through online job boards, and those listings are often more detailed than the two- or three-sentence ads you'd find in a newspaper. In addition to a job description and salary information, most online postings will contain company information and a link to where you can submit an application. Use the following tips to make the most out of your virtual resources:

- Look up career-focused and job listing websites such as CareerBuilder.com, Monster.com,

Your Resumé, Cover Letter, and Interview

Information on resumés, cover letters, and interviews fills entire books. To get you started, here are a few basic tips on giving yourself the best possible chance.

▶ **Resumé and Cover Letter:** Design your resumé neatly, using a current and acceptable format (look to books, career sites, or your career office for some standard formats). Make sure the information is accurate and truthful. Proofread it for errors and have someone else proofread it as well. Type or print it on high-quality paper (a heavier bond paper than is used for ordinary copies). Include a brief, to-the-point cover letter along with your resumé that tells the employer what job you are interested in and why he or she should hire you.

Prospective employers often use a computer to scan resumés, selecting the ones that contain keywords relating to the job opening or industry. When you construct your resumé, make sure to include as many keywords as you can. For example, if you are seeking a computer-related job, list computer programs you use and other specific technical proficiencies. To figure out what keywords you need, check out job descriptions, job postings, and other current resumés.[7]

▶ **Interview:** Arrive clean, neat, and appropriately dressed. Choose a nice pair of shoes—people notice. Bring an extra copy of your resumé and any other materials that you want to show the interviewer, even if you sent a copy ahead of time. Avoid chewing gum or smoking. Offer a confident handshake. Make eye contact. Speak honestly about yourself. After the interview, no matter what the outcome, follow up right away with a formal but pleasant thank-you note.

Being on time to your interview makes a positive impression—and being late will almost certainly be held against you. If you are from a culture that does not consider being late a sign of disrespect, remember that your interviewer may not share that perspective.

America's Job Bank, BilingualCareer.com, Job-BankUSA, and futurestep.com. Many sites offer resources on career areas, resumés, and online job searching in addition to job listings.

- Access job search databases such as the Career Placement Registry and U.S. Employment Opportunities.
- Check the Web pages of individual associations and companies, which may post job listings and descriptions.

If nothing happens right away, keep at it. New job postings appear, and new people sign on to look at your resumé. Plus, sites change all the time. Search using the keywords "job sites" or "job search" to see what sites are up (quintcareers.com has a listing of the top fifty best job sites).

Use an Organized, Consistent Strategy

Organize your approach according to what you need to do and when you have to do it. Do you plan to make three phone calls per day? Will you fill out one job application each week? Keep a record—on 3-by-5 cards, in a computer file or smartphone, or in a notebook—of the following:

- People you contact plus contact information and method of contact (e-mail, snail mail, phone)
- Companies to which you apply
- Jobs for which you apply, including any results (for example, a job that becomes unavailable)
- Responses to communications (phone calls to you, interviews, written communications), information about the person who contacted you (name, title), and the time and dates of contact

Keeping accurate records enables you to both chart your progress and maintain a clear picture of the process. If you don't get a job now but another opens up at the same company in a few months, well-kept records will enable you to contact key personnel quickly and efficiently.

Being able to imagine and plan for a path beyond college can make each step along the way a little more meaningful. Though it may still be years off, start imagining graduation and beyond today. You'll thank yourself tomorrow.

How WILL YOUR LEARNING IN THIS COURSE BRING SUCCESS?

Throughout *Keys to Success Quick* you have developed critical, creative, and practical thinking skills that you have applied to academic and life situations, putting them together to solve problems and make decisions. You are only just beginning your career as a thinker, problem solver, and decision maker. Over time, you will continue to discover the best ways to use your thinking skills to achieve meaningful goals.

You leave this course with far more than a final grade, a notebook full of work, and a few credit hours on your transcript. You leave with a set of skills and attitudes that will open the door to success in the 21st century.

Lifelong Learning and the Growth Mindset

With knowledge in many fields doubling every 2 to 3 years and with your personal interests and needs changing all the time, what you learn in college is just the beginning of what you will need to learn throughout your life to succeed. With a growth mindset—the attitude that you can always grow and learn—you are as ready to achieve the goals you set out for yourself today as you are to achieve future goals you cannot yet anticipate.

If you look back at the Partnership for 21st Century Skills grid on page 12, you will see that you have built skills and knowledge in each quadrant. As a lifelong learner, you will continue to build them long past graduation.

Flexibility Helps You Land on Your Feet

As a citizen of the 21st century, you are likely to move in and out of school, jobs, and careers in the years ahead. You are also likely to experience important personal changes. How you react to change, especially if it is unexpected and difficult, is almost as important as the changes themselves in determining your future success. The ability to "make lemonade from lemons" is the hallmark of people who are able to hang on to hope.

Your thinking skills will help you stay flexible. As planned and unplanned changes arise, you analyze them, brainstorm solutions, and take practical action. With these skills you can adapt to the loss of a job or an exciting job offer, to failing a course or winning an academic scholarship. Consider the following strategies for making the most of unpredictable changes:[8]

- *Focus on what* is *rather than what is supposed to be.* Planning for the future works best when you accept the reality of your situation.
- *Use your planning as a guide rather than a rule.* If you allow yourself to follow new paths when changes occur, you'll be able to grow from what life gives you.
- *Be willing to accept surprise.* Great creative energies can come from the force of a surprise. Instead of turning back to familiar patterns, explore new possibilities.

As you come to an end of your work in this course, use everything you've learned about yourself to define a meaningful life path.

How CAN YOU CREATE AND LIVE YOUR PERSONAL MISSION?

Dr. Stephen Covey, author of *The Seven Habits of Highly Effective People*, defines a *personal mission statement* as a philosophy outlining what you want to be (character), what you want to do (contributions and achievements), and the principles by which you live (your values). He describes the statement as "a personal constitution, the basis for making major, life-directing decisions."[9] The following mission statement was written by Carol Carter, one of the authors of *Keys to Success Quick*.

> My mission is to use my talents and abilities to help students of all ages, stages, backgrounds, and economic levels achieve their human potential through fully developing their minds and their talents. I aim to create opportunities for others through work, service, and family. I also aim to balance work with people in my life, understanding that my family and friends are a priority above all else.

To begin to formulate a personal mission statement, think about Covey's definition:

- *Character.* What aspects of character do you think are most valuable? When you consider the people you admire most, what qualities stand out? These could include attributes like ambition, compassion, determination, leadership, and integrity.

Fill in Your 21st Century Skills Resumé

Use the grid below to create a resumé of skills for yourself—skills you have built through reading this book and doing the work necessary for this course. For each quadrant (Core Areas; Information, Media, and Technology Skills; Learning and Innovation Skills; and Life and Career Skills), list a total of four specific skills you have acquired or developed (four per quadrant). It does not matter if you have one skill listed per bullet point or four skills linked to one bullet point in each quadrant. The point is for you to measure your progress in each general area.

Core Areas

- Global Awareness
- Financial, Economic, Business, and Entrepreneurial Literacy
- Civic Literacy—Community Service
- Health Literacy

Information, Media, and Technology Skills

- Information Literacy
- Media Literacy
- Technology Skills

Learning and Innovation Skills

- Creativity and Innovation
- Critical Thinking and Problem Solving
- Communication and Collaboration

Life and Career Skills

- Flexibility and Adaptability
- Initiative and Self-Direction
- Social and Cross-Cultural Skills
- Productivity and Accountability
- Leadership and Responsibility

- *Contributions and achievements.* What do you want to accomplish in your life? Where do you see yourself in 5 years? 10?
- *Values.* What is important to you? Family and friends? Success in the workplace? Education? What in your mission could help you live according to what you value most?

Because what you want out of life changes as you move from one phase to the next—from single person to spouse, from student to working citizen—keep your personal mission statement flexible and open to revision. Use it as a road map for your journey, helping you to infuse your daily activities with integrity and meaning.

With a growth mindset, you will always have a new direction in which to grow and a new challenge to face. Live each day to the fullest, using your thinking skills to achieve your most valued goals. Create your own life by seeking to improve and grow in the ways that are most meaningful to you—and grow as much as you can. By being true to yourself, a respectful friend and family member, a focused student who believes in the power of learning, a productive employee, and a contributing member of society, you can change the world.

quick! SKILL BUILDING

Think Back

Solidify your knowledge and prepare for tests with this review. Answer the following questions on a separate sheet of paper or electronic file.

▶ Revisit the chapter-opening questions on page 160. Scan the chapter and write a short answer for each.

▶ Go back to the Quick Check self-assessment. From the list, choose one item that you want to develop further. Set a specific goal based on what you read in the chapter. Describe your goal and plan in a short paragraph, including a time frame and specific steps. See if you can accomplish it in between this term and the next.

Analyze, Create, Practice

Assess Your Motivation

Analyze You assessed your motivation in Chapter 1. How motivated do you perceive yourself to be now, at the end of the term? Take the assessment again to find out.

	1 Not at All Like Me	2 Somewhat Unlike Me	3 Not Sure	4 Somewhat Like Me	5 Definitely Like Me
Please highlight or circle the number that best represents your answer:					
1. I am able to translate ideas into action.	1	2	3	4	5
2. I am able to maintain confidence in myself.	1	2	3	4	5
3. I can stay on track toward a goal.	1	2	3	4	5
4. I complete tasks and have good follow-through.	1	2	3	4	5
5. I avoid procrastination.	1	2	3	4	5
6. I accept responsibility when I make a mistake.	1	2	3	4	5
7. I independently take responsibility for tasks.	1	2	3	4	5
8. I work hard to overcome personal difficulties.	1	2	3	4	5
9. I create an environment that helps me to concentrate on my goals.	1	2	3	4	5
10. I can delay gratification to receive the benefits.	1	2	3	4	5

Now look back at page 13 for your original scores. Analyze the difference between the two sets. What changes do you see, and why do you think they happened? What positive effects do you think they'll have for you in school and as you pursue a career?

....
....
....
....
....
....
....
....
....

Create. Using Covey's three-part definition, write your own personal mission statement. Consider this to be your personal manifesto—the statement by which you will live your life and accomplish your dreams. To generate ideas, consider the following scenarios, and brainstorm your answers using a mind map or a separate sheet of paper.

1. First, imagine you are at your own retirement dinner after a long, successful career. Your best friend stands up and talks about five aspects of your character that contributed most to your success. What do you think they are?
2. Second, you are preparing for a late-in-life job change. Updating your resumé, you need to list your contributions and achievements. What would you like them to be?

Write your completed mission statement here:

....
....
....
....
....
....
....
....
....

Practice. Think about your personal mission statement, and consider your level of motivation as you finish this course. Define three actions that you will take between now and the time you start your next term that will make a difference for you in school as well as in life.

....
....
....
....
....
....
....
....

When you've finished with this exercise, make a copy, type it into a computer file, or simply rip out this page. Then post it in an obvious location—somewhere you'll be sure to see it every day—so that you can remind yourself of both your big-picture mission and the everyday actions that will help you accomplish it.

Multiple Intelligences in action

Write three intelligences in the left-hand column—two that are highly developed for you and one you would like to build. Then in the right-hand column, brainstorm a strategy for career exploration that relates to each intelligence.

Intelligence

Example: Interpersonal

Use MI Strategies to Come Up with Solutions

Build a LinkedIn profile and send invitations to all of your friends. After you build a set of contacts, explore them to see whom they in turn are connected with.

....

....

....

....

....

....

Endnotes

Chapter 1

1. Information in this box from the following sources: U.S. Census Bureau, "Average Earnings of Year-Round, Full-Time Workers by Educational Attainment: 2007," Current Population Reports Series, P60-235, August 2008; U.S. Department of Labor, Bureau of Labor Statistics, Office of Employment and Unemployment Statistics, "Employment and Earnings," January 2005; Institute for Higher Education Policy, "Reaping the Benefits: Defining the Public and Private Value of Going to College," Washington, DC: The New Millennium Project on Higher Education Costs, Pricing, and Productivity, 1998.
2. "Attitudes and Characteristics of Freshmen at 4-Year Colleges, Fall 2007," *The Chronicle of Higher Education: 2008–9 Almanac*, 55, issue 1, p. 18. Data from "The American Freshman: National Norms for Fall 2007," University of California at Los Angeles Higher Education Research Institute.
3. Robert J. Sternberg, *Successful Intelligence: How Practical and Creative Intelligence Determine Success in Life*, New York: Plume, 1997, pp. 85–90; and Carol S. Dweck, *Mindset: The New Psychology of Success*, New York: Random House, 2006, p. 5; Susanne Jaeggi, Martin Buschkuehl, John Jonides, and Walter J. Perrig, "Improving Fluid Intelligence with Training on Working Memory," 2008, *Proceedings of the National Academy of Sciences USA*, 105, pp. 6829–6833.
4. The Society for Neuroscience, *Brain Facts: A Primer on the Brain and Neurosystem*, Washington, DC: The Society for Neuroscience, 2008, pp. 34–35.
5. Based on Sternberg, *Successful Intelligence*.
6. Gina Kolata, "A Surprising Secret to a Long Life: Stay in School," *New York Times*, January 3, 2007, www.nytimes.com/2007/01/03/health/03aging.html.
7. Carol Dweck, "The Mindsets," 2006, www.mindset online.com/whatisit/themindsets/index.html.
8. Dweck, *Mindset: The New Psychology of Success*, p. 16.
9. Ibid.
10. From "Facts About Plagiarism," 2007, Plagiarism.org, www.plagiarism.org/facts.html.
11. John D. Mayer, Peter Salovey, and David R. Caruso, "Emotional Intelligence: New Ability or Eclectic Traits?" September 2008, *American Psychologist*, 63, no. 6, p. 503.
12. Adapted from Mayer, Salovey, and Caruso, pp. 505–507.
13. Mayer, Salovey, and Caruso, pp. 510–512.
14. Based on Sternberg, pp. 251–268.

Chapter 2

1. Dr. John Medina, *Brain Rules*, Seattle, WA: Pear Press, 2008, p. 39.
2. Paul Timm, *Successful Self-Management: A Psychologically Sound Approach to Personal Effectiveness*, Los Altos, CA: Crisp Publications, 1987, pp. 22–41.
3. Jane E. Brody, "At Every Age, Feeling the Effects of Too Little Sleep," *New York Times*, October 23, 2007, www.nytimes.com/2007/10/23/health/23brod.html.
4. Jane B. Burka and Lenora M. Yuen, *Procrastination: Why You Do It, What to Do About It*, Reading, MA: Perseus Books, 1983, pp. 21–22.

Chapter 3

1. Derek V. Price and Angela Bell, *Federal Access Policies and Higher Education for Working Adults*, October 2008, www.americanprogress.org/issues/2008/10/pdf/access_policies.pdf.
2. Howard Gardner, *Multiple Intelligence: New Horizons*, New York: Basic Books, 2006, p. 8.
3. Gardner, *Multiple Intelligence*, p. 180.
4. National Center for Learning Disabilities, "LD at a Glance," May 2003, www.ncld.org/LDInfo Zone/Info-Zone_FactSheet_LD.cfm.
5. National Center for Learning Disabilities, "Adult Learning Disabilities: A Learning Disability Isn't Something You Outgrow. It's Something You Learn to Master" (pamphlet), New York: National Center for Learning Disabilities.
6. Dr. C. George Boeree, "Carl Jung," 2006, http://webspace.ship.edu/cgboer/jung.html.

Chapter 4

1. Vincent Ruggiero, *The Art of Thinking*, 2001, quoted in "Critical Thinking," July 2006, http://success.oregon state.edu/criticalthinking.html.
2. Richard Paul, "The Role of Questions in Thinking, Teaching, and Learning," 1995, accessed April 2004, www.criticalthinking.org/ resources/articles/the-role-of-questions.shtml.
3. Sharon Begley, "Critical Thinking: Part Skill, Part Mindset and Totally Up to You," *Wall Street Journal*, October 20, 2006, p. B1.
4. Adapted from "Questions That Probe Reasons and Evidence" (www-ed.fnal.gov/trc/tutorial/taxonomy .html), based on Richard Paul, *Critical Thinking: How to Prepare Students for a Rapidly Changing World*, Santa Rosa, CA: Center for Critical Thinking, 1993;

and Barbara Fowler, "Bloom's Taxonomy and Critical Thinking," 1996, Longview Community College, http://mcckc.edu/longview/ctac/blooms.htm.

5. Robert Sternberg, *Successful Intelligence*, New York: Plume, 1996, p. 128.

6. Dennis Coon, *Introduction to Psychology: Exploration and Application*, 6th ed., St. Paul: West, 1992, p. 295.

7. Roger von Oech, *A Whack on the Side of the Head*, New York: Warner Books, 1990, pp. 11–168.

8. Adapted from T. Z. Tardif and R. J. Sternberg, "What Do We Know About Creativity?" in *The Nature of Creativity*, R. J. Sternberg, ed., London: Cambridge University Press, 1988.

9. "The Best Innovations Are Those That Come from Smart Questions," *Wall Street Journal*, April 12, 2004, B1.

10. Sternberg, *Successful Intelligence*, p. 212.

11. Ibid., p. 236.

12. Robert J. Sternberg and Elena L. Grigorenko, "Practical Intelligence and the Principal," Yale University Publication Series No. 2, 2001, p. 5.

Chapter 5

1. Alamo Colleges, "Survey, Question, Read, Recite, Review (SQ3R)," www.alamo.edu/sac/history/keller/accditg/sssq3r.htm.

2. www.pugetsound.edu/x30366.xml.

3. Jane C. Neale, June 29, 2010, http://info.org.il/english/books_on_the_floor.html.

4. Robert Harris, "Evaluating Internet Research Sources," June 15, 2007, Virtual Salt, www.virtualsalt.com/evalu8it.htm.

Chapter 6

1. Alina Tugend, "Multitasking Can Make You Lose . . . Um . . . Focus," *New York Times*, October 25, 2008.

2. "Note-Taking and Listening," www.eiu.edu/~lrnasst/notes.htm.

3. System developed by Cornell professor Walter Pauk. See Walter Pauk, *How to Study in College*, 10th ed., Boston: Houghton Mifflin, 2011, pp. 236–241.

Chapter 7

1. University of California–Irvine, "Short-Term Stress Can Affect Learning and Memory," *ScienceDaily*, March 13, 2008, www.sciencedaily.com/releases/2008/03/080311182434.htm.

2. Herman Ebbinghaus, *Memory: A Contribution to Experimental Psychology*, trans. H. A. Ruger and C. E. Bussenius, New York: Teachers College, Columbia University, 1885.

3. Bulletpoints from Kenneth C. Petress, "The Benefits of Group Study," 2004, *Education*, 124.

4. Dartmouth College Academic Skills Center, "How to Avoid Cramming for Tests," 2001, www.dartmouth.edu/~acskills/handouts.html.

5. "Study Shows How Sleep Improves Memory," *Science Daily*, June 29, 2005, www.sciencedaily.com/releases/2005/06/050629070337.htm.

Chapter 8

1. Ben Gose, "Notes from Academe: Living It Up on the Dead Days," *The Chronicle of Higher Education*, June 8, 2002, http://chronicle.com/article/Living-It-Up-on-the-Dead-Days/8983/.

2. Raymond Trevor Bradley et al., "Reducing Test Anxiety and Improving Test Performance in America's Schools," Institute of HeartMath, 2007, www.heartmath.org/templates/ihm/section_includes/education/pdf/tends_report.pdf.

3. From Paul D. Nolting, *Math Study Skills Workbook, Your Guide to Reducing Test Anxiety and Improving Study Strategies*, Boston: Houghton Mifflin, 2000. Cited in "Test Anxiety," West Virginia University at Parkersburg, www.wvup.edu/Academics/more_test_anxiety_tips.htm.

4. Adapted from Ron Fry, *"Ace" Any Test*, 3rd ed., Franklin Lakes, NJ: Career Press, 1996, pp. 123–124.

Chapter 9

1. National Center for Cultural Competence, "Conceptual Frameworks/Models, Guiding Values and Principles," 2002, http://gucchd. georgetown.edu//nccc/framework.html.

2. Information in the sections on the five stages of building competency is based on Mark A. King, Anthony Sims, and David Osher, "How Is Cultural Competence Integrated in Education?" Cultural Competence, May 2004, www.air.org/cecp/cultural/Q_integrated.htm#def.

3. Department of Justice, Immigration and Naturalization Service, "Immigrants to U.S. by Country of Origin," www.infoplease.com/ipa/A0201398.html.

4. Betsy Israel, "The Overconnecteds," *New York Times*, November 5, 2006, Education Life, p. 20.

5. Tina Kelley, "On Campuses, Warnings About Violence in Relationships," *New York Times*, February 13, 2000, p. 40.

Chapter 10

1. mtvU and Associated Press College Stress and Mental Health Poll Executive Summary, Spring 2008, www.halfofus.com/_media/_pr/mtvU_AP_College_Stress_and_Mental_Health_Poll_Executive_Summary.pdf.

2. T. H. Holmes and R. H. Rahe, "The Social Readjustment Rating Scale," 1967, *Journal of Psychosomatic Research*, 11, no. 2.

3. CBS News, "Help for Sleep-Deprived Students," April 19, 2004, www.cbsnews.com/stories/2004/04/19/health/main612476.shtml.

4. Gregg Jacobs, "Insomnia Corner," Talk About Sleep, 2004, www.talkaboutsleep.com/sleepdisorders/insomnia_corner.htm; also see Herbert Benson and Eileen M. Stuart, *The Wellness Book*, New York: Simon & Schuster, 1992, p. 292.
5. Mike Briddon, "Struggling with Sadness: Depression Among College Students Is on the Rise," Stressedoutnurses.com, April 22, 2008, www.stressedoutnurses.com/2008/04/struggling-with-sadness-depression-among-college-students-is-on-the-rise.
6. Boynton Health Service, "Health and Academic Performance: Minnesota Undergraduate Students," July 2008, www.bhs.umn.edu/reports/HealthAcademicPerformanceReport_2007.pdf.
7. mtvU and Associated Press College Stress and Mental Health Poll Executive Summary.
8. National Eating Disorders Association, "Learning Basic Terms and Information on a Variety of Eating Disorder Topics," 2010, www.nationaleatingdisorders.org/information-resources/general-information.php#facts-statistics.
9. Centers for Disease Control and Prevention, "Alcohol and Public Health," September 3, 2008, www.cdc.gov/alcohol/index.htm.
10. Joel Seguine, "Students Report Negative Consequences of Binge Drinking in New Survey," *The University Record*, University of Michigan, October 25, 1999, www.umich.edu/~urecord/9900/Oct25_99/7.htm.
11. Substance Abuse and Mental Health Services Administration, Office of Applied Studies, *Results from the 2007 National Survey on Drug Use and Health: National Findings*, NSDUH Series H-34, DHHS Publication No. SMA 08-4343, 2008, Rockville, MD: Author.
12. "Definition of Birth Control," Medicine.net, www.medterms.com/script/main/art.asp?articlekey=53351.

Chapter 11

1. Jim Hanson, "Your Money Personality: It's All in Your Head," University Credit Union, December 25, 2006, http://hffo.cuna.org/012433/article/1440/html.
2. Ibid.
3. "Attitudes and Characteristics of Freshmen at 4-Year Colleges," Fall 2007, *Chronicle of Higher Education*.
4. FinAid.org, "Defaulting on Student Loans," 2010, www.finaid.org/loans/default.phtml.
5. Anne Ryman, "Defaults on Student Loans Rising," *The Arizona Republic*, March 7, 2010, www.azcentral.com/12news/news/articles/2010/03/07/20100307student-loan-defaults-CP.html.
6. Ben Woolsey and Matt Schulz, "Credit Card Statistics, Industry Facts, Debt Statistics," CreditCards.com, January 15, 2010, www.creditcards.com/credit-card-news/credit-card-industry-facts-personal-debt-statistics-1276.php#youngadults.
7. Nellie Mae, "Undergraduate Students and Credit Cards in 2004," May 2005, www.nelliemae.com/library/research_12.html.

Chapter 12

1. Self-Directed Search, www.self-directed-search.com.
2. National Service Learning Clearinghouse, "Service Learning Is . . . ," 2004, www.servicelearning.org/article/archive/35.
3. University of California at Los Angeles Higher Education Research Institute, "The American Freshman: National Norms for Fall 2007." Cited in the *Chronicle of Higher Education: The 2008–9 Almanac*, 55, no. 1, p. 18.
4. "The Hot Jobs with High Pay," February 2007, Career Prospects in Virginia, www.careerprospects.org/Trends/salary-high.html.
5. U.S. Department of Labor, Bureau of Labor Statistics, "Number of Jobs Held, Labor Market Activity, and Earnings Growth Among the Youngest Baby Boomers: Results from a Longitudinal Survey" (news release), August 25, 2006, www.bls.gov/news.release/pdf/nlsoy.pdf.
6. Bureau of Labor Statistics, Economic News Release, "The 30 Fastest Growing Occupations Covered in the 2008–2009 Occupational Outlook Handbook," December 18, 2007, www.bls.gov/news.release/ooh.t01.htm.
7. Job Interview and Career Guide, "Resume: Keywords for Resumes—Keywords List," December 8, 2009, www.job-interview-site.com/resume-keywords-for-resumes-keywords-list.html.
8. Margaret J. Wheatley and Myron Kellner-Rogers, "A Simpler Way," 1997, *Weight Watchers Magazine*, 30, no. 3, pp. 42–44.
9. Stephen Covey, *The Seven Habits of Highly Effective People*, New York: Simon & Schuster, 1989, pp. 108, 309–318.

Index